124
AF522685

HUMAN RESOURCE PLANNING

Edited by

Dr. M. Sudhir Reddy
Project Officer,
NTMIS Nodal Centre,
JNTU,
Hyderabad (A.P.)

Dr. P. Murali Krishna
Associate Professor,
SKIM, SK University
Anantapur (A.P.)

Dr. K. Ramakrishna Reddy
Professor
Management & Member
Executive Council
SK University
Anantapur (A.P.)

Dr. K. Lal Kishore
Director
Academic & Planning
JNTU
Hyderabad (A.P.)

DISCOVERY PUBLISHING HOUSE
NEW DELHI-110002

First Published - 2005

Reprinted - 2017

ISBN: 978-81-8356-033-7

© Author

Human Resource Planning

Published by:

DISCOVERY PUBLISHING HOUSE PVT. LTD.

4383/4B, Ansari Road, Darya Ganj

New Delhi-110 002 (India)

Phone: +91-11-23279245, 43596064-65

Fax: +91-11-23253475

E-mail: discoverypublishinghouse@gmail.com

sales@discoverypublishinggroup.com

web: www.discoverypublishinggroup.com

Printed at:

Infinity Imaging Systems

Delhi

Dedicated to

All the Participants
Resource Persons
And
The Staff

Preface

The globalisation initiatives and process there of, had brought several visible changes in our Economy, Culture and Practice. Of all the changes, one factor that continuously and radically rededicating itself is Human Resources in India. It is not exaggeration to assert that the organisations are facing turbulent times in planning their Human Resource requirements. The human being is increasingly becoming capable of absorbing the information and technology Tsunami all over the world. This enhanced profile and competence of human resource leads to higher challenges and priorities for the organisations.

We have been hearing stories from the corporate world that many companies have initially downsized that human strength and subsequently have increased the number, of course with different patterns and practice of management. We followed large sizing, down sizing and today smart sizing. Hence, what should be actual size of human resource that will help organisations? It is a debatable question even today. In the same way one more aspect of human resource that drives organisations, researchers and thinkers to evolve new dimensions, models, techniques and tools that come in handy to organisations in estimating their human resource requirements. Towards this objective in importance we have made an attempt to gather views from human resource professional all over the country. This book "Globalisation and Human Resource Planning", is a result of a seminar jointly organised by the NTMIS, Delhi and JNTU, Hyderabad.

The views expressed by the contributors in the book and their own on different issues and aspects of manpower. There are about 33 articles written by contributors from across the nation. The variety in articles has been concentrated upon in choosing the articles. There are case studies, practical experiments, specific incidents, and committee assignments in the area of human resource planning.

We express on sincere thanks to Prof. H. Ramachandran, Director, IAMR, Delhi for Choosing AP Nodal Centre at JNTU for organising the seminar we are sincerely thankful to Prof. Y. Venkatrami Reddy, VC, JNTU for his constant support and encouragement Er. Anil Kumar, Chief, NIMIS, IAMR has been a source of support and motivation to us in conducting the seminar. We thank him for the same. We are extremely thankful to Mr. Tilak Wasan of Discovery Publishing House, New Delhi for publishing this book within a reasonable time. Our thanks are also due to all participants, resource persons authors and the staff that made this publication possible.

M. Sudhir Reddy

P. Murali Krishna

K. Ramakrishna Reddy

K. Lal Kishore

Contents

1

Technical Manpower Planning in the Knowledge Era

The Challenges and Solutions

*C.D.Balaji**

ABSTRACT

Technical manpower planning in the networked economy of today hinges on developing a resource base of skilled and knowledgeable manpower of high caliber. But there are several key challenges such as lack of educational access to a substantial proportion of the population, doubtful quality of technical education due to inadequate infrastructure, staff shortages and unprecedented proliferation of technical institutions. Government's share in R & D expenditure is still around 75 per cent, unlike the developed countries where the corporate world accounts for a major portion of R & D investment. There has been an alarming drop in the quantity of scientific research in the country. Due to lack of interest and awareness of patenting the researchers do not enjoy the monetary benefits arising out of their research whereas the West is extremely patent savvy.

* **Panimalar Institute of Management Studies and Computer Science, 20, Railway Colony Second Street, Nelson Manickam Road, Chennai- 29, Email: cdbalaji2004@rediffmail.com**

Key Words: Education, Higher education, Illiteracy, Lack of industry-institute interaction, Patents, R & D, Technical education.

INTRODUCTION

Technical manpower planning in the networked economy of today hinges on developing a resource base of skilled and knowledgeable manpower of high caliber. India has the unique opportunity to gain from the global requirement of talent by leveraging its human resources. It has a once in a life time opportunity to usher in a talent driven economic revolution. The country should make up for missing the industrial revolution. India has every opportunity to emerge as a significant economic power by developing its professional resources, have proved that they are second to none in the global arena.

But in developing such a resource base there are several key challenges such as:

Illiteracy

Lack of educational access to a substantial proportion of the population remains a key challenge. According to National Sample Survey Organization overall literacy rate in the country is only 62 per cent. The expenditure on elementary education has declined from 55 per cent of the total for the sector in the 1950's to less than 35 per cent in the 1990's. As a result over 40 per cent of India's population is illiterate. An average Indian spends just about two years in school, while a Chinese spends five and a South Korean Nine. 59 per cent of the students never complete 5th standard, secondary enrolment is 58 per cent, but of those that enroll, 54 per cent never complete 8th standard. Only a small proportion of youth receive vocational training and less than 1 per cent of the population is computer literate.

The problem is further compounded by the fact that in many schools function with just a couple of teachers. A World Bank Study published startling findings regarding the high absenteeism rate of primary school teachers which in effect means that very little of teaching takes place in many primary schools.

Table—1.1 Proportion of vocationally trained among youth by labour force–Intl. Comparison

Country	Age group	Vocationally Trained (% of those in Labor Force)
India developing	20-24	5.06
Botswana	20-24	22.42
Colombia	20-29	28.06
Mauritius	20-24	36.08
Mexico	20-24	27.58

Source: Ministry of HRD.

Table—1.2 Absentee rates from primary schools 2003 (%)

State	Absenteeism Rates
Andhra Pradesh	31
Assam	31
Bihar	26
UP	26
Uttaranchal	25
Karnataka	23
Gujarat	21
West Bengal	21
Haryana	19
Kerala	18
Punjab	18
Tamil Nadu	17

Source: World Bank.

In 1966, the report of the Education Commission (1964-66) stipulated that 6 per cent of GNP should be allocated for education; this was reiterated by the Majumdar Committee in '99 in the context of making education a fundamental right. In 1993, the ruling of a five member bench of the Supreme Court declared that education must be adequately provided for "irrespective of the economic capacity of the State". From being just another development goal, UEE was elevated to the status of an undeniable right that the

State has to provide for. The Union Cabinet set up a group of experts to estimate the financial requirement for UEE for the 6–14 age groups.

In absolute terms the figure quoted in the 1999 Tapas Mazumdar Committee Report is gigantic: Rs. 1,36,822 crores to be spent over a period of 10 years, in addition to what India is currently spending on education, for the age group of 6–14 years. Expressed as a percentage of GDP, this equates to spending only an average yearly additional 0.7 per cent of the GDP over and above the current expenditure on education.

Inspite of the realistic and practical suggestions of the above said report, the educational expenditure of the government edged up only marginally from 3.84 per cent of GNP in 1990-91 to 4.3 per cent in 2000-01.Of this meager public expenditure, a little less than one-third or 1.5 per cent of GNP is spent on primary education. This is the prime reason for the non-attainment of the goal of universal primary education by 1990, as visualized in the New Educational Policy of 1986. Policy makers would do well to remember the words of Adam Smith while planning allocations for the education sector. He said in his Wealth of Nations (1776), "The expenses of the institution for education (are) no doubt beneficial to the whole society and may, therefore, without injustice be defrayed by the contribution of the whole society".

It is not only on the low spending volume that has led to inefficiencies in the education sector but also on the parameter of productivity the country's record is far from satisfactory. India spends around 4 per cent of GDP on education and achieved only 52 per cent literacy. China spent only 2.5 per cent of GDP but has achieved more than 90 per cent literacy. Indonesia spends a tiny 1.4 per cent of GDP on education, but focuses this on efficient delivery of primary education and so has achieved 90 per cent literacy for males and over 80 per cent for females.

Higher Education

The higher education sector has witnessed a 13-fold increase in the number of universities, 25-fold increase in the number of colleges and 30-fold increase in the enrolment of students since independence.

Table—1.3 Decadal growth in number of universities and colleges

Year	Universities/University Level Institutions	Colleges
1950-51	32	695
1960-61	56	1542
1970-71	102	3604
1980-81	133	4722
1990-91	190	7346
2000-01	256	12342

Table—1.4 All India growth of students enrolment since (1950-51)

Year	Total Enrolment	% Increase Over Preceding Year
1950-51	1,73,696	–
1960-61	5,56,559	15.6
1970-71	19,53,700	9.0
1980-81	27,52,437	3.9
1990-91	49,24,868	7.0
2000-01	83,99,443	4.3

Source: Ministry of Human Resource Development.

By the last count—on November 25, 2002—the Indian higher education system was catering to the needs of 88,21,095 students being taught by 4,26,817 teachers in around 13,150 colleges and 294 universities all over the country. But despite this multifold growth, the access to and quality of higher education remains limited. The 10 per cent access parameter that they have set for this plan period is way below the access parameters of the developed world, with the US boasting a high 59 per cent, Canada 54 per cent, the UK 22 per cent and Israel 30 per cent.

Technical Education

In consonance with the growing demand for technical education during the late 1980's and 1990's the number of institutions offering technical education has expanded at a pace not witnessed in the last 50 years. The government unable to finance the increased demand, allowed private investments in the self financing mode. The number of new engineering colleges increased from 838 in 2001 to 1265 in 2003. Annual engineering seats which were around 1.25 lakhs in 2001 expanded to over 3.25 lakhs in 2003.

Many of these institutions lack basic facilities like classrooms and labs. This has led to the poor performance of the students in the University exams. The performance of the students from the various engineering colleges in Tamilnadu illustrates this phenomenon:

Table—1.5 Pass percentage of students in Tamil Nadu engineering colleges (2003-04)

Pass % Range	No. of Colleges	No. Appeared	No. Passed	Average %
80-100	0	–	–	–
70-80	5	6,669	4,983	74.7
60-70	21	24,826	15,872	63.9
50-60	22	21,861	11,866	54.3
40-50	31	24,457	11,168	45.7
30-40	66	42,502	15,087	35.5
20-30	52	26,680	6,926	26.0
10-20	27	10,364	1,629	15.7
0-10	5	1,343	132	9.8
Total	**229**	**1,58,702**	**67,663**	**42.6**

While on the one hand the performance of the students is poor, many students passing out these institutions lack knowledge of current technologies and emerging trends in the industry and are unemployable. The unprecedented proliferation of institutions has led to shortage of qualified teaching faculty. Even in IIT Delhi against a sanctioned strength of 690 staff members currently there are only 455 staff members. In many self-financing institutions a lot of unseats remain unfilled. In Tamil Nadu for the year 2002 nearly 21,000 seats remained unfilled in various engineering and many of them face survival problems. This phenomenon repeats itself with unfailing regularity in many institutions offering technical education.

LOW HUMAN DEVELOPMENT

The UNDP commission HDR 2004 which focuses on three measurable dimensions of human development; living a long and healthy life, being education and having a decent standard of living assigned India among the medium human development putting it in the 127th slot, a notch higher than Botswana but lower than Namibia.

Table—1.6 Medium human development

HRI Rank	2002	2001
Russia	57	63
Mauritius	64	62
Thailand	76	74
Maldives	84	86
China	94	104
Sri lanka	96	99
Iran	101	106
South Africa	119	111
India	127	127
Bangladesh	138	139

LOW INVESTMENT IN R & D

It is now a well recognized fact that investment in R&D is the sine-qua-non for innovation and growth. But in our country the government's share in R&D expenditure is still around 75 per cent of the total R & D spend whereas in the developed countries, the corporate sector accounts for a major portion of R&D investment. An important indicator reflecting the status of R&D in any country is the per capita R & D investment (or R&D to GDP ratio). Against a global annual expenditure on R&D of $500 0- 600 billion, India spends a mere $2.5 billion which is slightly above what Merck a US based pharma firm, spent($2.1 billion) in 1999. The annual R & D spend of the US is $265 $85 billion.

Poor Track Record of the Corporate Sector

Indian Co., track record in R & D investment is quite poor. According to a study conducted by the Hyderabad based Administrative Staff College of India(ASCI) on R & D in India – 86 per cent of the country's joint stock co., out of the total 8,334 reported zero spend on R& D in their annual reports for the year 2001-02. Of the 8,334 firms only 644 have shown active involvement in R & D while the rest of the industries totalling 7,690 have not reported that they are carrying out any R & D activity. During the 1990's only chemicals & pharma co., and the IT sector increased their R & D spend as a ratio of output.

Table—1.7 Expenditure on R & D as a percentage of total output

Industry	1990–91	1999–2000
Chemicals & Pharma	0.33	0.39
IT	–	3.5
Electricity gen. & distn.	0.53	0.01
Tea, Sugar, Jute	0.09	0.04
Cotton Textiles & Rayon	0.05	0.08
Engg, Motor Vehicles & Transport	0.38	0.31

Source: RBI

Lack of Industry–Institute Interaction: Barring a few exceptions like the IITs most of the research in Indian universities has no link with the needs of the industry. The most important reasons for this state of affairs are:

Lack of any industrial experience, choice of research topics mainly based on the interest of the supervisor, Publication oriented research with an eye on promotion and monetary incentives, outdated research labs and equipment, Lack of skills to market their products.

Table—1.8 Factors hindering synergies between university and industrial research

	University/Academic Style	Industry Style
Nature of Organization	Non-profit	Profit oriented
Research Type	Open activity, valuation through publications	Closed type, valuation through patents or revenue through restriction on communication and publication.
Research Aim	Expansion of knowledge	Exploitation of knowledge in product/process form.
Speed of Research	No emphasis on urgency	Short term goals with high pressure on time.
Nature of Research	Undirected and Fundamental	Directed/strategic and applied/ad-hoc
Research Activity	Mainly part-time	Full time

Source: Adapted from Zaky and El-Faham (1998)

The outcome of all these is that there is a complete mismatch between industry's needs and academic research. Many a times the industry is unaware of the research being carried out in the academic institutions. History is replete with instances where academic through constant interaction with industry played a prominent role in fostering its growth and competitiveness. Silicon Valley is one such example where the Stanford University and the University of California, Berkeley not only created an industry but also played an active role in its growth. It is therefore imperative that there is a proper interface between the academia and the industry. Developed countries like the US, the UK and France understood the dynamics of this gap and created institutions/agencies leading to an effective interface. CNRS in France, SERC (Scientific and Engineering Research Council) in the U.K and federal agencies in the U.S such as NASA have acted in the past and continue to act as an effective interface between industry and academia.

Fostering Closer Industry-Institute Interaction

The following initiatives from industry will go a long way to reduce the gap between it and the academia:

(a) Specifying what kind of skills and human resources it would require in the future;

(b) Providing support for student projects;

(c) Sponsoring long term research;

(d) Holding periodic seminars in colleges and encouraging industrial visits;

(e) Sharing equipments and facilities with the academic world.

The following initiatives from the academic side would also help to bridge the gap between academic research and industry requirements:

- The academic world should have regular interaction and close contact with the industry to understand industry's requirements;
- Understanding the fact that engineering skills alone are not sufficient but students passing out should be effective communicators and should understand the linkages between science and commerce;
- Inviting industry to participate in periodic review of syllabi and course content to suit industry requirements.

Industry-Academia Tie-ups

Some instances of these are:

(a) Synopsis India, an electronic design automation firm has tied up premier engineering colleges and the co., provides software tools to labs at these colleges;

(b) Sun Microsystems works with several IIT's and REC's to impart Sun Technologies for their academic and research purposes;

(c) Wipro has tied up with Birla Inst. of Technology, Pilani, for its Wipro Academy of Software Excellence Course;

(d) IBM has tied up with IIT,Roorkee; IIM,Delhi and Lucknow and the Visvesvaraya Technical University, Karnataka for this purpose.

INDIAN RESEARCH—LOSING IT'S SCIENTIFIC TEMPER

There has been an alarming drop in the quantity of scientific research in the country. In terms of research output, India fell from 8th place in 1980 to 13th in 1995 and is at present ranked 15th. In the last 20 years the number of scientific papers produced in India has gone down from 15,000 to 12,000; contrast this to China's performance in the same period which has gone up from 1000 to 22,000.

Table—1.9 Number of scientific papers published

Country	1980	2000
India	14,983	12,217
China	924	22,061
South Korea	175	12,013
Brazil	2,215	9,565
Israel	5,733	9,292

Source: Science Citation Index, Institute for Scientific Information, Philadelphia

Efforts are being made to rectify the situation. The idea is to promote greater involvement of scientists in academic programmes. To begin with the partnership would be between CSIR labs and 40 academic institutes including the IIT's for sharing of research facilities for maximum efficient use.

LACK OF A PATENTING CULTURE

"Arth Karicheye Vidya"–create wealth from knowledge asserted Chanakya, King Chandragupta's pragmatic advisor ages ago. In this age of patents it is surprising to find that the Indian psyche is still not very comfortable to create wealth from knowledge. Consider the following facts:

1. Prof. C.N.R.Rao, former director of the Indian Institute of Science (IISc) published more than 1000 research papers without filing a single patent;

2. The CSIR with 5,400 scientists working with annual funding of $225 million, has been granted patent applications by the US Patent and Trademark Office (USPTO) during 1991-2000. In contrast the IBM research division with 2700 scientists filed over 900 patent applications;
3. Inspite of having hundreds of professors and students the seven IIT's, the All India Institute of Medical Sciences (AIIMS) and the IISC have filed only 84 patents with the USPTO during 1991-2000;
4. India lags the US, Japan and Germany in terms of converting government expenditure on R&D into valuable patents.

WEST—PATENT SAVVY

The West is extremely patent savvy as can be judged from the following instances:

(a) Guglielmo Marconi filed the world's first patent in 1896, for a system of telegraphy using Hertzian waves, and founded the world's first wireless telegraphy using Hertzian waves, and founded the world's first Wireless Telegraph and Signal Co., in 1897.

(b) Alexander Graham Bell patented the telephony system in 1876. In 1877, two businessmen financed him to create Bell Telephone co., that later became AT & T;

(c) Thomas Alva Edison sold his first invention–an unpatented stock quotation printer – for $40,000(Rs.18.4 lakh). He utilized this to start a lab in 1876 that lead to 1093 patented inventions, one of which helped the installation of the world's first large central-electric power station (in New York) by the Edison General Electric Co., today's GE."The introduction of patent laws" said Lincoln "was one of the three most developments in the history of the world" and " the patent system adds the Fuel of Interest to the Fire of Genius"

Due to lack of awareness and interest in patenting the researchers are not able to enjoy the monetary benefits arising out of their research which is one of the prime reasons for the alarming drop in the percentage of science students from 32 per cent in 1950 to 15 per cent now. Against an average 149 research scientists and engineers in India for every million population, the three largest spenders on S&T–US, Japan and Germany have, on an average 3,805 research scientists and engineers.

According to a survey done by the Patent Facility Centre(PFC) of the Technology Information Forecasting and Assessment Council(TIFAC) global corporations accounted for nearly 85 per cent or 2320 out of the total 2711 applications filed by corporates and individual innovators with the Indian Patent Offices during the three year period of study by the PFC. For India, the only encouraging feature was the trend of increasing number of patent applications being filed by both co., and innovators during 1999-2001 against around 100 in the previous four years. MNC development centers in India filed for 763 patents by March 2003, whereas Indian IT services firms filed for only 82.

CONCLUSION

The 4th century philosopher and historian Seneca said "If you do not know to which port you are sailing, no wind is favourable". This in essence sums up our problems here in India; we have not set our objectives clearly. Let us begin to ask the right questions to arrive at the destination at which we would like to be. India has the ability to build technology and knowledge competencies. About two-thirds of incremental global GDP is expected to come from technology domains and the country has the opportunity to leverage technology for economic progress and development. From deriving benefits from innovation we should be the drivers of innovation to achieve sustained economic progress.

2

Development of Engineering Entrepreneurs in India

*V. Veeraswamy**

ABSTRACT

Engineering is a learning profession rather than a learned profession. Engineering education has to respond to the needs and aspirations of the society, in discharging its duties of training technical manpower. In any country, engincers are supposed to play a vital role in industrialization. The 21st century will bring with it new challenges to the field of production technology, quality control, management and above all employment. The share of Indian goods in the world market is practically negligible as compared to many South-East Asian Countries despite the fact that India has today the third largest technical work force in the world. In India, engineering education lacks creativity and training to meet future challenges. It is therefore, necessary to introduce entrepreneurship development as an integral part of engineering education to transform engineers from "Job seekers to job creators" by establishing their own industries in the near future. In this paper, the author focused on developing a large number of young engineering entrepreneurs for accelerated industrial development in India.

* **Electrical and Electronics Engineering Section, ESC Government Polytechnic, Department of Technical Education, Government of Andhra Pradesh, Nandyal – 518 501, E-mail: vemulaveeraswamy@rediffmail.com**

Key Words: Engineering Education, Entrepreneurship, Industrialization, Technical Manpower.

INTRODUCTION

Engineering is a learning profession rather than a learned profession. Engineering education has to respond rapidly and properly to the needs and aspirations of the society in discharging its duties of training technical manpower. The technical manpower has to support the industrial revolutions and for this we have to equip ourselves with capabilities and calibre commensurate with the world standards.

In India, the response of the engineering education system to the demands of the over growing industry and needs of the society has been extremely slow. It is necessary to reframe our engineering education system to relook and redefine our goals and priorities relevant to our requirements. Engineering education should produce competent engineers to inspire self-confidence and creativity for building an infrastructure. The technologies should be chosen that are relevant to our needs for development and prosperity of the entire country[1].

Today's world is becoming more and more global. At the same time, modern societies are also becoming more and more science-intensive. The technological change in the coming decade is going to be driven by the highly sophisticated scientific areas like Energy, Space, Materials Science, Information Technology, Robotics and Artificial Intelligence, Bio-Technology and Environmental Imperatives. The links and Interactions between countries and regions are developing rapidly and the need to integrate different kinds of expertise is a must for successful implementing any project, be it a development project, a public action or a private business. This is especially true of "emerging" countries like India. In India the engineering education is not comprehensive. The engineering education must have direct relevance to industry and society as a whole. This lack of meaningful rapport between technical institutions and industries is a matter of grave concern. Engineers as a vehicle of industrial growth, which can compete in the world market, are a distant dream. The infrastructural facilities are far from satisfactory in many cases and facilities available are highly under utilised[2].

Entrepreneurship development activity is perhaps the most critical factor in the industrial and economic growth of any country. Entrepreneurs play a catalytical role in utilizing the resources in an optimal manner. Therefore, one of the important prerequisites for a healthy industrial and economic growth is the availability of effective and efficient entrepreneurs. A successful entrepreneur should follow the motto of "Think Globally Act Locally"[3].

NEED FOR ENGINEERING ENTREPRENEURS

Post-independence era experienced industrial revolution leading in involvement of government in establishing public sector units in the area of heavy industries. The total emphasis in the country has been revolving round the concept that the "entrepreneurs cannot be made, but are born". Eventhough there were several private sector industries that came into being, their activities were handling business and it was only a shift from the business activity to industrial activity. As the market shifted from sellers market to buyers market because of higher level of industrial activity, the need for planned approach increased. Further, the concept evolved by behavioural scientists that entrepreneurs can be prepared by structured approach led to several organizations taking up entrepreneurship development activities.

With the advent of ISO 9000, a quality system standard, every industry has to come under the umbrella of this standard if it wants to compete in the international market. Those corporations which are trying to come under ISO 9000 will also look up to vendors who are in tune with their thought process in-terms of total quality management conforming ISO 9000. This calls for developing entrepreneurs who have engineering/technology background, who can understand the various strategies of quality management. There will be a great need in future of engineering/technology entrepreneurs who can not only manage the enterprise, but also provide product conforming to the requirement of the concern.

Further, the concept of major organization to produce every thing in-house is shifting towards developing more vendors and keeping main activity of assembly and quality assurance to themselves. This is where the need for engineering/technology entrepreneurs will be on the increase[4].

The globalization of the market place with the liberalized industrial policy has created an impetus to the development of more and more entrepreneurs with engineering/technology background, to face the challenges specially to meet the quality standards in the international market. The development of engineering/technology entrepreneurs as to be looked in the perspective of not only managing the manufacturing activities, but also, in terms of delivering the products fulfilling the user requirements.

DEVELOPMENT OF ENGINEERING ENTREPRENEURS

Entrepreneurship in a broader sense can be described as a creative and innovative response to the environment. Entrepreneur is an innovator who introduces something new into the economy, a new method of production which has not yet been tested in manufacturing, a product with which the consumers are not familiar or of new market hither-to-unexploited and other similar innovations.

Now the time has come when engineers should leave fancy for white-collared Government Jobs. Considering the present socio-economic factors, Government Jobs are bound to reduce. With employment opportunities in other Asian and African Countries reducing every year, one will have to make his/her place in one's own country. With liberal economic policy of Central Government, our export horizon has widened. Thus, there is unprecedented scope for export provided that quality and cost are maintained. The industrialist with engineering technology background and knowledge in entrepreneurship development has better chances of exporting his/her goods as compared to the one without technical background. The theory of "survival of fittest" stands valid even today and would continue in future also[5].

It is interesting to note that the findings of Dr. E. Paul Torrance, an authority on creativity. He studied 15,000 students from Nursery to Sixth Class and found that most children start life with a "valuable creative potential but have it knocked out of them by the time they reach the Fourth Class". The condition is still worse in India. Education in India is so academically oriented that it leaves little room for creativity. Creativity and entrepreneurship are inter-linked. Thus, the school education reduces the entrepreneurial traits in students. It is, therefore, important to change school education to have more stress on creativity and aesthetics. Till such time, entrepreneurship development should find an important place in engineering education. Such education should have cognitive outcomes, equipping the students with skill of logical thinking, critical analysis, decision making and above all an integrated view of knowledge needs that have not been fulfilled by the traditional education system.

One of the main aims of technical education after independence was to produce a select band of young engineers who would establish their own industries. They are supposed to be "Job creators rather than Job Seekers". It was expected that these engineers or technocrats to transform India into an industrialized country, which can compete in the world market. Unfortunately, the share of India in international market is abysmally low. The tiny islands like Taiwan, Hong Kong and Singapore are individually having more export than India. The main reason is that Indian goods are costlier and having poor quality. This trend can be reversed if a large number of engineers or technocrats are inspired to go for entrepreneurship[6].

The entrepreneurship development should be made as an integral part of curriculum of technical education for all branches of engineering. Entrepreneurship has a very vast scope and technical knowledge imparted during engineering education may constitute only 20 per cent. It includes the management of men, material and money. The Financial and Personnel Management, is perhaps, the most difficult for engineers. This is one of the main reasons, why many engineers are not successful entrepreneurs. This handicap can be removed by exposing the engineering student to the course of entrepreneurship development. It is recommended that this exposure should be done at the initial level. The whole idea is to "catch them young". The seed sown at the initial stage would grow to the full tree by the time the student completes his/her studies. The old myth that entrepreneurs are born, does not hold good now. The entrepreneurs can be developed by proper training and guidance. Hence, the role of technical institutions in this field can not be over-emphasized.

CONCLUSION

It is found that entrepreneurs without engineering technology background do not respond spontaneously to available business opportunities despite various incentives and inducements. Now the time has come to introduce entrepreneurship development as an integral part of engineering education for developing a large number of engineering entrepreneurs who would set up their own industries in the areas to which they belong, thereby converting the surplus engineering manpower into an employment creating force. This would go a long way in solving, to some extent the problem of unemployment and would provide a much needed boost in hi-tech industries in the near future.

REFERENCES

1. V. Veeraswamy, *How to Instill Quality in Technical Education – A Practical Approach*, AICTE, New Delhi, 1999.
2. V. Veeraswamy, *Engineering Education in India: Perspectives and Prospects*, IEEE, ACE'93, Hyderabad, 1993.
3. Devinder K. Banwet and Vinay Kumar, *Technology Transfer – Select Issues for Technical Entrepreneurship*, NATWOTE-92, IIT Delhi, 1992.
4. Abid Hussain, *Industrial Policy and Technological Innovation*, Mail Stream, Nov. 28, 1987.
5. L.N. Sapru, *Building up Technologists as Entrepreneurs, Productivity*, Vol. XII, No.1, April–June 1971.
6. B.S. Rathore, *Entrepreneurial Development*, Entrepreneurship Development Training Material, TTTI, Chandigarh, 1988.

3

Developing R & D Manpower Through Training

A Case Study

*Sunil K Dhawan**

*Santanu Roy***

INTRODUCTION

Organizations engaged in Research and Development (R&D) activities have several distinct characteristics that make them different from business and service organizations. First, the work environment involves a high degree of uncertainty surrounding the projects. The uncertainties could be a result of pushing the state of art or could be because of changes in the project's direct cost and priorities. Secondly, the management of R & D and expenses involved in it, have a substantial amount of "risk" element. The gains from successful R & D projects can be substantial or may result in financial loss[1]. Thirdly, there is a certain amount of, what one can say, "sheer faith" in ideas and initiatives of scientists involved. Fourthly, managing R&D calls for a great

* National Institute of Science, Technology & Development Studies, PUSA, K S Krishnan Marg, New Delhi-110 012, Email: sunilkdhawan@yahoo.com

** National Institute of Science, Technology & Development Studies, PUSA, K S Krishnan Marg, New Delhi-110 012, Email: rsan58@yahoo.co.uk

amount of tolerance of "creative individualism" which is not always possible to control or check by using any of the modern principles of management[2]. Finally, it is not always possible to work out the productive benefits or impact of R&D on the society in simple economic language.

Despite its unique nature, the concepts of modern management are as applicable to R &D institutions as to any other organization. The managerial terms such as goal setting, planning, organizing, coordinating, controlling and so on are relevant and used in R & D institutions. Thomas listed four reasons that make it important to use management tools in R&D institutions[2]:

- Whether it is a country or an individual business, its long-term ability to keep pace with others and, more so, to overtake others will depend on its innovative skill, and the single largest source of innovation is R&D. Therefore, managing R&D resources is as crucial to success as managing finances or human beings.
- In the modern world, R&D is more of a team effort than the effort of brilliant individuals. Where people work together, the need for, and the benefits of, applying principles of management become more real.
- R&D is becoming more sophisticated and therefore more expensive as years go by. This again makes it important to subject it to the principles of management; otherwise it can become a serious liability.
- As the main resource in R&D is people, the result of an unmanaged group effort can be aimless and demoralization. Demoralized and non-achieving R&D manpower is worse than having no R&D because the former has a debilitating influence on the whole organization. Management of R&D is necessary to avoid this danger.

Once it is agreed that principles of management are relevant for R&D institutions, the next step is how to bring these principles into actual practice in the organization. The most important resource in R&D is the scientist himself. Therefore, a very important part of the management of R&D is understanding management of scientific manpower and developing them in managing their work more effectively through utilization of management techniques. One way of doing this is to organize specific training programmes for this scientific manpower. Social scientists can help them in team building, organizational diagnosis, and by carrying out specific research projects and sharing the results in the training programmes.

One should mention here that little attempts have been made in this direction and even literature does not provide sufficient insight into the conceptual framework that one should adopt in training programmes. Side by side, whatever little efforts have been made by some R&D institutions, it is not possible to evaluate whether such attempts have resulted in any meaningful change or effectiveness in scientists' work. The increase in the productivity of scientists depends, in addition to the management training, on factors such as policy guidelines at national and organizational level, work climate and interaction with users of research.

The present paper is an attempt to examine the type of training programmes carried out in an R&D organization and highlights issues emerging out of this effort. The R&D organization under study is the Council of Scientific and Industrial Research (CSIR). The paper is divided into three parts: Part-I provides detail of the development of training programmes in CSIR. Part-II highlights the problems and issues of training. The last part provides an alternative approach of looking at Management of R&D system and alterations in the training programmes that are necessary for creating an effective management training system.

Before we pass on to the main theme of the paper it will be appropriate to give some background of the R&D organization CSIR.

CSIR was set-up in 1942 as a registered society under the Registration of Societies Act of India (Act No. XXI of 1860). The main functions assigned to it were promotion, guidance and coordination of scientific and industrial research in India. It started with a few laboratories of its own and slowly built up the infrastructure necessary for any R&D organization. Side by side, through review committees, it tried to modify its work system more towards the goals and objectives laid down in the charter and as suggested by the Government of India.

CSIR administers 39 national laboratories/institutes. The laboratories and institutes are divided into five groups: Physical sciences, Biochemical sciences, Engineering sciences, Biological sciences and Information sciences.

TRAINING PROGRAMMES

The need for having a separate training wing in CSIR was felt as early as in 1971. This was the period when a high-powered committee emphasized the need of creating a "collegiate culture" among scientific manpower and recommended a number of steps for reorganization of the structure of CSIR. It was considered desirable at the top-level that in order to implement the recommendations of the committee, regular training programmes should be conducted for the scientists and other staff for their continuing education in modern management techniques.

A training unit Centre for Management Development (CMD) was established at the headquarters of CSIR in 1975. The main objectives assigned to it were:

- To impart knowledge and techniques in the modern concept of management to different levels of staff in CSIR laboratories;
- To develop scientific and modern systems for R&D efforts in general, and its various supporting functions in particular;
- To study, in a continuous process, the systems of R&D so as to reshape the future training programmes;
- To provide consultancy services to laboratories and others in the field of organizational and management development.

Since then, training has become a regular feature in CSIR. Training is given in four areas: R&D Project Management, Materials Management, Financial Management and Administrative Management.

CONCEPTUAL APPROACH AND PROGRAMME DESIGN

The conceptual approach to the training programmes is two-fold. First, understanding the existing system of management of R&D, its linkages with internal and external environment and the constraints which the existing system is putting on to the effective carrying out of projects. Secondly, once the gaps in the system are determined, developing alternative ways of doing the work through participative style in the training programmes.

One should mention here that R&D organizations and in particular, the scientific manpower have a different set of values, norms and climate under which they work compared to other business organizations. They take/use inputs from the environment for a purpose, which often is in an inchoate form, and develop some output suitable or otherwise for the environment. The inchoate form of goals of projects often clashes with the modern management theory, where the emphasis is on systematic planning and organizing. Even for examining the existing practices, the trainer has to be cautious about this fact, and develop a programme design accordingly. The programmes are mainly consists of three parts: raising "awareness", "learning" from others' experiences, and developing "skill".

Let us take-up the programme on R&D Project Management as an example. Under "awareness", the topics include group dynamics, motivation, conflict management, leadership style, etc. Under "skill" development are items like Cost-Benefit analysis, Network analysis, Costing and Budgeting, Monitoring and Evaluation. Under "learning", faculty from outside CSIR share their experience on Organizational Development activities and use of Management By Objectives.

OBJECTIVES OF THE PROGRAMMES

The broad objectives of the programmes organized by CMD are basically in line with its own objectives i.e. imparting attitudinal changes among participants towards acquiring R&D culture, role clarity and the responsibilities of scientists in lieu with organizational goals/rules, organizational diagnosis techniques so as to make participants understand their work system; various sub-systems and the interlinkages, and making them aware of modern techniques of management.

In line with these broad objectives, specific objectives are framed for each programme. Details of objectives for the four areas—administrative management, materials management, project management, and management of R&D are given below:

Administrative Management Programme

- To clarify the role and functions of administration as service agency in R&D
- To guide the participants in identifying their functional objectives with the overall objectives of R&D
- To equip the participants with knowledge and applicability of modern concepts in management science so as to enable them to realize their functional objectives
- To provide the necessary background of policies, procedures and rules concerning various matters such as service conditions

Programme on Materials Management

- To highlight the importance of materials management in R&D and identify its place in overall R&D Management
- To clarify the role and functions of purchase and store officers
- To expose the participants to modern concepts and techniques of inventory management
- To provide the necessary background of policies, rules and procedures

Programme on Project Management

- To highlight the need and method of correlating the R&D efforts with national socio-economic goals
- To develop professional attitude and skill in the application of the tools of planning and management of R&D

- To evolve a common attitude and understanding among the laboratory sub-systems for an efficient implementation of R&D programmes

Programme on Management of R&D

- To provide a framework of knowledge about the concepts of management and the relevance of 'the management approach' to the problems of the R&D laboratories
- To familiarize the scientists with some important techniques of management which are relevant for project coordinators and heads of research departments

METHODOLOGY

Each training programme conducted by CMD involves a number of steps. First, the participating laboratories are chosen for the preparation of case studies. Take for instance a recent programme on Performance Budgeting. Before the programmes, its members were busy in preparing case studies on the subject from the concerned laboratories. To create a high-level of participation, one of the participants from each laboratory had been given the responsibility of preparing the case and presenting it to the audience during the programme.

Secondly, whatever work CSIR has done on the subject plus some other literature is distributed to the participants in advance as background material. In the training programmes, sessions are held using the lecture discussion method, small group discussions, and exercise playing. Finally, the outcomes of each programme are shared with the top management of CSIR and a list of recommendations is also given to them. For instance, a common suggestion from the participants is the rigidity in following rules and regulations that they perceived are relevant for government departments and not for CSIR. As an outcome of this suggestion, CMD has been asked to prepare manuals on four areas: R&D Management, Financial Management, Administrative Manual, and Materials Management.

CONSTRAINTS IN MANAGEMENT CHANGES

The main objective of training programmes in CSIR is to improve the management system. To achieve this, one must concentrate on problems and issues faced by the scientists so that training efforts should focus on minimizing the constraints in their work system. Through personal interviews and survey of some reports of the review committees and other literature on CSIR, we have prepared a list of issues faced by the scientists.

Specific Problems of Scientists

- Scientists find themselves confused and ineffective because the goals and objectives of the organization are not clearly defined.
- In some cases the organizations have been growing so fast that their structure remains continuously fluid and the scientists are not able to find their position and their role in these institutions.
- Scientists usually have great difficulty in obtaining inter-divisional cooperation as well as cooperation from administration and service departments.
- Scientists are not fully aware of the industrial applicability of the R&D work in their group, because market survey data are not available.
- They do not know the priorities of the various projects in their group or of other projects in the research institute.
- Scientists are not able to ensure the effective working of research projects because comprehensive project plans are usually not prepared.
- They are not able to perform their function as reviewer of projects and in deciding about their continuance/discontinuance because project management practices are not yet widely prevalent.
- Scientists have almost no process at their disposal to motivate the scientific workers in their group.

- They find it almost impossible to generate team spirit among the people.
- Inter-personal and inter-department conflicts are frequent and they seem to be beyond the control of the research managers.
- Scientists think that purchase and store procedures as well as the administrative procedures in the laboratories are a great hindrance to effective conduct of research.

Ideas Associated with Colleague/Other Scientists

- People don't take much interest in work/apathetic behaviour
- Some scientists have been given more facilities-funds, staff and space
- Lack of guidance from Senior Scientists
- Majority of scientists want to work on their own projects and show less commitment to research suggested by others i.e. more towards 'individualism' than institutional orientation
- When lower-level scientists are given a chance to participate in a high level committee they keep quiet if senior scientists are also present
- If top is heavy and people with similar grade are more, coordination becomes a problem unless the Head is very highly competent or aged (hierarchy feelings)

Issues Related to Management of Systems

- Bureaucratic procedures create delays
- Rigidity in following rules and regulations
- Organization of common services/instruments is arbitrary
- Lack of proper delegation of power with authority
- Communication gap
- Poor Budgeting

- Lack of Project Management Schemes
- No Project or proposal evaluation scheme
- No policy-making in laboratories
- Problems with Purchase and Stores department

Issues related to Work Environment

- Polluted atmosphere
- No proper space
- Lack of welfare activities
- Lack of incentives
- Poor transport arrangements to visit other places
- Lack of trust
- Harassment
- Mutual support and help is lacking

Organizational Related Issues

- Inadequacy of the budget allocation to the division
- Unsatisfactory appointments at senior levels
- Inadequate assessment, credits go to other party
- Irrational policy for foreign assignment & training

TRAINING ALTERNATIVES

In part-I and part-II, we have examined the type of training programmes being conducted at CSIR and highlighted issues emerging out of this effort. In this part, our focus is to develop an alternative style of training programmes in the context of R&D environment.

One important factor controlling the training needs in an R&D institution is the structure of that institution. Structure, in fact, determines the linkages among various sub-groups/sub-systems within the organization and as scientists themselves are the most important component, their internal and external linkages become vital for determining gaps, if any, in the training programmes and its design.

An alternative way of looking at the structure of R&D organization is presented in Figure—3.1. This is a modified version of Garg[3]. We have divided the structure into four parts: policy-makers, senior scientists as managers, scientists in the sub-committees, and scientists; the doer. These four groups can have some overlapping, i.e., members of sub-committees could be senior scientists also or senior scientists could be member of policy-making group. Further, the four groups are interconnected in a "Z" form as shown in the figure.

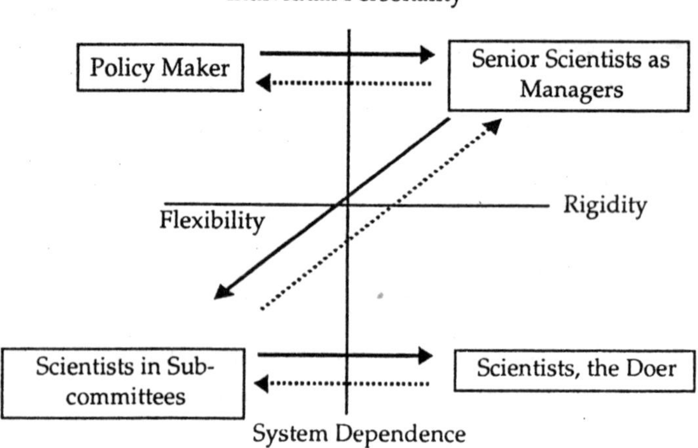

Fig. 3.1: Structure of R & D Organization

We are hypothesizing that the policy makers function within the boundaries of "flexibility" on the one side, and "individual personality" on the other side. If we look at the membership of the policy-making group, we will find that a majority of them are top-level executives/Heads of institutes/senior-most scientists. They bring with them, along with new knowledge, "personality component" and each tries to influence his area of specialization. Further, the working of policy-makers involves high level of flexibility as their main role is to develop/modify policy issues.

Coming to the senior scientists as managers, we are basically, referring to the Headquarters managers, members of executive bodies, etc. Again, we are assuming that this group enjoys some sort of "personality component" and this component sometimes imposes "rigidity" in their thinking/behaviour and in the system.

Scienusts in the sub-committees are normally appointed to create a sense of participation among them. They are given the responsibility of providing guidelines to the executives, in which flexibility comes, but side by side, they are bound with the rules and regulations and other systems of the organization. In reality this group gets caught in the double-mind. If they act within the structural constraints, they are labelled as lacking initiatives. If they act with initiative, they are viewed as stepping on somebody's toes.

Scientists, the doer, could be senior level scientists or junior level scientists. Our focus in this category is on junior level scientists. Our assumption is that senior scientists are members of one or the other committee. Our hypothesis for the junior level scientists is that they are subjected to the rigidity of senior scientists on the one side and system dependence on the other. They feel underutilized and burdened with routine type of work only.

There are several issues that emerge out of this structure. First, if there is a continuous change in the policy guidelines in terms of priorities to an area or even otherwise, the issue becomes to what extent the structure of the R&D organization is flexible enough to accommodate these changes. If we look at the history of R&D efforts in India, we will find several instances where the main goals of R&D have undergone major changes. Unless the structure is flexible, such changes will result in nothing but "confusion" among scientists. Therefore, one major area to be covered in training programmes is the evolution of linkages between the policymaking group and the management of R&D institutions. One can study historical events and the ways in which R&D institutions have reacted to such changes. "Learning" from such experiences will help in building "stability" in the organization.

Secondly, if the policy makers decide to cut funds of a particular area or of the institution, it becomes the headache of the management to allocate funds and reallocate priorities. The total system gets disturbed by this. Therefore an important part in training programmes is "skill development" towards optimum utilisation of resources. Performance Budgeting and Project-wise allocations are some new techniques which can help the management to deal with such situations.

Finally, but not lastly, sub-committees are generally formed to create a sense of participation among members of the organization. However, scientists in sub-committees often find themselves in a helpless position and instead of getting the feeling of "part of the executive functions" see themselves as a redundant part of the system, A systematic work-flow study will help the actual needs of sub-committees, clarify its role, objectives, responsibility and authority. Feedback of such studies in the training programmes will help the laboratory management to have a second look at their functioning style and modify the system accordingly.

REFERENCES

1. Baillie, A.S., Management of Risk and Uncertainty, *The International Journal of Research Management*, Vol. XXIII, No.1, 1980.

2. Thomas, T., Management of Research and Development, paper presented at the 18th CIOS Conference on *Management Perspectives for Economic Growth and Human Welfare*, 5-8 December 1978, New Delhi.

3. Garg, P.K., Organization: Structure, Design and Development, *Toward Continuing Education*, Vol.3, No. 5, 1981.

4

Labour Market for Engineers and Technicians in Kerala

*Joseph Alexander**

ABSTRACT

This Paper discuss the current facilities for Technical Education in Kerala in terms of the number of institutions, intake and outturn. The labour market situation and its trend in terms of the absorption patterns and size of unemployment is also discussed for Diploma, Degree and P.G. Courses in Engineering for the batches from 1985 to 2000. The estimate of the size of unemployment for 2004 is also presented.

INTRODUCTION

In Kerala there are 56 Polytechnics and 81 Engineering Colleges. Out of this, 49 Polytechnics and 31 Engineering colleges are govt. institutions. About 27 courses are offered at diploma level, 24 at degree level and 16 courses offered at P.G. level in different institutions. The sanctioned intake in Engineering at diploma level is 10285 in 2003 . At degree level the sanctioned intake is 19932 and at P.G. level the sanctioned intake is 880. The outturn during 2003 at diploma level is 5135 while for degree it is 3944 and for P.G. it is 612.

* **Project Officer, Nodal Centre, Cochin University of Science & Technology, Kochi 682 022, Phone: 0484- 2577405, 2576141, Email: kernodal@md4.vsnl.net.in**

INTAKE

The sanctioned intake of 3778 in 1988 has increased to 10285 in 2003 at diploma level. Electronics Engineering has the highest intake of 1775 among all disciplines. The intake in CD & DM has been discontinued from 1994 and the recent additions in the courses are Medical Electronics, Information Technology and Telecommunication Technology.

In degree courses there is a drastic increase in intake during the last 15 years from 2580 to 19932. In degree courses Computer Engineering has the highest intake of 4466 among all branches. At P.G. level, the admission capacity has increased from 288 in 1988 to 880 in 2003. The new additions to disciplines are, Information Technology, Bio-technology, Electronics and Telecommunication Technology, Marine Engineering and Safety Engineering at degree level and Computer Aided Structural Analysis and Design and Industrial Catalysis at PG level.

OUTTURN

The outturn of diploma courses has increased from 2995 in 1988 to 5135 in 2003. The increase in outturn of Computer Engineering and Electronics is remarkable. During the 15 years, outturn of degree courses in Engineering has increased from 2016 to 3944. The outturn of P.G. Courses also increased from 147 to 612 during this period.

ABSORPTION RATE

The percentage of absorption of engineers show a wide variation among the branches of Diploma courses. The rate of absorption of CD & DM was very low and hence the course has been discontinued. Branches like Architecture, Computer Hardware Maintenance, Medical Electronics, QS & CM, and Tool and Die showed high rate of absorption. Cent per cent of the degree holders passed out in 2000 in disciplines like Bio-Medical, Computer Science, Electronics, Electronics and Communication Engineering, Industrial Engineering, Information Technology, Naval Architecture and Ship Building and Polymer Science and Rubber Technology were absorbed within two years of passing out. Another notable information is that, the rate of absorption in conventional branches like Civil, Mechanical and Electrical is steady over these years. In the case of P.G. Degree, the percentage of absorption is above 70 per cent during the first year and 100 per cent during the first two years in most of the disciplines.

SECTOR OF EMPLOYMENT

The sector-wise tabulation of Diploma, Degree and P.G. Degree holders shows that nearly 70 per cent were employed in private sector while the employment in Central Govt. and State Govt. is showing a declining trend.

SIZE OF UNEMPLOYMENT

The size of unemployment shows that there will be 1330 unemployed diploma holders in Civil Engineering during 2004, 1208 in Electrical, 2373in Electronics and 1661 in Mechanical. But we can notice a decrease in unemployment in disciplines like Civil and Electrical . But in Electronics, the size of unemployment has increased from 330 in 1989 to 2373 in 2004. In the case of degree courses, there is not much change in any discipline during the past 10 years . The size of unemployment in Civil Engineering has come down from 704 in 1989 to 333 in 2004. For Electrical Engineering the size is between 250 and 400 during 1989 to 2004. For Mechanical Engineering it is varying within the range of 250 to 530. For the other branches the unemployment rates are not high. The overall size of unemployment of 1420 in 1989 is changed to 1638 in 2004. The size of unemployment at P.G. level is almost steady.

SUMMARY AND CONCLUSION

Among diploma courses, branches like Architecture, Computer Hardware Maintenance, Medical Instrumentation and Tool and Die find good employment opportunity. Hence there is scope for increase in intake in these disciplines. In the case of degree almost 100 per cent absorption is observed in several branches during the first two years after passing out. At P.G. level also there is scope for increase in intake in most of the branches in Engineering due to good employment chances.

Table—4.1 Percentage absorption of Diploma holders in engineering during first two years

Discipline	Years										
	1985	1986	1989	1990	1993	1994	1995	1996	1997	1998	1999
1	2	3	4	5	6	7	8	9	10	11	12
Applied Electronics					85	100	100	90	75	78	72
Architecture			87	55	100	100	15	43	59	68	67
Automobile	44	31	38	55	74	68	67	64	72	58	50
Chemical	54	38	35	44	62	21	34	43	67	25	54
Civil	40	39	41	38	43	46	45	51	48	38	41
Costume Design and Dress Making	7		10								
Commercial Practice	25	23	22			35		26	25	23	22
Computer			71	62	75	100	65	81	69	68	63
Computer Appln. & Business Management									45	50	40
Computer Hardware Maintenance					100	100	100	86	73	100	70
Electrical	28	37	40	43	45	52	47	45	49	42	38
Electronics	50	51	42	45	45	52	55	48	44	47	40
Electronics & Avionics									36		
Electronics & Communication									43	55	31
Electronics & Instrumentation									55	47	30

(Contd...)

1	2	3	4	5	6	7	8	9	10	11	12
Electronics & Production Tech.									87	62	51
Instrument Tech.	38	52	40	28	32	48	43	40	23	39	29
Mechanical	50	47	39	43	50	61	71	68	53	53	38
Medical Electronics					59	79	100	73	100	100	100
Polymer Tech.	70	30	63	100	80	100	100	100	82	66	42
Printing Tech.	47	43	41	22	50	72	54	71	45	78	47
Quality Survey & Construction Management									90	100	62
Textile Technology	50	48	35	71	48	39	100	79	83	62	49
Tool & Die		50	77	100	80	100	100	100	76	65	71
Wood Technology		62		64	100	72	100	100		100	60

Table—4.2 **Percentage absorption of degree holders in engineering during first two years**

Discipline	Years											
	1985	1986	1989	1990	1993	1994	1995	1996	1997	1998	1999	2000
Applied Electronics & Instrumentation		100		52	100	100	100	100	100	81	82	74
Architecture	100	83	85	58	83	100	100	100	100	80	100	84
Bio Medical					65	100	100	100	100	100	100	100
Chemical	78	48	78	100	62	82	100	70	91	100	64	69
Civil	53	57	58	60	56	75	75	75	76	70	54	74
Computer Science & Engineering			90	100	100	100	100	100	100	100	86	100
Electrical & Electronics	77	65	70	64	63	100	62	86	84	83	80	81
Electronics	100		94		100	100	100	100	100	100	85	100
Electronics & Communication		100		88	65	100	100	100	100	100	90	100
Industrial Engineering			65	100	64	100	100	100	100	100	60	100
Information Technology											82	100
Instrumentation & Control	95	67	100	90	100	79	100	86	100	53	100	86
Mechanical	86	90	85	74	81	80	100	84	85	81	75	84
Naval Architecture & Ship Building	100	100	100	100	100	100	100	100	100	100	100	100
Polymer Science & Rubber Technology	92		90		100		73		100		100	100
Production Engineering	81	90	90	75	73	100	100	100	100	77	79	76

Table—4.3 Percentage absorption of P G Degree holders in engineering during first two years

Discipline	Years									
	1969	1990	1993	1994	1995	1996	1997	1998	1999	2000
Applied Chemistry	67	50	100		75	100	87	100	100	60
Architecture							100	100		100
Chemical	100		100	100	100	100	87	100	100	100
Civil	100	72	100	100	100	100	100	100	100	100
Computer	100	100	100	100	100	100	100	100	100	100
Computer Aided Structural Analysis & Design							100			
Electrical	85	100	72	100	100	100	100	100	100	100
Electronics (M.Tech)	100	100	100	100	100	100	100	100	100	100
Electronics (MSc.)			100	100	74	80	87	100	100	89
Mechanical	100	100	100	100	100	100	100	100	100	100
Polymer Tech.	100		100	100	71	100	100	100	100	100
M B A		100	100	100	100					
M C A		100	100	100	100	100	100	82		

Table—4.4 Estimates of size of unemployment of Diploma holders in Engineering

	Years											
Discipline	1989	1990	1993	1994	1997	1998	1999	2000	2001	2002	2003	2004
1	2	3	4	5	6	7	8	9	10	11	12	13
Applied Electronics					23	12	28	38	56	56	68	192
Architecture			7	13	1	2		66	62	23	22	
Automobile	141	218	264	156	78	78	111	134	110	202	259	229
Chemical	63	92	102	112	56	123	90	122	48	159	81	159
Civil	1447	1407	1390	1690	892	651	973	952	1087	1644	1641	1330
Costume Design & Dress Making	216		141									
Commercial Practice	274	324	356			234		399	516	438	397	423
Computer			111	129	76	35	286	171	392	399	513	779
Computer Hardware Maintenance					5	31	39	55	138	59	183	375
Electrical	1572	1330	1220	1369	890	687	843	1136	434	1440	1554	1208
Electronics	330	370	806	764	705	510	659	921	1188	915	1082	2373
Electronics & Avionics									81			65
Electronics & Communication									275	138	262	348
Electronics & Instrumentation									182	202	291	355
Electronics & Production Tech.									21	55	78	122

(Contd...)

1	2	3	4	5	6	7	8	9	10	11	12	13
Instrument Tech.	72	66	92	136	87	54	72	101	115	133	159	126
Mechanical	950	931	1218	1438	762	485	556	708	559	1122	1532	1661
Medical Electronics					23	12	7	13	12	20	5	41
Pharmacy								397				
Polymer Tech.	16	46	27	15	12	9	26	21	64	72	96	75
Printing Tech.	57	73	70	150	66	19	79	30	79	36	83	35
Quantity Survey & Construction MGT									2	3	19	3
Textile Tech.	67	86	103	52	53	44	12	51	47	92	139	126
Tool & Die		25	18	5	5	6	15	8	31	32	21	42
Wood Tech.	12	7		12		6			2	4	25	9
Total	**5217**	**4975**	**5925**	**6041**	**3734**	**2998**	**3796**	**5323**	**5501**	**7244**	**8510**	**10076**

Table—4.5 Estimates of Size of Unemployment of degree holders in Engineering

	Years											
Discipline	**1989**	**1990**	**1993**	**1994**	**1997**	**1998**	**1999**	**2000**	**2001**	**2002**	**2003**	**2004**
Applied Electronics & Instrumentation				46	17	10	0	22	6	47	46	90
Architecture	4	22	42	65	37	6	0	0	0	33	9	26
Bio Medical					32	4	0	3	3	4	2	6
Chemical	51	108	42	17	50	53	25	42	14	20	61	65
Civil	704	596	583	474	450	262	257	247	258	329	332	333
Computer Science & Engineering			44	31	52	53	51	66	38	124	285	117
Electrical & Electronics	305	394	327	396	367	178	384	236	252	320	322	311
Electronics	67	46	144		18	7	48	51	13	49	100	42
Electronics & Communication				149	191	55	64	78	109	116	207	187
Fine Arts								48	42	36	36	18
Industrial Engineering			19	9	18	3	3	2	1	6	27	2
Information Technology											21	35
Instrumentation & Control	9	25	9	9	14	13	11	16	4	42	15	15
Mechanical	250	263	285	315	247	312	205	313	313	408	528	348
Naval Architecture & Ship Building	5	3	6	5	10	8	5	6	0	0	0	0
Polymer Science & Rubber Tech.	1		2				11				3	0
Production Engineering	24	37	81	51	50	18	22	27	0	34	27	43
Total	**1420**	**1494**	**1584**	**1567**	**1553**	**982**	**1086**	**1157**	**1053**	**1568**	**2021**	**1638**

Table—4.6 Estimates of Size of Unemployment of P G Degree holders in Engineering

	Years									
Discipline	**1993**	**1994**	**1997**	**1998**	**1999**	**2000**	**2001**	**2002**	**2003**	**2004**
Applied Chemistry	24	14	1		7	1	5		2	6
Chemical	6								1	0
Civil	12	24	8	21	7	6	1	22		10
Computer	5	3	2		4	0	3			0
Computer Aided Structural Analysis & Design							2			
Electrical	31	3	18	7	5	10	0			7
Electronics (M.Tech)		3				0	4			0
Electronics (MSc.)			5	10	10	9	8		4	8
Mechanical	6	6	7	10	8	10	0	12	16	12
Pharmacy						1				
Polymer Tech.	1		2		9	0	0		4	4
M B A		4	11		11					
M C A		22	7	22		24	19	71	77	59
Total	**85**	**79**	**61**	**70**	**61**	**61**	**42**	**105**	**104**	**106**

5

Human Resource Planning in Rourkela Steel Plant (RSP)

*P. K. Mohanty**
*S. K. Mahapatra***

ABSTRACT

The Human Resource Planning exercise in SAIL/RSP has gone much beyond the traditional concept of manpower planning. At SAIL, Planning and Changing the work culture is an important aspect of HRP during transition. The exercise was more of a culture building process than a game of numbers based on plain cost-economics. Communicating the transition strategies and tactics to the people was the critical factor for success of HR Plan. Maximisation of the contribution of each employee (asset) to the prosperity of the organization has been a priority of the HRP policy.

Key Words: Broadbanding, Compatmentalisation, Capacity Utilisation, HRIS, QAS, Restrictive Work Practices, Team Work

* **Department of Business Administration, Utkal University, Bhubaneswar-751 004. E-mail- pkmohanty55@hotmail.com**

** **Xavier Institute of Management, Bhubaneswar**

INTRODUCTION

"It is not enough to understand what we ought to be, unless we know what we are; and we do not understand what we are, unless we know what we ought to be" once said T.S. Eliot[1]. Planning is knowing where one stands and where one wants to go. Human Resource Planning has been a function of management since the origins of the modern industrial organization. Economist Alfred Manshall observed in 1890 that the head of business must assure himself that his managers, clerks and foremen are the right men for their work and are doing their work well[2]. Division of labour, specialization, organization of management into levels, work simplification and application of standards for selecting employees and measuring their performance were all principles applied early in industrial management. Manpower is a decision taking resource. This is increasingly its most important characteristic. Yet it has often been over-looked in the past and some managers outlook it now. 'A company is merely a dusty legal framework. All its assets overt or hidden, are mostly inanimate, even intangible objects. Only people can breaths life into business and bring about the profitable exploration of the firms assets[3].

CORPORATE PLAN UPTO 2000 AD

The Corporate Plan for year 2000, adopted in May 1987 by SAIL was the first ever attempt at long-term planning. The plan for 2000 AD, earmarked nine priorities for human resources planning in SAIL.

- *Manpower Productivity:* to achieve 150T/MY by 2000 AD.
- *Manpower Planning:* to reduce numbers while improving the QAS-mix.
- *Organization Structure:* to reduce hierarchy for greater autonomy and shed non-core activities like running township and transport.
- *Work Culture:* to improve discipline, personal and technological and to have more productive work practices while eliminating restrictive ones.

- *Training and Management Development:* to improve quality and coverage.
- *Motivation:* to improve (rationalize) existing financial incentive schemes and give thrust to non-financial motivation schemes.
- *Systems, Rules and Procedures:* to debureaucratise and simplify for giving thrust on fast results rather than procedures.
- *Participation:* to elicit genuine participation of employees and unions.
- *Safety:* transit to new technology with due attention to safety and training.

The plan 2000 did not envisage any target in terms of numbers excepting perhaps manpower productivity, but set out a vision that would eventually get at the right numbers. Five years later, in February 1992, SAIL announced its second Corporate Plan for year 2005 AD. This Plan has been prepared while SAIL was in the midst of implementing a massive modernization project.

CORPORATE PLAN UPTO 2005 AD

The Corporate Plan for 2005 focused on six thrust areas for human resource planning while clearly outlining the organizational vision for Human Resources. The vision focused on two actionable directions:

- Continued human resources development (HRD) for modernization of mind and competence building; and
- Developing a culture of achievement with emphasis on performance and discipline.

The vision acknowledges weakness in areas of employee' attitude, competence, discipline and performance. The Plan envisaged six thrust areas for action:

- *Labour efficiency:* to achieve labour productivity of 170T/MY by 2005.
- *Manpower Plan:* to optimally utilize available manpower and to correct distortions in Organization Structure such

as improving Works/Non-Works ratio from 7: 3 to 9: 1, while rationalizing numbers to competition benchmarks. SAIL had manpower of 2,30,000 in 1992.

- *Recruitment:* to recognize the knowledge and skills for bringing innovation and abilities to manage change, and to make the recruitment process more scientific.
- *Training:* to focus on effective induction of new entrants and continuous development of employee capabilities (skill/knowledge/competence) with a thrust on building creative capacities.
- *Organization Structure:* to develop flexibility/mobility, broad-banding and horizontal interface for decision-making with sufficient role-clarity and result-orientation; and to achieve a flatter and flexible organization that is responsive to quick change in market demands for product-mix.
- *Systems and Procedures:* to reengineer job/role designs/profiles, succession planning and career development policies, employee involvement schemes and practices for making the organization culture more creative and competitive.

The Corporate Plan 2005, repeated five out of nine thrust areas outlined in the Plan 2000 document viz, Manpower Productivity, Manpower Planning, Training and Development, Organization Structure and Systems and Procedures. Recruitment was the new addition and issues like Work Culture, Motivation, Participation and Safety did not find exclusive focus although each of these issues was included as a running theme in some form or other.

COMMUNICATION: THE STRATEGY-IMPLEMENTATION LINK

Human Resource Planning in SAIL started as a system supporting the turnaround strategy of SAIL enunciated in 1985 by Sri V. Krishnamurthy, the then Chairman of SAIL he started with a plan to unleash the biggest ever communication exercise in India's corporate history to instill 'confidence', 'pride' and a 'fire in the belly' among two hundred and fifty thousand employees of SAIL. Taking out a monograph titled, "The Priorities for Action" with a very personal but open letter to every employee was the starting point. The document listed five distinct areas for improvement prioritized for action :

(i) Work Culture

(ii) Capacity Utilisation

(iii) Productivity

(iv) Profits through cost control

(v) Customer Service

Company wide deliberations were held in all these five priorities, and it was felt that the employees of the company held the keys for successful intervention in all the areas. Thus the HRP model of yesteryears dealing only with matching of numbers recruited or promoted against sanctioned vacancies had to undergo a sea change for bringing in qualitative insights.

HRP in SAIL/RSP was reinvented to address effectively all the priority areas. For example, in order to improve work culture, the issue of work intensity had to be addressed which demanded from the HR plan, setting of targets for reducing absenteeism, over-time, shift-change delay, work quota system, crew manning rigidity, spilling over of rest intervals etc. Similarly while addressing the issue of capacity utilization, HRP had to look at the awareness and involvement of employees about goals, tasks, targets and their capabilities to achieve. On the issues of productivity, cost control and customer service, the HRP had to address systems of communication, information management, work practices, quality assurance, and skill enhancement using training as a facilitating tool.

Combining all the challenges and issues before the HR Planning, a set of unique interventions emerged for respective ISPs of SAIL including one for RSP. The HRP for RSP thus began with the identification of broad issues and concerns, and formulation of broad objectives. Each objective could then be reduced to actionable plans with specific measurable tasks and targets.

IDENTIFIED ISSUES/CONCERNS FOR HRP IN SAIL

- The Labour Productivity in RSP was very low (49 in 1985)
- The capacity utilization of installed facilities was very poor. It was 83.51 per cent in 1976-77 & 61 per cent in 86-87
- The work-culture was full of unproductive practices
- The Qualification, Age and Skill mix profile of workforce was dysfunctional
- The morale of workforce was low
- The managerial hierarchy was dysfunctional
- There was no systematic approach to training—it had become a ritual

Addressing the above-mentioned concerns, the HRP objectives were formulated in RSP. These objectives were aligned with the over-all business rejuvenation goals of the company and the implementation strategies were formulated as coordinated approaches along side other functional area strategies as part of a grand business turnaround plan. The foremost business objective of RSP in 1985 was to make the best use of available installed capacity and progressively augment and exceed the rated capacity. Accordingly, all the installed facilities were examined and classified into three categories.

- Facilities which could be made better use of improved work practices alone;
- Facilities which could be made better use of through partial augmentation of process technology and improved work practices;
- Facilities, which had to be retired, and substituted/ augmented by new technology and new work practices.

Since prima-facie, fresh investment was necessary to improve capacity utilization and debottleneck existing capacity a proposal was moved for consideration of the Government of India (GOI). The proposal came to be popularly known as the plan for modernization of RSP, which sounded distinctly different from the previous attempt in 1962-69 for adding 0.8 MT capacity to the original 1 MT layout of RSP. The previous plan was known as Expansion, meaning mere addition of new facilities, whereas the modernization plan aimed at achieving and exceeding the rated capacity of RSP, primarily through technology and culture upgradation.

The process of finalisation of the modernization project report by the consultants M/s M. N. Dastur & Co, and getting the approval of GOI for going ahead with the projects was too long, which finally came in October 1989. During the four long years of bureaucratic delay, the 'Human Resource Planning' (HRP) could not proceed in a systematic way and had to limit focus to certain issues only, which could possibly facilitate later the smooth implementation of Modernisation. The task of preparing the cultural base for the success of modernization was taken up.

LAYING THE FOUNDATION FOR A SUPPORTIVE WORK CULTURE

These intervening years were devoted to plan intensive communication with the employees regarding the modernization plans and to negotiate with the unions for launching improved work practices and HR utilization. The HR Plan during these years focused upon addressing some critical issues related to workculture along with the unions:

- Elimination of 'Over-time', 'Quota System' and 'Crew System';
- Reduction of 'Absenteeism', and 'Shift-change delays';
- Elimination of 'Unproductive work practices';
- Introduction of 'Mobility and flexibility' in deployment;
- Improving 'Morale and motivation' of employees through:
  (a) Fostering teamwork, creativity and employee involvement
  (b) Revamping incentive/reward schemes
  (c) Providing career progression opportunities

(d) Human touch in dealing with grievances and welfare

(e) Fast and fair disciplinary action

Brick by brick the foundation was laid for the HRP super structure, which was to be erected along with the progress of modernization projects.

THE EARLY BREAKTHROUGH

The first major breakthrough achieved was stoppage of over-time in RSP excepting in two department, i.e., Refractory and Transport. The exceptions too fell in line a little later. The second and most important breakthrough was achieved on 16.5.88, when a bipartite agreement called the "Non Executive Promotion Policy" (NEEP) was signed with the recognized union (Rourkela Mazdoor Sabha) paving the way for ushering in teamwork, mobility, flexibility, job combination, job enrichment, broad banding, training for skill upgradation and growth opportunities for the entire non-executive workforce in RSP.

Besides, these breakthrough, considerable progress was made in the other areas of intervention as well. Year after year, absenteeism, shift-change-delay and employee grievances started failing. Employee involvement and creativity improved through launching of Quality Circle (QC), Shop Improvement group (SIG) and Individual Creativity Award (SRUJANI) schemes. Welfare facilities like Canteens, Restrooms, Drinking water points, Heat/Humidity/Dust control systems, Health check-up routines, Hospital facilities, Educational and Recreational provisions, were given thrust and improvements monitored in joint committees (JC) along with the recognized union (RU). New reward schemes were launched bringing monetary motivation to exceed departmental performance targets. Regular action planning with monitoring and review were institutionalized.

THE UNFINISHED AGENDA

In September 1988, after a thorough review of the progress in several fronts that were prioritized in the 'Priorities for Action', the unifinished tasks were complied and documented in a monograph called 'The Unifinished Agenda'. Reviewing the progress in developing a productive organization culture, the document noted with satisfaction considerable progress but also outlined the areas requiring further thrust. On the positive side, it was noticed that the overall work environment has become conducive to take a leap forward with a massive change in attitude of trade unions, environment as well as the employees, improvements in general discipline levels, welfare orientation, better grievance handling and reduction in unproductive practices like absenteeism and overtime. However, several shortcomings were also identified in the areas of 'Work Practices', 'Manpower Planning and Utilisation', 'Organization Structure and Systems', and 'Efficiency and Commitment'. Among the work practices needing further thrust for change were, 'shift handling over and taking over practices', 'overtime and absenteeism control', 'quota working systems', 'crew manning procedures', 'engagement of contract labour in jobs which could be departmentally handled', 'teamwork' and 'operational discipline'. An appropriate example would be the high rate of absenteeism prevailing in RSP since inception till 1987-88.

Although there was a fall in the rate of unauthorized absenteeism during 1986 to 1988, the extent of reduction was not significant. The progress in other work practices was equally slow and insignificant to have an overall impact on productivity.

'Manpower Planning and utilisation' was also a matter of key concern. In terms of reducing the 'numbers' alone, a long way had to be covered. But the document identified that reducing the numbers is not the real objective, which is actually, 'improving productivity'. 'The shift in planning should be towards upgrading our human resources, identifying better ways of doing things, planning for technological changes and improving human resource utilisation', revealed the document.

It was noticed that the Managers were still thinking short-term and pressing for more of unskilled labour. Thrust was to be given for recruiting "skilled and knowledgeable only" for 'proper utilisation' and wherever necessary 'redeployment' was to be resorted to. A "manpower planning manual" was developed for the first time in 1987 for SAIL addressing some of these concerns.

At the plant level, keeping in view the impending modernization, the manpower planning required a distinct approach, which was given in the form of a draft approach paper. The approach paper is fairly comprehensive and concerned about the implementability of the manpower plan. It takes into account predictable uncertainties in future, provides enough cushion for contingencies and it also includes a training and development approach embedded in the Human Resource Plan.

As regards the 'organization structure and systems' , SAIL had intended to speed up the decision making process by cutting down to size the hierarchy of reporting levels. The implementation was slow, sporadic and at best erratic, it was noted. The structure had to be lean and efficient and there was no alternative, but somehow the mindset of employees, especially at the executive level was not yet ready to accept 'broadbanding'. It was further noted that mere changes in structure would not suffice unless the attitude towards decision-making changed.

Finally, with respect to 'efficiency and commitment', it was felt that employees' involvement held the key to success of any strategy and not enough was happening on this front. People were holding back their ideas, their suggestions and their application of mind to solve the company's problems. To make this happen, positive interventions were necessary in the areas of communication', 'competence building' and 'motivation'. The NEPP discussed above had laid a platform to launch the competence building initiatives at RSP. A distinct road map emerged to steer the training activities for the next decade and a half towards achieving a lean, efficient and more productive workforce.

The foundation was laid strong for the incoming modernization. The formal nod for going ahead with the modernization came from the GOI in 1989. And the ground work for popular involvement being ready especially after the 16.5.88 agreement, the focus of HRP shifted to drawing up a meticulous plan for taking modernization through the process of transition with optimal deployment of workforce. Accordingly, a new set of HRP objectives was formulated for RSP.

THE HRPM OBJECTIVES IN RSP

- Achieving Labour Productivity of 97 at the end of modernization;
- Analysing the QAS Mix, identifying the gaps and meeting the shortfalls through planned interventions;
- Analysing managerial practices including delayering and work practices working methods and procedures, which would be necessary to introduce or alter for optimum utilization of manpower;
- Introducing productive and desirable work practices, and eliminating all unproductive/restrictive work practices;
- Preparing a succession plan for key/critical skill/ operations;
- Introducing systematic training to:
  - *(i)* Decriticalise skill requirements;
  - *(ii)* Prepare employers to shoulder higher responsibilities;
  - *(iii)* Inculcate an attitude among employees to respect and adhere to the desirable standard operating practices;
- Identifying employees for redeployment;
- Identifying employees, who are unproductive and who also can not be developed to perform up to expectation, and motivating them to seek voluntary separation.

The overall objectives of human resource (HRP) during the modernization posed a formidable array of activities for meticulous planning and proper implementation. The planning and implementation during a period of transition are like the two sides of a rolling coin. Both the aspects keep changing in relation to each other as they roll together over a period of time and through a period of rapid transition in their internal as well as external environments. In order to ensure that the set objectives of HRP get achieved, it was necessary to form an approach to attain the objectives in full.

The Approach-4 Key Steps

First, there was a need to match the objectives of SAIL and that of RSP, and to accept the ground realities that there could be differences. This called for formation of an apex group of planners comprising representatives from each unit of SAIL. For bringing in dynamism and cross-functional insights into the plan-discussion the apex team in each ISP undergoing modernization, was constituted with representation from the Personnel, Training, Industrial Engineering and Systems areas. The inter disciplinary group in each unit was to continuously interact with Line and Project officials and take their views into account along with the consultant's reports on manpower.

Second, the amount of data to be handled being vast and complex, it w as necessary to use the processing power of computers. Thus, as part of HRP, a new system of computerized MIS was to be developed called the 'human resources information system' (HRIS).

Third, it was felt necessary to come to a uniform yet unique rational approach for each plant, while sharing notes on experience of one another. The broad uniformity was to be with respect to the corporate HRP objectives and the uniqueness was to reflect the compromises that were necessary to adapt to local variables such as level of technology, environment, work-culture etc.

Fourth, and the most important approach were to take the plan to the people who would be affected by the plan. It was felt mandatory to undertake a massive communication exercise to present to and discuss the plan with the rank and file employees of the organization. All the why's, how's and what's of the transition that employees were to see, had to be explained to get their total involvement and full commitment.

Action Planning for the HRP

The scope of HRP flowing out of the objectives of modernization of RSP was delineated in terms of several actionable points as mentioned here under:

1. Assessment of manpower linked to changes in technology and physical facilities;

2. Target setting for improvement in performance indices from pre modernization to post modernization scenario;
3. Analysis of existing manpower profile vis-à-vis assessed requirements during and after modernization, and arriving at short falls;
4. Planning for meeting the shortfalls in terms of QAS requirement and deployment of right number of people at right time;
5. Developing an allocation model for redeployable employees;
6. Identification of unproductive work practices, analysis thereof and planning for elimination of the restrictive practices;
7. Developing a systematic training plan (STP) consisting of :
   (i) Need identification;
   (ii) Module preparation;
   (iii) Calendar preparation with names of participants and duration of training;
   (iv) Monitoring effectiveness of training and calendar for refresher course.
8. Developing a comprehensive plan for managing the transition from pre-modernisation to post-modernisation processes. The transition management plan would attune the scope of each one of the aforesaid action points with the environmental dynamics.

As may be seen above, the action planning went much beyond mere manpower planning, straying into the areas of developing a supportive work culture, training mechanism and a comprehensive plan for managing the grand transition at RSP.

'Work Culture' Planning

Before we delve into the arithmetic of manpower planning, notice must be taken of the plan to improve some of the specific work practices and work methods. A general policy statement was made under the title of "Principles for Work Organization After Modernisation". The preamble of the Policy read as follows:

"It is axiomatic that improvement in work practices shall be a pre-requisite for modernization. Not only the restrictive practices, which have cropped up over the years need to be eliminated but also a new ethos of working, conducive to the needs of modrenisation, has to be evolved. The most prevalent restrictive practices which are to be removed are 'shift change delays', 'quota system', 'compartmentalization of jobs' etc. Besides, with modernization and new technological improvements, mechanization will help work to be done faster and more efficiently".

The policy further delineated 14 cardinal principles for bringing about desired improvements in the work culture at RSP:

- Compartmentalisation between jobs are to be replaced by cluster system of jobs, multi-skill training leading to flexibility of working and redesignation;
- Supervisors should willingly take up operating jobs as and when necessary;
- All maintenance crew should work in multi-trade;
- During shutdowns and capital repairs, idle manpower will be suitably redeployed;
- Operation crew can be involved in maintenance jobs of their own unit during repairs and shutdowns;
- Minor maintenance jobs and primary preventive maintenance checks like bolt tightening, lubrication etc. will be done by operation crew;
- Shift-in-charge or Supervisors can deploy and distribute the work. Working will not depend on group size and no one in a group should remain idle while others work;
- All working groups will carry their tools and tackles as necessary;
- Cleaning and other non-skill jobs arising out of an operation is to be done by the workmen of that place;

- High shift utilization in all units will be ensured;
- Common stores will function in shops for operation and maintenance;
- At technical discipline, norms and safety regulation be adhered to;
- Suitable persons of different discipline will be identified to constitute groups for project implementation;
- Supervisors and experienced skill hands will impart training to their juniors in all units.

CRITICAL APPRECIATION OF HUMAN RESOURCE PLANNING IN RSP

Officially, although all the modernization projects were completed, on ground, many hiccups remained which engaged the attention of Management even beyond the millennium. Project execution suffered from numerous delays and irregularities and invariably the valuable manpower readied for modernization through recruitment or redeployment, wasted their valuable time and training in sundry postings elsewhere. The unproductive work practices too crept into modernization units due to frequent interruptions in operation of the units, both planned and unplanned . Key and critical category workmen got used to extended relief hours in their work-shifts and started regimenting to formalize such practices through trade unionism. Genuine faults in technical execution of new projects also led to covering up exercises leading to deautomation and re-manualisation of work. Never-the-less, this study found many achievements quite significant and positive for the future of RSP.

Manpower

As on 31st March 1998, RSP had reduced its manpower strength to 31,677 excluding the Mines against the post modernization assessment of 31,641 including 3,990 for Mines. Thus RSP lagged behind the target for reduction in manpower by 4,026 numbers. If the revised manpower budget for post-modernization RSP is taken into account, then against a target of 29,809 (26,017 excluding 3792 for Mines), the surplus available was a staggering 5,660. The excess manpower adversely reflected in terms of lower Labour Productivity and higher Labour Cost.

On 29th May 1998, SAIL increased the retirement age of employees from 50 to 60 years, compounding the woes on account of excess manpower. Over 3500 contract labour were further regularized in RSP during 1995-96, due to Supreme Court orders that found their erstwhile engagement as permanent and perennial.

Inspite of all these hurdles and delays, the foundation that was laid by the historic agreement of 16.5.88 ushering in the era of multi-skilling in RSP, paid rich dividends a little later and RSP was able to downsize well below the target by 31.3.03.From a level of 39,635 in 1984-85, the manpower of RSP has comedown by 62 per cent to 24674 in 2002-2003. This is no mean achievement for a public sector company.

Labour Productivity

In 2002-2003 , the Works Labour productivity has reached only 77 tonnes/man-year leaving a yawning gap to be bridged. The failure to achieve the targeted labour productivity of 97 tonnes of crude steel per man-year was mainly due to poor capacity utilization of post modernization facilities. RSP did achieve the targets but the success often came late. The labour productivity has climbed up by 31 points from 46 to 77 but is still 20 points behind the target. This questions the existing level of labour efficiency and work intensity.

Voluntary Retirement

As far as implementation goes, the actual optimization could not strictly follow the microplan route, weeding out the scientifically identified real unproductive people or by deploying through redeployment or recruitment the identified skill-talent. However, to a great extent the manning norms have matched the standards set by the planners. SAIL and RSP could not forcibly retire or retrench even one unworthy soul from the rolls of the company but innovative strategies helped in weeding out considerable numbers of unproductive people through disciplinary removals as well as voluntary exits. Four schemes for voluntary separation were floated between 1986 and 2001 and a sizable strength exited through VR.

The data indicates that less than half the separations—around 46 per cent has occurred through normal retirements on attaining the superannuating age. Voluntary retirement schemes account for 32 per cent and medical reasons including untimely demise account for another 13 per cent of separations. The raising of the age of superannuation from 58 to 60 impacted adversely the normal retirements during 1998 to 2000 but the drive for motivating mostly aged and less productive employees to opt for voluntary retirement was successful to maintain the downsizing trend.

Training and Development

Undoubtedly, it can be said that still the number of employees without formal schooling is high for RSP but intensive training on technical literarcy has helpful RSP to best utilize the legacy of the past. Training of employees was a low priority since inception of RSP. Only about 1302 employees received training each year till 1984-85. In 1985-86 the training coverage was trebled to 3566 and the coverage strode fast to reach peak coverage of 19,447 persons in the year 1992-93. The training ratio was below 5 per cent of manpower before 1985-86, which rose to 9.03 per cent in 85-86 and peaked at 63.7 per cent in 1992-93.

The qualification, age and skill mix of works employees have improved considerably but the qualification of people is not translating fully to the quality of their work. Training has become methodical and purposeful but has not yet yielded the desired competence. The work culture has improved multiskilling has been agreed to; many restrictive work practices have been jettisoned but employee utilization has many question marks still. While labour productivity was targeted, there was no target set for labour cost. As a result the efforts for improving labour productivity has remained confined to stabilizing new technology capacity and reducing the numbers.

CONCLUSION

J.F. Kennedy, Ex-President of USA said 'to fail to plan is to plan to fail. RSP did plan for the numbers but it did not plan for the future human resources. There were too many loose ends in the plan. The short-comings of the plan were not sought to be removed during planning but was planned to be taken care of during implementation.

REFERENCES

1 Vetter Eric, The Nature of Managerial Manpower Planning of High Talent Manpower, University of Michigan, Graduate School of Business Administration, 1967.

2. Mahapatra, S.K., Human Resource Planning During Transition : The Challenges of Right Sizing—A Case Study of Rourkela Steel Plant, Unpublished, Ph.D. Thesis, Utkal University, 2003, p. 118.

3. Mishra, T, Manpower Planning in Steel Industry with Reference to Rourkela Steel Plant, Unpublished Ph.D. Thesis, Utkal University, 2002, p. 12.

Annual Reports of SAIL (1985-2001), SAIL Corporate Plan-2000AD, SAIL Corporate Plan 2005AD, Accelerating Change in SAIL, A SAIL Monography 1997, Detailed Project Report (DPR) for Modernisation of RSP, by M/s Dastur Co.

6

Developing Entrepreneurial Workforce for Sustenance of Small-Scale Engineering Industries in India

V. P. Wani[*]
T. K. Garg[**]
S. K. Sharma[***]

ABSTRACT

The fast changing industrial scenario has posed various challenges to the small-scale engineering industries in India. The challenges are in the form of shorter product life-time cycle, fast chaniging technology, entry of multinationals, and awareness of by customer due to deep penetration of media. It is the fact, these units are facing numerous problems resulting to their sickness. This has necessitated them to be competitive for their sustenance. On the other hand, the opportunities have come in the form of access to better technology, availability of a variety of raw materials and components, impetus to quality, efficiency, and opportunities to restructure and diversify. To face these challenges

* **Workshop Supdt., National Institute of Technology, Kurukshetra-136119, (Haryana) India, vpwani@rediffmail.com**

** **Professor, National Institute of Technology, Kurukshetra-136119, (Haryana) India, tkgargnitk@yahoo.com**

*** **Professor, National Institute of Technology, Kurukshetra-136119, (Haryana) India, sksharmanitk@yahoo.com**

and grab the opportunities, an entrepreneur has to adopt innovative product process, productivity improvement techniques, and effective technology management for sustainability of the unit. Here the innovative approach will be the remedy for an entrepreneur for sustainability. For sustainable growth of this sector, the latest technology and knowhow for application of technology has arisen as necessity of time.

In recent years, the development of entrepreneurship programmes for engineering students has gained considerable momentum. An engineer through entrepreneurship can bring a technical revolution that can meet the challenges. Simultaneously, the mushroom growth of engineering institutions will be producing thousands of engineers per annum. The addition of thousand of engineers per year will increase the unemployment problem for the students. This increasing unemployment problem has forced the policy makers in India to explore new avenues in the smallscale sector and take necessary steps to encourage engineering students towards selfemployment/entrepreneurship in their early career. Engineering and engineering education have undergone significant changes in the recent past. The lead-time in education, in general, and engineering education, in particular, is long; and unless we plan ahead reasonably and accurately, we would be unable to fulfill our obligations effectively. In the changing environment where world is becoming a global village, engineering education must not only teach the fundamentals of engineering theory, experimentation, and practice, but also be relevant, attractive, and connected. It should be conducive to prepare students for a broad range of careers and life long learning.

This paper discusses a comprehensive strategic approach for developing entrepreneurial capabilities among engineers. Objectives are to foster an increasingly entrepreneurial culture that helps students and faculty to understand the fundamentals and feasibility of forming technology enterprise, to help them establish and manage sustainable ventures and to accelerate commercialization of technologies developed.

Key Words: Entrepreneur, Technopreneur, Sustenance of SME, , Sickness

INTRODUCTION

The major outcomes expected from universities are research results and graduates. Basic prerequisite for usability of these outcomes is a good interaction between industry and university. The interaction must be able to cope with a dynamic industrial and technological change, which is often very difficult for rigid university planning.

Development of new industrial organizations require engineers with entrepreneurial skills, with significant communication and persuasion skills, the ability to lead and work effectively in a multidisciplinary team, and an understanding of the non-technical factors that profoundly affect engineering decisions. In fast changing environment, wherein the technology is changing at faster rate and product lifetime cycle is shrinking, technical entrepreneurship has assumed a central place for economic growth of a nation. Technical entrepreneurship can play a pivotal role in the process of industrialization through innovations, product development, and improvement in productivity. Therefore technical education synchronized with the systematically planned entrepreneurship development programme can be useful in molding engineer in entrepreneurial fold.

SME'S IN INDIA: PRESENT SCENARIO

In developing countries like India, small-scale industry is the potent way by which maximum employment can be generated with comparatively low investment. It is also helpful in removal of regional imbalance in industrial development. Even in developed countries, like USA, employment by small firms contributed 53 percent of total employment during the period 1976-1990[1]. Birch[2] in his seminal research, empirically showed how this small entrepreneurial companies had created 80 per cent of the new jobs in the United States from 1969 to 1976.

Small enterprises serve as the seedbed of entrepreneurship due to following features:

- It creates more employment opportunities with comparatively low capital investment;
- SSI unit is generally local resources/demand based;
- They can be located anywhere more easily, resulting in horizontal growth and removal of regional imbalance;

- This sector gives quick returns and has a shorter gestation period;
- These units help to maintain / retain traditional skills and handicrafts;
- These units assist large and medium industries by acting as ancillaries.

The small-scale sector has emerged as the most dynamic and vibrant sector in recent times. It currently contributes about 40 per cent of the industrial production, 35 per cent of total exports and provides employment to over 18.6 million persons in India[3]. Inspite of this development, it is a fact that SSI Sector has not been developed to its fullest potential. The sickness in this sector is widespread, and is growing at a fast rate, resulting in huge loss at different levels. The units in this sector were operating in sheltered markets and majority of them has paid little attention to technology up-gradation, quality improvement, and cost reduction during last several decades. This has resulted in large number of units being sick with little scope for any improvement in future.

The changing economic environment has posed challenges to the Small-Scale Industrial (SSI) sector. To face these challenges, an entrepreneur has to adopt innovative product process, productivity improvement techniques, and effective technology management for sustainability of the unit. Here the innovative approach will be the remedy to an entrepreneur for sustainability. In today's competitive world, it is the technology that drives the economy. Since engineers create this stuff, they are the real masters of the society. Therefore, development of an effective engineer with entrepreneurial approach is a need of hour for sustenance of small-scale sector.

CHALLENGES AHEAD OF SSI SECTOR

Contemporary transformation of the business environment, due to liberalization, privatization, and globalization has increased competitive pressure on the small-scale enterprises in India. Small-scale enterprises are facing an entirely new paradigm of competitive threats:

- Major shift in product and process technology;
- Changes in preference from customer segment etc.

Under the changed circumstances, ability to generate and utilize knowledge is the only way to sustain one self. Technological innovation is a key to survival and growth for small-scale enterprises in India[4]. The technopreneur can be useful in industrial development through innovations in product/process development, increased productivity, production process and systems[5], with the application of knowledge he gained.

In India, the performances of small scale sector in terms of critical parameters such as no. of units, production, employment generated and export during the last decade is as indicated in the Table—6.1 below:

Table—6.1 Year-wise growth of SSI units in India

Year	No. of Units (Million nos.)	Production (Rs. In Billion)	Employment (no. in million)	Export (Rs. In Billion)
1990-1991	1.94	1553.40	12.53	96.64
1991-1992	2.08	1786.99	12.98	138.83
1992-1993	2.24	2093.00	13.40	177.85
1993-1994	2.38	2416.48	13.93	253.07
1994-1995	2.57	2939.90	14.65	290.68
1995-1996	2.72	3562.13	15.26	364.70
1996-1997	2.85	4126.36	16.00	392.49
1997-1998	3.01	4651.71	16.72	439.46
1998-1999	3.12	5275.15	17.15	489.78
1999-2000	3.22	5784.70	17.73	Not available

Source: Laghu-Udyog, Volume xxv, April-September 2001 (6)

Basic accent of India's policy for small-scale sector has been defensive, aiming to protect it from dynamics of the competitive growth. The new environment for this sector consists of challenges emerging from the ongoing process of economic reforms confirming to the WTO agreement and to the fast changing economic, technological and information environment. In this process[7], it has posed certain challenges and provided opportunities to the small-scale sector. The challenges are in the form of increased competition; reduced protection due to lowering of tariffs and market determined rates of interest. Opportunities have come in the form of access to better technology, availability of variety of raw materials and components; impetus to quality, efficiency and opportunity to restructure and diversify. Further the challenges posed in front of the small-scale sector are as follows;

- Increased competition in most of the spheres of manufacturing activities including those in rural area;
- Increased penetration of branded consumer products in rural area from large-scale units;
- Deep penetration of media increased awareness of consumers leading to:
    - — Quality consciousness;
    - — Preference for branded products;
    - — Wider choice of brand/products and services to satisfy similar needs;
- Limited scope for quality price trade off;
- Increased purchasing power among the rural populace/masses.

To accept the challenge and sustain the growth of SSI sector, the entrepreneur need to be creative, innovative, well acquainted with the latest technology, sophisticated machines and equipments so that his industrial venture can compete in this cut throat competitive market and have the sustainable growth.

SICKNESS IN SMALL-SCALE SECTOR

In spite of growth and development, it is a fact that small-scale sector has not been developed to its fullest potential. This sector is beset with a number of problems, which have impeded the development of this sector. The sickness in this sector is widespread and growing at a fast rate, resulting in huge losses in different shapes.

Sickness in the small-scale sector is a matter of great concern and debate. Sickness in industrial sector results in locking up of resources, wastage of capital assets, loss of production and increasing unemployment. In addition, it affects the circulation of bank credit. As per Reserve Bank of India, the magnitude and nature of sickness and its growth in the last ten tears is reflected in the Table—6.2 below.

Table—6.2 Sickness in SSI Sector in India

As at the end of the year	Sickness units Details		Potentially viable unit details	
	No. of units	Outstanding amount (Rs. in crores)	No. of units	Outstanding amount Rs. in crores
1991	2,21,472	2792.00	16,140	693.12
1992	2,45,575	3100.67	19,210	728.90
1993	2,38,176	3432.97	21,649	798.79
1994	2,56,452	3680.37	16,580	685.93
1995	2,68,815	3547.16	15,539	597.93
1996	2,62,376	3721.94	16,424	635.82
1997	2,35,032	3609.20	16,220	479.31
1998	2,21,536	3856.64	18,686	455.96
1999	3,06,221	4313.48	18,692	376.96

Note: These units include village industries also.

Source: Annual Report of SIDO 1999-2000[8]

The Small Industries Development Bank of India (SIDBI) in its annual report[9] analyzed the causative factors for sickness among the small industries with the investment range of 10-15 lakhs as follows:

- Technological obsolescence;
- Inadequate marketing efforts and facilities;
- Lack of infrastructure;
- Paucity of working capital;
- Management inadequacies; and
- Delay in settlement of receivables.

Even for the small industries with higher investment there is only variation in intensity and not the kind. The genuine reasons for sickness of industries as observed by Mukharjee[10] are technological obsolescence, lack of planning, and failure in timely modernization, and loss of market. Over and above the lack of: work culture, good management culture, and committed workers led by a responsible trade union.

Raju[11] has given certain indicators for sickness to SSI sector as follows:

- Shortfall in projected turnover;
- Withdrawal of stocks and reduction in capacity utilization;
- Raw material and or finished goods stocks pile up;
- Erosion in margins;
- Return of bills/cheques;
- Non-maintenance/poor maintenance of account books/stock registers;
- Arrears of loan instalments and interest more than two quarters consecutively

No doubt by this indicators, the number of probable sick units would increase substantially, but that will bring into sharp focus the need to take corrective measures at an early stage for bringing potentially viable units back to health[12].

Data on sick units in the country is compiled by Reserve bank of India. According to its report, number of causes, internal and external, often operating in combination are responsible for sickness of industrial sector. The main causes include deficiencies in planning, mismanagement, shortage of inputs, labour strikes, marketing etc. The RBI report[13] mentions change in government policy as one of the external factor. Report highlighted the magnitude of the causes of sickness in terms of percentage as follows:

Mismanagement	52%
Faulty planning	14%
Marketing difficulties	23%
Shortage of inputs	09%
Labour strikes	02%

Juneja identified the causes of sickness in SSI unit as internal as well as external[14]. The external factors are increased competition, technological obsolescence, labour problems, changing government policies, power cuts etc. The internal factors are inherent financial weakness, diversion of funds, technological obsolescence, inadequate management competence and inept marketing strategies. Juneja has given main reasons for sickness and magnitude of these factors for sickness of small-scale industrial units in terms of percentage is detailed in the table follows:

Table—6.3 Percentage of various factors in sickness to SSI sector in India

S. No.	Reasons for sickness	% of sick units
1.	Marketing problems/inadequate product demand	19
2.	Managerial incompetence/failure	35
3.	Dispute among partners/directors	04
4.	Diversion of working funds	11
5.	Poor quality of product	21
6.	Change in government policy	01
7.	Delayed payment frcm customers	04
8.	Technological obsolescence	03
9.	Non availability of raw material	01
10.	Labour prcblems	01

In nutshell 86 per cent of sick units are sick due to internal factors.

As per Neelamegam[15] the reasons of sickness in small-scale industrial unit are: insufficient amount of working capital, late receipt of working capital and heavy dependence on other sources of finance. This sector is vulnerable to sickness mainly due to financial insufficiency. Therefore, Neelamegam assumes the greater significance of proper finance management in SSI sector.

Pandey[16] see that starting a business of one's own is appealing to many people, but it is also fraught with risks. A large number of small businesses fail each year. The reason: would be entrepreneurs are often unaware of and are ill equipped to handle the many problems they will have to face. The reasons for sickness in SSI as observed by Pandey are as follows:

- Excessive optimism;
- Inability to delegate authority;

- Negligence in developing subordinates;
- Inability to recognize what business they are in;
- Understanding of economic effects;
- Doing things that they like;
- Failure to grow with business;
- Improper selection of associates;
- Unwillingness to make sacrifices;
- Failures to monitor results and take necessary action.

DEVELOPING ENGINEER AS ENTREPRENEUR

In fast changing technological environment, role of technical entrepreneurship assumes a central place. Entrepreneurship means the ability to create new values through a reordering of reality. The science based entrepreneurial engineer aims, by means of technical intervention (invention, innovation, planning and management organization) to exhibit to produce new products/ services or market that can be recognised as valuable by society[17]. The necessity of developing creative design, methodology, or several of them to suit individual idiosyncrasy is unquestionable. Its usefulness for developing creativity in students has been verified by many teachers. The methodology of creative thinking alone cannot turn as engineer into an entrepreneur, unless he has the required amount of insight. To develop necessary insight, Karune[18] has emphasized on only one method, and that is presenting the principles from known to unknown, from old concepts to new one, involving several laws. This will give the students right insight and develop his confidence in meeting new situations with initiative and originality.

Farr and Merino[19] recommends that the educators has to overcome the traditional disciplinary barriers for what it is a multi-disciplinary approach with heavy emphasis on economic, business and entrepreneurial skills. Baburao[20] gives the favourable factors for the engineer as entrepreneur. Engineer who learns sufficient science and engineering acquire capabilities to know why and how of various theories and can design products and services based on their knowledge and skill competencies.

PROBLEM FORMULATION

The objective of the investigation was to analyze the prospects of small-scale engineering units in the context of liberalization, privatization, and globalization. For this, the objective was divided in three steps as follows:

- To study and analyze the factors responsible and affecting the performance of small-scale engineering units;
- To study and analyze the entrepreneurial characteristics and entrepreneurial capability of the engineering students;
- To study and analyse the input by faculty in developing engineer as effective entrepreneur.

From this, to identify as to how the entrepreneurial capability of the engineering student is dependent on the qualitative and quantitative input of faculty in engineering institution. For this hypothesis were set as follows:

Hypothesis—1

The performance of an industrial unit in small-scale industrial sector is dependent on the factor viz. managerial, technical, financial, and personal capability of an entrepreneur. To test the hypothesis a questionnaire was prepared incorporating factors affecting the performance of SSI unit. In the questionnaire the entrepreneur was to give his opinion about the significance of factors affecting performance of his individual unit.

Hypothesis—2

Engineering students do possess the entrepreneurial characteristics and capabilities. To test the hypothesis a questionnaire was prepared incorporating the checks for measurement of entrepreneurial attributes. In the questionnaire students were to mention their choice over various entrepreneurial attributes.

Hypothesis—3

Teacher does have the knowledge, skill, and understanding of the entrepreneurial education to engineering students.

To test the hypothesis a questionnaire was prepared incorporating the various factors for assessment of knowledge of the faculty, input by faculty for developing effective engineer, learning attitude and receptive mind of faculty, and entrepreneurial awareness as well as the industrial exposure of the faculty. In the questionnaire, teachers were to provide their views over various factors.

TESTING OF HYPOTHESIS

Hypothesis—1

Response of Entrepreneurs having Technical Background

- In facilitating factors leading to entrepreneurship technical factors are rated as on first followed by personal, managerial and then motivational factor;
- For success of unit respondent considers technical factor as first followed by personal, managerial, and financial;
- For difficulties while running the unit, priority is for financial followed by managerial and then technical;
- For sickness of unit, financial factor is important, followed by personal, managerial, and then technical factor.

Response of Entrepreneur not having Technical Background

- As regards facilitating factors leading to entrepreneurship, the personal factors are rated as first followed by motivational, managerial, and then personal factor;
- Respondents for success of unit considers personal factor as important, followed by managerial, financial and technical;
- For difficulties while running the unit, entrepreneur gives priority for technical followed by financial, and then managerial.

For sickness in the unit, respondents consider technical factors as most important, followed by financial, managerial, and then personal factors.

Hypothesis—2

From the response of final year students opting self/wage-employment as career option, it can be observed that:

- No. of students opting self-employment is lower to no. of students opting wage-employment as career option;
- Entrepreneurial characteristic of the students is on higher side as compared to their entrepreneurial capability;
- The entrepreneurial characteristic of the students opting self-employment is on higher side than students opting wage-employment as career option;
- The entrepreneurial capability of the students opting self-employment is on higher side than students opting wage-employment as career option.

Hypothesis—3

From the analysis of the response from faculty it is observed that factors/input by faculty do have significance for developing engineers as entrepreneurs as follows:

- As regards to the knowledge of faculty is concerned, it is on highest side with respect to other factors/input;
- The input by faculty for developing personality of students as an engineer is on the second preference;
- The learning attitude/receptive mind of the faculty is on third preference;
- The industrial exposure and entrepreneurial awareness of the faculty is at last number.

OBSERVATIONS

1. For non-technical background entrepreneurs technical, financial and then managerial are the most important inhibiting factors affecting the growth of a SSI unit. Whereas, technical entrepreneurs financial, personal, and managerial are the most important inhibiting factors. Thus, for sustainable growth of the SSI sector, a technical entrepreneur can be more effective. The

technical person needs to be developed in entrepreneurial fold along with managerial, financial knowledge for development of SSI sector.

2. The engineering students do have the entrepreneurial concept and capability. The entrepreneurial capability of student can be increased by appropriate input. This will enable student for better understanding of science and technology and its application for socio-economic development.

3. There is scope for improvement in the two factors namely: learning attitude/receptive mind and industrial exposure/entrepreneurial awareness among faculty. Improvement in these factors will enhance the entrepreneurial capability of the students.

CONCLUSION

In the small-scale engineering industry, the entrepreneurial success and failure depend not only on what entrepreneurs know, but also on what they can do with what they know. Since they often deals with uncertainty and change, their comfort and insight with intuitive judgements and action are as important as their deliberative decisions and implementations.

Due to the protection from the government, there is significant growth of small-scale sector in India in past several decades. The changing environment needs this sector to be competitive for its sustenance. For remaining competitive, units have to response to the changing technological advancement, customer demands, and changing product life cycle. For this engineer as entrepreneur can be the viable alternative. In this context, the engineering educators have to give proper emphasis on developing engineer as entrepreneur for sustenance of small-scale engineering units in India.

REFERENCES

1. Small Business Administration, the State of Small Business: A Report to the President of the USA.
2. Abu-Khalaf Aziz M., "Improving Thinking Skills in the Unit Operations Laboratory", International Journal of Engineering Education, Vol. 17, No. 6, 2001, pp. 593-599.

3. Prasad C. S., "The Third Census of SSI Units", Laghu-Udyog, Volume XXV to XXVI, April-September 2001, pp. 14-20.

4. Wani V. P., Garg T. K., Sharma S. K., "Effective Technological Innovation Necessity for sustainable Development of Small-scale Enterprises in India", International Conference on SME's in a Global Economy' University of Wollongong, Wollongong NSW Australia, July 2002.

5. Wani V. P., Garg T. K., Sharma S. K., "Developing Technoentrepreneurial Workforce for Effective Technological Innovation Necessity for Sustainable Development of SSI's in India", International Journal of Entrepreneurship and Innovation Management, Vol.3, Nos.5/6, 2003, pp.492-508.

6. Laghu-Udyog, Volume XXV, April-September 2001.

7. Vasundhara Raje, "Taking SSI Towards New Millennium—Message of Hope", Laghu- Udyog, Volume XXIV to XXV, April-September 2000, pp. I-VI.

8. Aranha Jose Alberto, Bueno J.A. Pimenta, Luiz Carlos Scavarda do Carmo and Marcos A Da Silveira, "Entrepreneurship in the Engineering Curriculum Some Initial Results of PUC Rio's Experiment", Proceedings of ASEE2002, Conference, Berlin October 2002.

9. Small Industries Development Bank of India, Annual Report, 1990-1991.

10. Mukharjee Deepankar, "Industrial Sickness and Work Culture" <http//www.ganashakti.com/old/1998/981207/featureeco.htm>

11. Yerram Raju, "Ailing Sn...ll Industry Sector A Clinical Approach Suggested" http://www.smeindia.com/article4.htm

12. Report of the High Level Committee on Credit to SSI, Chairman R. L. Kapoor, RBI, 1998.

13. Kapila Uma, "Suggestions Small Scale Industries: Maladies and Remedies", Ed. Kapila Uma, Understanding the Problems of Indian Economy, Academic Foundation. <http//www.technopreneur.net/timeis/technology/sctechjuly-aug/small_industries.htm>

14. Juneja J.S., "Management Excellence SME's Imperative in the New Millennium", Abhigyan, Vol.XVII, No.1, 1999, pp. 15-26.

15. Neelamegam R, and Maria Inigo, "Management of Working Capital in Small Scale Industries in India", Abhigyan, Autman 1996, pp. 59-62.

16. Pandey U., "Why Small Business Fail", Trainers Training Programme on Entrepreneurship Management", IIT, Delhi November-December 1998.

17. Carmo, L.C.S. do, Pimenta-Bueno, J.A., Aranha, J.A., Costa T.S.,da, Parise J.A.R., Davidocich, M.A.M., da Silveria, M.A.: "The Entreprenurial Engineer: A New Paradigm for the Reform of Engineering Education", Proceedings of the ICEE97, Vol. 1 Southern Illinois Un. At Carbondale, Carbondale, Illinois, USA, 1997, pp. 398-408

18. Karune S., "Entrepreneurship Characteristics and Fostering Entrepreneurship Among Engineers", Indian Journal of Technical Education, Volume 10, No. 2, July1987, pp. 30-33

19 Farr J.H., and Merino D.N., "Educating Entry Level Engineers: are Broad-based Business Managerial Skills a Key to Sustaining the US Innovation-based Economy", International Journal of Engineering Education, Vol. 19, No. 2, 2003, pp. 252-259.

20. Baburao G., "Promotion of Technical Entrepreneurship: Role of Humanities and Social Sciences", Journal of Engineering Education, Jan.1999, pp. 7-11.

7

Human Resource Management in R & D Institutes

A Case Study of CSIR Institute

*Rathore S.K.S**
*Sharma Rajeev***
*Gupta R.N****
*Katiyar Deepti*****

ABSTRACT

Human Resource Management is an important sector in general and very important, if we are talking about R&D Institute in specific. National Botanical Research Institute under the broad umbrella of CSIR (Council of Scientific and Industrial Research), which has a total manpower of 20.985 including 5,112 Scientist under the Department of

* **Scientist E I, R&D Planning and Monitoring, National Botanical Research Institute, Rana Pratap Marg, Lucknow-226001, email : sanjai1962@yahoo.com**

** **Scientist E I, R&D Planning and Monitoring, National Botanical Research Institute, Rana Pratap Marg, Lucknow-226001**

*** **Scientist E I, R&D Planning and Monitoring, National Botanical Research Institute, Rana Pratap Marg, Lucknow-226001**

**** **Management Trainee of Institute of Management Studies, A-8B, Institutional Area, Sector 62, Noida,U.P. email: deepti_2159rediffmail.com**

Scientific and Industrial Research (Ministry of Science and Technology, Govt of India), is a premier research Institute of the Country. The Institute is engaged in basic and applied research of multidimensional aspects of Plant sciences. NBRI has come out with number of green technologies. Many of them have been licensed.

Human Resource Management is a subsystem of the total management system. It provides specialized concepts, methods, techniques for the integration and coordination of human resources in general and S&T personnel in specific. It requires management of available manpower in a quantitative as well as qualitative manner leading to achieve the ultimate goal of the organization. Ultimate goal consists of gaining supremacy not only in academics but also generation of ECF (External Cash Flow), EBR (External Budgetary Resources) and LR (Lab Reserve) for the organization. Further, societal development and services sector should also be there. Human Resource Management also requires critical analysis of demand and supply of the Manpower vis-a vis demand and supply ratio of the research.

National Botanical Research Institute, Lucknow with a total staff of about 473 persons (including 94 Scientists,89 technical personnel besides staff in Administration, Finance and Purchase) is engaged in various activities of plant science research viz. Biodiversity, Bioinformatics, Biomass Biology, Biotechnology, Conservation, Ethnopharmacology, Floriculture, Plant Physiology, Genetics & Plant Breeding, Molecular Biology & Genetic Engineering, Microbiology, Natural Product development etc.

Key Words: ECF, EBR, LR, CSIR.

INTRODUCTION

Few years back for science graduate, which are the future backbone of the technical Manpower in the country, the option was any combination of subject among from Chemistry, Zoology, Botany, Physics, Maths and statistics. Even in Post-graduate courses in science was either Botany, Zoology, with the specialization in particular areas like Genetics, Biotechnology etc. However due to rapid transformation in industry emphasis in R&D, job/market oriented courses, one can see that this specialization has percolated down to graduate level like B.Sc. in Genetics, Biotechnology, Bio-informatics, Molecular biology,

Microbiology, Industrial Microbiology and so on. With this scenario there is need for technical manpower planning in Research and Development Institute. Technical Manpower Planning would be ultimately useful for getting better results in the area of academics and also enhancing the technical skill in the country.

Council of Scientific and Industrial Research (CSIR) comes under Department of Scientific and Industrial Research (DSIR) under Ministry of Science and Technology, Government of India (Fig. 7.1).

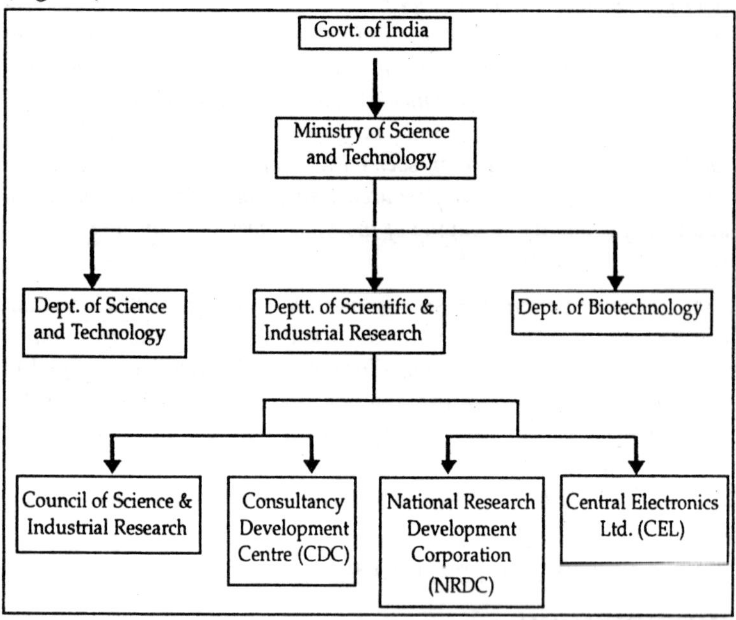

Fig. 7.1: Status of Council of Scientific and Industrial Research (CSIR)

The Council of Scientific and Industrial Research (CSIR), constituted in 1942 by a resolution of the then Central Legislative Assembly, is an autonomous body registered under the Registration of Societies Act XXI of 1860. CSIR structure is as shown in Fig. 7.2.

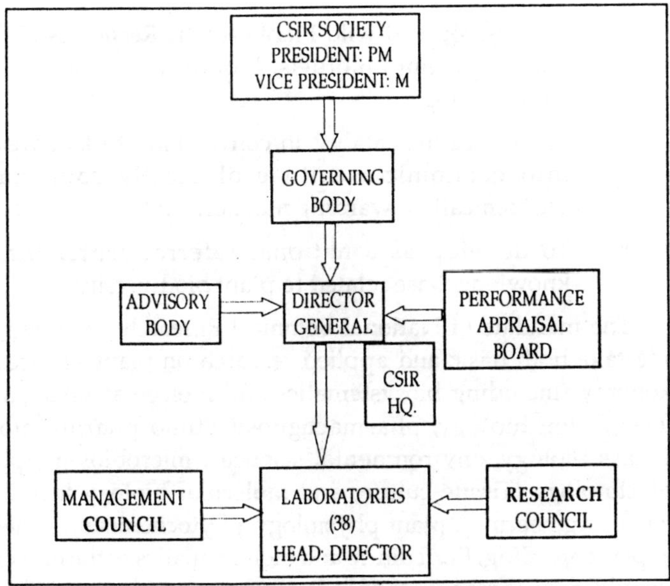

Fig. 7.2: CSIR Organizational Structure

NBRI is the premier national plant research center for India under the umbrella of CSIR known Sikander Bagh, the legendary royal garden of the erstwhile Oudh kings who ruled the region of century before it was taken over by the British in 1857.CSIR took over National Botanic Garden in 1953 and expanded the scope of the multidisciplinary plant research center and renamed it in 1975 as the National Botanic Research Institute. NBRI is now an internationally well-known research center in India and it focuses on both basic and applied aspects of plant sciences. While working on Biodiversity, Bioinformatics, Biomass biology, Conservation, Ethnopharmacology, Floriculture, Plant Physiology, Genetics and Plant Breed Biology amd Genetic Engineering, Natural product development, etc., it caters to the need of aspect of plant research in South Asia region in general and India in particular.

The vision of NBRI is:

- To be a premier national and international center on plant sciencc research development in the areas of plant biodiversity, conservation and sustainable utilization of non-crop and wild Plant Genetic Resources (PGR), bioprospecting, biofuels, bioinformatics and plant biotechnology;

- To be a prime catalyst in conversion of plant wealth into economic wealth ecologically sound and economically rewarding manner;
- To develop as a national referral center for all knowledgebase related to plant biodiversity.

The mandate of National Botanical Research Institute is to undertake both basic and applied research on plant sciences in taxonomy (including biosystematics and molecular taxonomy), conservation biology, pharmacognosy Ethno pharmacology, biomass biology, environmental sciences, microbiology, plant biotechnology (Tissue culture and molecular biology including genetic engineering), plant physiology, phytochemistry, genetics and plant breeding, floriculture and bioinformatics of the non-crop and wild genetic resources of India

Method

In the present study, CSIR has been taken up for the study in general and National Botanical Research Institute, Lucknow has been taken up specifically. CSIR has got its credit for number of technologies. Further, it has got the distinction of filing largest number of patents from India among the Research Sector in general from Govt. of India.

Three basic parameter were taken in to account while assessing the success of Technical Manpower Planning. The success in the area of academics, success in Business and success for societal benefits due to the output of the working of the Institute. The secondary parameters which are indicators for the these three basic parameters were also taken into account. Like for Publication , the number of publication was taken in to account. For societal benefits the technology and training part was considered and for Business ECF(generating External Cash Flow) was considered. Four years data (2000-2001 to 2003-04)were taken for study purpose. However in some cases three years data has been taken like in training(2000-2001 to 2002-2003). In some cases data for more years has taken in to account like in case of publication. Some of the indicators are interlinked and applicable to more then parameters.

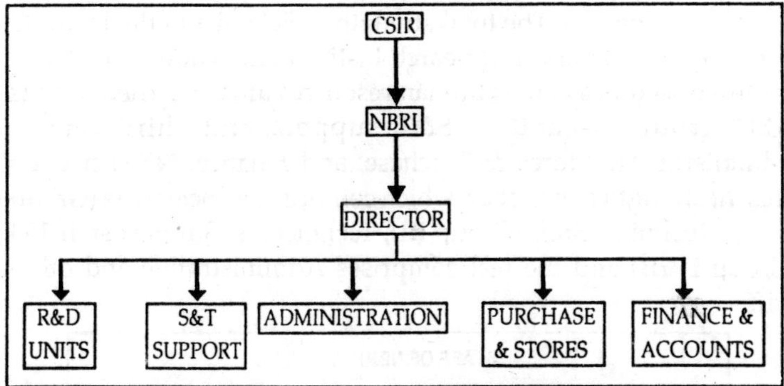

Fig. 7.3: Organizational Structure of National Botanical Research Institute, Lucknow

The working of NBRI is reflected in Fig. 7.4.The working of NBRI gets the support of Management Council (MC) and Research Council(RC).

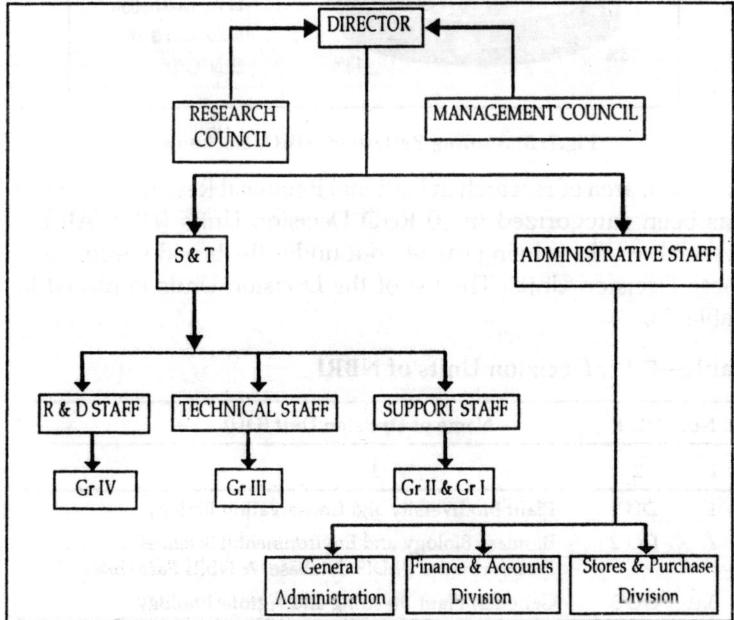

Fig.: 7.4: Management of National Botanical Research Institute, Lucknow

National Botanical Research Institute is having a total staff strength of 478 persons. The classification under different category is shown in Fig. 7.5. The total strength of Scientist in the Institute is 94.National Botanical Research Institute, Lucknow (NBRI) has got three sectors as far as human resources are concerned. One is R&D group, second is S&T support and third one is Administration, Stores & Purchase, and Finance. NBRI has the present strength of 473 staff, which comprises 94 Scientists (Group IV), 43 Technical Staff (Group III), Technicians/Support staff 133 (Group I &II) and the rest comprises Administrative and other staff.

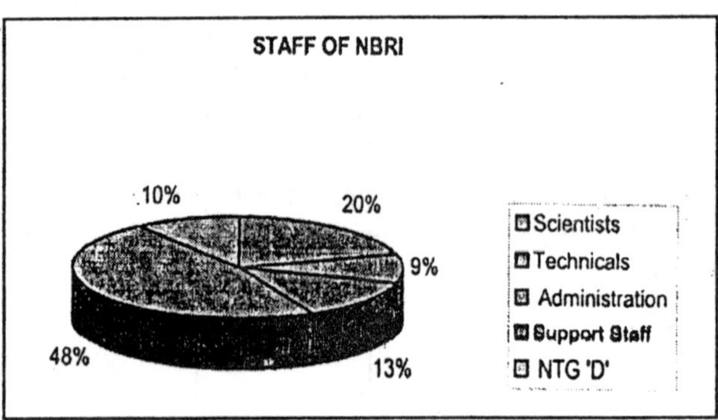

Fig.7. 5: Staffing Pattern of NBRI, Lucknow

The area of research in National Botanical Research Institute has been categorized in 10 R&D Decision Units (DU). All the research works is being carried out under the broad spectrum of these Decision Units. The list of the Decision Units is placed in Table 7.1.

Table—7.1 Decision Units of NBRI

Sl. No.	DU #	Name of Decision Unit (DU)
1	2	3
1.	DU 1	Plant Biodiversity and Conservation Biology
2.	DU 2	Biomass Biology and Environmental Sciences, Bioinformatics (ILDIS database) & NBRI Farm Sites
3.	DU 3	Genetics, Plant Breeding and Agrotechnology

(Contd...)

1	2	3
4.	DU 4	Plant Conservation and Eco-education
5.	DU 5	Molecular Biology and Genetic Engineering
6.	DU 6	Pharmacognosy and Ethnobotany
7.	DU 7	Phytochemistry
8.	DU 8	Botanic Garden and Floriculture
9.	DU 9	Biotechnology and Plant Physiology
10.	DU 10	Herbarium

Support services comprise Planning, Information, Library, Technology Transfer and Business Development Group etc.

RESULTS

Academic Excellence

The academic excellence can be judged by the number of publications and also by the Impact factor of the publication. The publication number shows the incremental growth. Like wise the Impact factor has also shown the incremental growth (Fig. 7.6). The number clearly indicates the incremental growth from 97 in year 98-99 to 141 in 2003-04. This shows the success of Technical Manpower Planning in the Institute for the academic field.

The Impact factor has also been increased during the period. Impact Factor denotes the importance of publication.

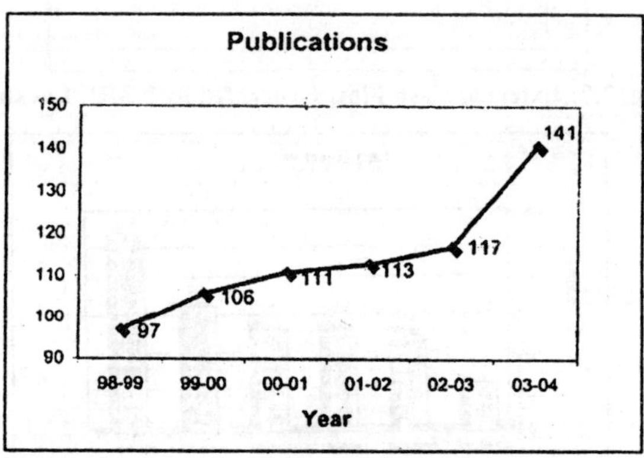

Fig. 7.6: Number of Publication Yearwise from National Botanical Research Institute, Lucknow

Business

In terms of Business External Cash Flow, Lab Reserve and External Budgetary Resource . External Cash Flow is also related to Academic Excellence as it comes from the funding agencies leading to increase ih number of projects.

The External Cash Flow is the money received from the outside funding agency (other then CSIR Hq) is considered as External Cash Flow. This amount does not include the training component and also sample analysis and other miscellaneous amount received the Institute. In fact most of the ECF comprises money received for research purpose under different project mode like Grants-in -aid, Consultancy, Sponsored, Collaborative. In the CSIR system they are considered and GAP, CNP, SSP and CLP projects respectively. Other receipts form Lab Reserve. The addition of Lab Reserve and External Case Flow is considered as External Budgetary Resource.

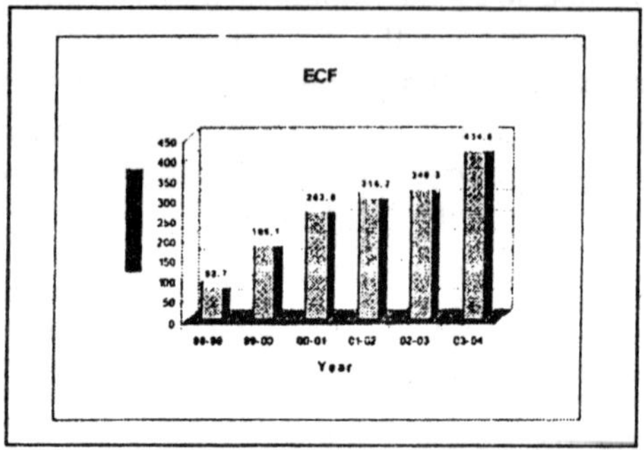

Fig. 7.7: External Cash Flow Generated by NBRI, Lucknow

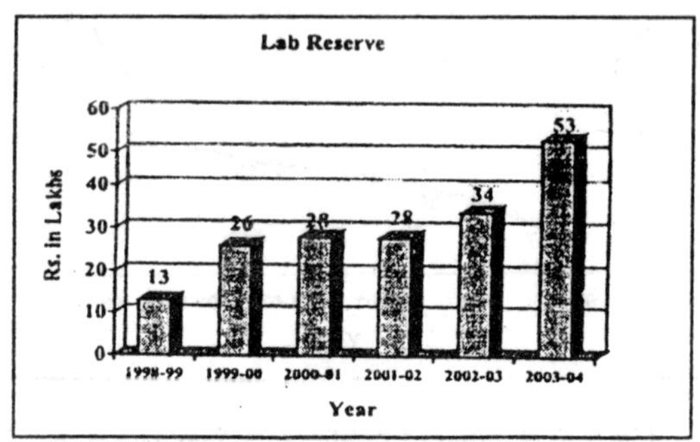

Fig. 7.8: Lab Reserve Generated by NBRI, Lucknow

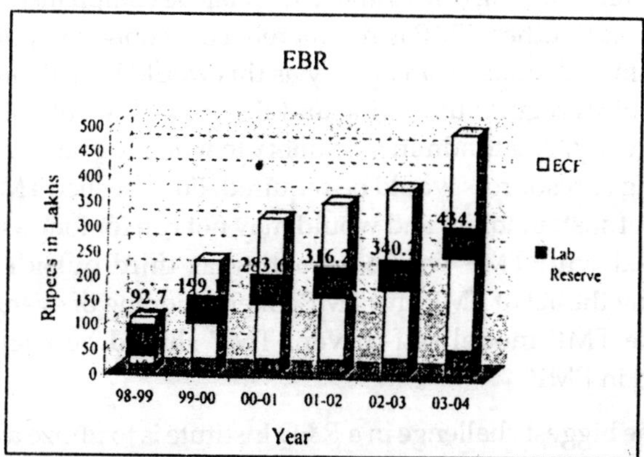

Fig. 7.9: External Budgetary Resources Generated by NBRI, Lucknow

External Cash Flow , Lab Reserve and External Budgetary Resources show the incremental growth during the period from 1998-99 to 2003-04. ECF increases from 92.7 lakh in 1998-99 to 434.7 lakh in 2003-04 (Figs. 7.7 and 7.9). Situation at Figs.7.8 and 7.9 denote about the Lab Reserve and EBR growth in the Institute.

Societal Benefits

National Botanical Research Institute, Lucknow has total 19 green technologies. 15 of them are already transferred either commercially or for the benefit of society by way of training. NBRI, Lucknow has developed a garden for Visually Challenged Persons for the societal benefit besides other extension activities which are being carried out regularly. For societal benefits extension activities are being carried out by NBRI in the area of Biodiversity based vocation, upliftment of weaker section and Environmental Securities.

CONCLUSION AND DISCUSSION

Technical Manpower Planning (TMP) provides proper utilization of our resources in education planning to cater to need of growing and expanding industry/market. TMP operates at two level the supply side is Education Manpower Planning (EMP) and demand side is market/Industry manpower planning. For a successful/operational TMP, it is imperative that Educational

Manpower Planning (EMP) and TMP shall be complementary and dovetail each other. TMP is not merely collection/compilation of data from both ends by an agency as this would be a gigantic task that requires regular up-dating and this process would also adds up to already/create admin machinery to whom sustain additional pumping of resources would be required. Further such TMP being devoid of sustainability and would may not run for long as agency entrusted with TMP would be acting as third outside player balancing the act of EMP and TMP for envisioning of overall TMP. To make TMP model self-driven, TMP should be encrusted/ studded in EMP.

The biggest challenge in a R&D Institute is to utilize available human resource in a proper and sustainable basis. The ultimate goal of an Institute is to get the proper recognition in the field of Research and Development without compromising the quality and also with optimum use of resources whether it is human resource or financial resource. The three parameters are of utmost important in assessing the growth of an Institute in this sector. They are Academic excellence, generation of External Cash Flow (ECF), generation of External Budgetary Resources (EBR), and societal benefit. These four sectors decide the growth of R&D Institute. A model has been developed to denote the success of a Research and Development Institute, which is shown in Fig. 7.10. There is an urgent need to cater the demand of Technical Manpower in the important sector. The model shows how the different parameters for proper Technical Manpower Planning are interlinked. In fact every aspect has it's own weightage and value, which would be ultimately useful in the TMP.

For proper Technical Manpower Planning the training for the staff of Institute is also very important. This would give a platform for capacity building for future growth of the Institute. NBRI provides ample opportunity for their staff to undergo training for different area. The number of trainings received by the Scientist of the Institute shows an increase from 12 in 2000-01 to 21 in 2002-03 (Fig. 7.10).

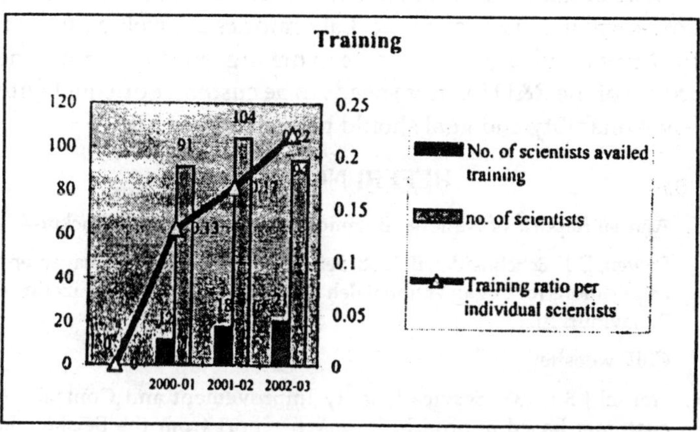

Fig. 7.10: Number of Trainings received by the Scientists of NBRI

Hensel (1988) reported about the improved systems based on better technology the possibility and motivation for both employees and customers to handle their part in the service production process. NBRI also undertakes Customer Satisfaction Exercise with the strength of green technologies and strong R&D base. Brown and Schneider (1988) also favoured that all the aspects of organization design have to be geared to the creation and delivery of the system. In large organization the abundance of staff makes accurate and up-to-date decision making even harder. States Peters(1988):Then comes the praetorian guards of central corporate staff. The corporate center is rightly is tightly protected...by a phalanx of brilliant, MBA trained, virgin (no line-operating experience), analysis driven staff. NBRI also does not believe in having overstaffing of the Institute and takes the staff only when there is a demand of the work and within the sanctioned strength of CSIR.

The beauty of NBRI Manpower Planning is that it is linked with overall CSIR planning .HR planning in NBRI takes into account, employment trends, replacement needs, productivity and expansion and Growth, work load analysis, skill analysis. Well-organized concept of job description, job specification, job evaluation and performance appraisal are the integral part of

Manpower Planning. Selection method includes screening method for shortlisting the candidates includes the best possible methods of test, seminars, discussions etc. Laboratories are well-equipped, fully automated and conducive working environment. The approach of the R&D Institute needs to be customer oriented with self-sustainability and goal should be societal benefit.

REFERENCES

1. Annual Reports of National Botanical Research Institute, Lucknow.
2. Bowen, D.E. & Schneider, B. 1988. Service Marketing and Management: Implications for Organizational Behaviour. Research in Organizational Behaviour, 10.
3. CSIR website.
4. Hensel,J.S. 1988: Service Quality Improvement and Control : A customer-based approach, Research report from the Seisheimer Symposium on Business: The Integration of Organizational Behaviour and Marketing—Implications for Service Management. Freeman School of Business at Tulane University, New Orleans, Nov. 11-12.
5. Katiyar, Deepti, 2004: Project Report on Human Resource Development: A Case Study of NBRI.
6. Peters, T. 1988: Restoring American Competitiveness: Looking for New Models of Organization. The Academy of Management. Executive, No. 2.

8

Beyond the Horizon

Adding Value of Certification for TQM

Achintya[*]

ABSTRACT

The gains to be drawn from the globalisation are dependent on the quality and the discipline with which we adapt and practise the requirements of standard in our daily conduct. The success is top driven; similarly the failure, should it ever result, is due to the lack of perception and leadership of the same function. The committed leadership in disseminating technical education always encourage incremental improvements through quality circles, suggestion schemes, brainstorming sessions, and organizing seminars and workshops. In this chapter, the significant factors such as ISO certification, etc. which influence the competitive edge and operational efficiency of the technical manpower planning in the present era has been highlighted.

Key Words: ISO Certification, Leadership, Quality, Technical Education and Manpower.

* **Associate Professor, Department of Civil Engineering, Muzaffarpur Institute of Technology, Muzaffarpur, Bihar– 842 003, Email: drachintya@rediffmail.com**

INTRODUCTION

Galileo said long back, "*Count what is countable, measure what is measurable and what is not measurable, make measurable.*" As a matter of fact, development of technical education and so the technical manpower— all are quantifiable, provided a sincere attempt is made. Once such an attempt is made that every item can be quantified, then the subjective opinion of resource identification of technical manpower planning can be evaluated and consequently, corrective and/or preventive measures, if any, could be taken up with accuracy and precision. Once the production terminologies and other relevant terms in technical education are properly understood, attempts are required to be made to find the leader, the system/process and the goals of progress i.e. the output as technical manpower.

ISO certification gives significant leverage on many factors affecting operational effectiveness which influences the competitive edge depending on a given demand/supply situation and product leadership. The following are the benefits derived from ISO certification:

- Formal structure and mechanism towards pro-active action;
- Awareness of need for quality and consequent flexibility in thinking;
- Common thread and common language for action;
- Quest for more benefits;
- Workplace of quality improvement;
- Increased interest towards integration;
- Improved calibration/certification management;
- Increased training leverage through documentation.

In all the above and, the role of the management as the motivator and benchmark-setter cannot be ignored. An enlightened management would not jump for quick gains from the process, rather consolidate and improve continuously for the quality, added value and therefore, the profitability. Quality means conformance, customers' satisfaction, even delight; and system means method, strategy we may claim to be working to a quality system only when we cater to the customer in an efficient way. The ISO 9001-1994 standard provides ample regulatory controls and indicators to achieve this. Organizations should evolve means for conducting periodic self-assessments of value gained through implementing the ISO 9000 quality systems.

TOTAL QUALITY MANAGEMENT (TQM) AND ISO STANDARDS

Visualising a technical institution in the form of an industry helps to identify typical areas for improvement. The enormous benefits being experienced by manufacturing organizations provide motivational effects for the organization of various nature. In technical institutions, for a successful implementation of Total Quality Management (TQM) concepts and hence to gain competitive advantage, it is said as essential to adopt various industrial techniques where TQM improvements are possible.

ISO 9000 are set of standards – 9001/2/3–concerning QMS (Quality Management System). They do not concern specifications of products or service. They concern management process and systems employed in order to deliver product or service conforming to agreed requirements between the supplier and customer. ISO 9000 per se does not guarantee quality. Through somewhat exaggerated for the sake of emphasis, one can say that it is theoretically possible for the certified technical institutions/ technical education group/company to continue with inefficient process, have high reject rates and complaints provided this is well documented at all stages, including voluntarily post-complaint producers. But for the globalisation, the technical institutions wanting to initiate TQM in both letter and spirit, comprehensive documentation of processes, producers, work instruction and job descriptions forced by ISO 9000 standards are an essential basis for the purpose of continuous improvement, otherwise it is difficult to improve a process or its implementers. Relevant jargons of TQM as per ISO-9000 are as follows:

Process	—	Series of actions or activities that produces result
	—	Blending of inputs that produce output
	—	All work is a process
Inputs	—	Information received in order to operate a process
Outputs	—	Results of a process, product, service or processed information provided to immediate or ultimate customer
Suppliers and Customers	—	Providers of inputs are suppliers whereas receivers of outputs are Customers
	—	They both are either internal or external to an organization
	—	All people within an organization have simultaneous suppliers and customer roles

Just as the product quality is realized through manufacturing process, customer satisfaction is achieved through management process. ISO 9000 systems concern all such management processes which impact the quality of product or service delivered to ultimate customers. This is illustrated in Fig. 8.1.

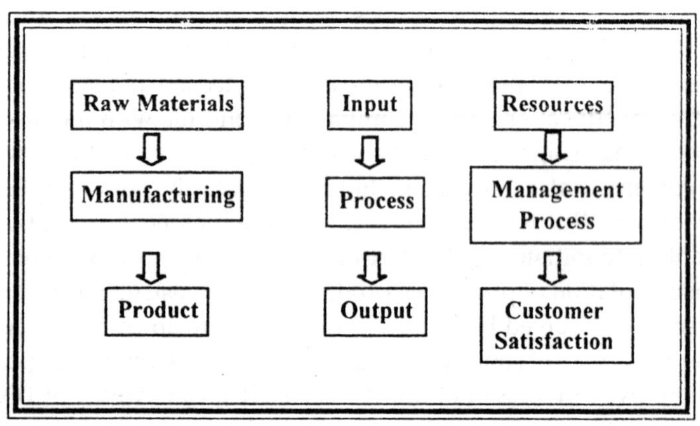

Fig. 8.1: How is Quality Achieved

Every process consumes one or more of the inputs and delivers one or more of the outputs as shown in Fig. 8.2.

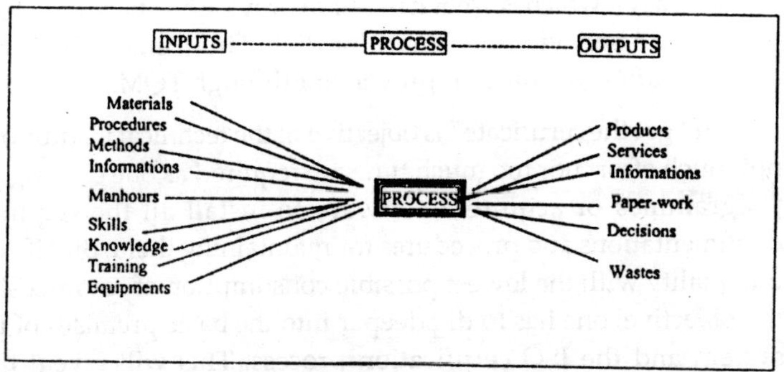

Fig. 8.2: Inputs, Process and Outputs

The entire technical education setting can also be put in the form of a process as shown in Fig. 8.3. Once the process approach is complete, for each of its components, list of factors which affect the quality of the process as a whole (which can be quantified and measurable) have to be developed. For example, consider teaching faculty as a component under consideration. The list of factors that influence the quality can be classified and categorized as qualification, experience (academic and/or industrial), papers published, awards received, etc. And these factors can be quality indicators which have bearing on the output of the process, i.e. technical manpower. A continuous monitoring of the performance of a technical institution with respect to the TQM dimensions will no doubt help the technical institution to gain competitive advantage in the present competitive market place.

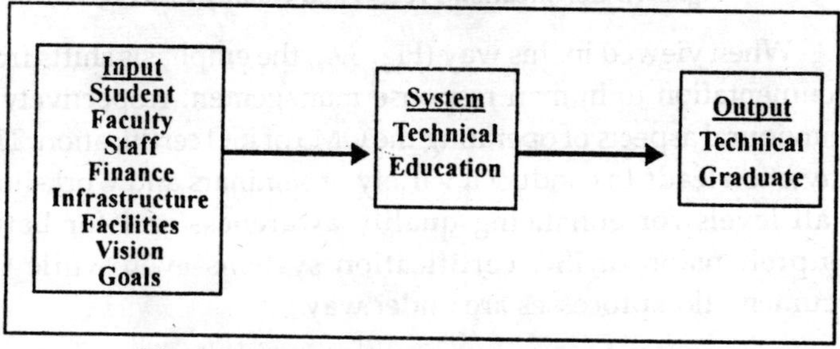

Fig. 8.3: QFD Model for Technical Institution

ISO CERTIFICATION—PHILOSOPHY OR BUREAUCRACY

ISO 9000 system has all the potential to remain an excellent bureaucracy – which is what it is—or to provide an effective vehicle to achieve a behavioural climate for Right First Time (RFT) habits and thereafter to launch improvement through TQM.

If "get the certificate" is objective of the technical institutions, not much effort nor too much time are required as one can engage programmes or acquire a software to install all the required documentations and procedures for maintaining them. But, if "get the quality with the lowest possible consumption of resources" is the objective, one has to dig deeper into the basic premises of the system and the ISO certification process. This will reveal that quality human response is an inseparable element of both TQM and ISO 9000, which makes the latter as much a philosophy as the former.

CERTIFICATION PROCESS				
Documented Proof of Establishment	+	Documented Proof of Maintenance	=	ISO Certification
QUALITY PROCESS				
Documented ISO 9001	+	Right First Time Culture	=	Total Quality

Fig. 8.4: Certification Process and Quality Process

When viewed in this way (Fig. 8.4), the emphasis shifts from documentation to human response management respectively to behavioural aspects of operating the QMS of ISO certification. This conviction leads to conduct a variety of seminars and workshops at all levels for enhancing quality awareness and for better comprehension of ISO certification systems even while the documentation processes are under way.

CONCLUSION

Final documentation of ISO certification system including the rationalized networks and processes is the first important step. This activity itself would prepare the people to recognize the need and the benefits of change, and inform them what, how and why of right first time. This is a solid foundation from which to launch for behavioural transformation needed for TQM.

The moral of the above analysis is clear. One may replace *systems* by *strategy* or *structure* and have all the three developed well ahead of your nearest competitor. But the key to *quality* will ever remain with *people*, their skills, style and above all shared values. It is to remember that ISO certification system is only a part of TQM process. Through the systematic approach and discipline required, it will form however the backbone for an overall quality philosophy that aims at preventing, instead of correcting, errors and failures.

Last but not the least, ISO certification systems provide effective, if not indispensable, instrument for TQM. The lifeline of TQM is with the leadership and his team who must lead by example for creating TQ culture for behavioural transformation. There is probably nothing worse in business to work for a boss who does not want to win.

9

Role of Professional Societies in Continuing Education and Quality Upgradation

Debabrata Maji[*]

INTRODUCTION

The National Policy on Education-1986 stipulates a variety of efforts for improving the quality of education, promoting social relevance and contributing effectively to the socio-economic development of the country. The policy amply recognizes the importance of continuing education in implementing the various programmes which should ideally play the major role in the development of learning, resource materials, consultancy and interaction with industry, research and development including innovation, extension services to the community and acquisition and development of expertise in different field.

In general, the professional societies have shown interest in the promotion of quality and standards in continuing education. It is the wheel of development that hastened the progress of education and resulted in a revolution in the realms of commerce, industry and social progress, in terms of development of human

* North-eastern Regional Institute of Science and Technology, Nirjuli (Itanagar)-791 109, Papum Pare District, Arunachal Pradesh

civilization and economic progress in any country. It offers opportunities for higher education to all those who desire and seek it. The learner is free to choose the pace of study according to convenience. Thus, rigidity is absent. It makes lifelong learning a reality. It is built on the concept aimed at democratising higher education.

Looking into the entire education process of these societies, the rooms of upgradation have been identified in this chapter. They are introducing technician education, examination reform, introducing training scheme both general and company specific, monitored professional development scheme, curriculum development and development of instructional materials. A separate section has been devoted to elaborate each of these topics. A critical estimate has been included for bringing uniformity in the course curricula country wide with the guidelines provided by the central bodies like AICTE or UGC.

FEATURES AND OBJECTIVES

The innovative and significant features of continuing education are: relaxed entry rules, study according to the learner's own pace and convenience, flexibility in choosing the combination of courses from a wide range of disciplines; study from the student's own chosen place and use of modern educational and communication technology.

The policy of continuing education has been established to advance and disseminate learning and knowledge by a diversity of means. It aims at:

(a) providing opportunities for higher education to large segments of population and seeks to achieve the educational well-being of the community;

(b) providing access to higher education to the disadvantaged groups and individuals and to unlock opportunities for upgrading knowledge and skills;

(c) promoting National integration and integrated development of the human personality;

(d) providing high quality education at the University level with continuous updating and standardising its own scope.

THE CAREER-BUILDING SECRET

Let us have a dialogue with one's self regarding his/her own career and try to identify some useful answers in an interactive narration.

Are you satisfied with your present job and future prospects? Do you see yourself as "a going concern" or are you just drifting ? One way to find out the truth is to ask yourself, how your employer would react if you resign this very day. Would he/she:

(a) accept it without comment?

(b) accept it with some regret but do nothing about it?

(c) try to persuade you to stay?

If the answer is (a) or (b) you are probably not "a going concern" and you should be very much critical about the way things are going.

There may be nothing specifically wrong with your job, yet somehow you feel it is not well. Why it should happen?

The answer is that you are not satisfied about your present way of life because you feel it could be better. Before you feel any real satisfaction from your professional career, certain basic conditions must be fulfilled:

(a) It must bring in enough money not merely to provide for your needs but also to give you the financial freedom to acquire some of the things you have always wanted;

(b) The work must be interesting to you and offer full scope for your abilities;

(c) It must be a job with a future;

(d) It has to be a job that requires some special skill or knowledge. Ideally, it should be such that very few will be able to do it and hence, you have a feeling of security that you can not be replaced easily.

This is where complete self honesty comes in. You have to measure your present success and see how you rate among your colleagues. The answer may disturb you but it can provide the vital spark that will send you speeding towards some real achievement.

The receipe for the kind of success you want is straight forward. All you have to remember is:

(a) Your employer buys a service from you;

(b) There is a gap in supply and demand;

(c) Untrained or unskilled labour is always available;

(d) Trained ability and specialized knowledge are in short supply;

(e) According to the degree of your specialized ability and knowledge you can frame your own terms and in most of the cases the employer will agree to it for your valued service.

The great secret of successful career building is to acquire specialized knowledge—something that your colleagues do not have. This is the down to earth realistic approach that makes sense to a hard headed employer.

IMPORTANCE OF PROFESSIONAL SOCIETIES IN TECHNICAL EDUCATION

The Planning Commission, the Union Ministry of Education (then) and the University Grants Commission (UGC) gave careful thought to the problem of expending and equalizing educational opportunities in order to scope with the rapidly increasing demand for technical expertise. Technical education is a specialized form of education dedicated to practical ends so that there will be enough qualified persons to plan, design, operate and service a vast complex of new and existing machinery, devices and techniques. It is basically an education for a career and carries with it a practical incentive—the promise of a new, better paid, more progressive and more interesting job. Therefore, demands rapidly increasing for technical persons. So the professional societies are partially fulfilled the ongoing demand of technical manpower. Unlike the technical Universities and Institutions, the professional societies impart advanced training to the target population, a large fraction of that are already in the profession which helps enhancing the skill also. This is because the man in the job knowing "what I am doing" is upgraded when he/she knows "why I am doing". Here lies the significant difference between the two parallel streams of technical education in our country.

SUGGESTIONS FOR UPGRADATION

Introducing Technician Education

For the last few years, there have been many observations from local organizations and from various visiting teams from abroad that the polytechnic system in India could not meet the need of technicians in a modern economy[1]. During these years there was very little modernisation of infrastructure as far as this need is concerned.

Every one admits that technician education is the backbone of the industrial sector. If countries like Japan, South Korea, Singapore, Hongkong and Taiwan have prospered in the industrial sector, it is mainly due the efficient use and assimilation of technology. Why have we not succeeded in assimilating technologies as fast as is being done in these countries? The answer is that we do not have the right type of trained manpower engaged in our industrial sector. Technician education has to concentrate more on technology development and assimilation and on supervisory skills. It should develop its own identity and status as an important component of technical education.

Therefore, it is very much needed to introduce such type of education in professional societies by the following agenda:

(a) Introducing a system for technician education as is done in most of the developed and developing countries;

(b) It may design for technician education a more technology and supervisory skill oriented curriculum to suit the needs of the industry and the rural economy instead of the existing diluted version of the degree curriculum;

(c) A detailed study/research is to be made on the technician education system by examining the systems in other countries and by getting feedback from employing agencies on the following aspects:

- concepts and definitions of technician education;
- role of technician, based on activity analysis;
- structure, standard and content of courses and programmes;

— practical training of students;

— linkage with industry and community.

EXAMINATION REFORM

In India, students are coming from diverse environments and social backgrounds with widely varying value systems and interests. On the other hand the technology is changing continuously. To match with today's trend in technology, the curriculum also having been changing accordingly, keeping in mind its acceptability and appropriateness to the diversity mentioned above. Therefore, it is the duty of any professional society to reform system of existing examination system on an urgent basis. The most compelling reason for examination reform comes from academic consideration. Examination is an aspect of educational process which is intimately linked with its other important aspects like learning. Hence learning processes are bound to be affected by a defective examination system.

Therefore, it is proposed to organize a series of workshop/ seminar on the subject of examination reform with the following points:

(a) review of the work done by UGC and other centralized bodies on examination;

(b) problems introducing examination reform;

(c) establishing a logical equivalence of absolute and relative grading systems;

(d) objective type questions Vs short and long answer questions;

(e) establish examination as an integral part of learning;

(f) improvements in question paper setting;

(g) reforms in evaluation methods.

INTRODUCING TRAINING SCHEME

General Training

In every phase of practice wherever an engineer works general training is essential to improve and update his/her skill and knowledge. It should link the conceptual analytical abilities with their wide practical application in industry and provide a sound base for professional development.

The training should serve to help the learner to learn quickly about the use of knowledge gained through the courses:

— by experiencing at first hand that success as an engineer depends on team work and good human relations;

— by experiencing that industrial problems rarely have a unique solution and the optimum use of alternatives is important;

— by experiencing that cost and time are vitally important in all engineering activities;

— by experiencing and understanding the processes of design and manufacture;

— by experiencing the need to satisfy customers through product quality and reliability and timely delivery;

— by experiencing the need for a company to remain competitive and profitable;

— by understanding the role of engineers in industry and society.

The main aims of the training suggested above are as follow:

(a) *Resources* : to develop an understanding engineering resources and the skills used in utilizing them effectively.

(b) *Interdependence* : to develop an understanding of the inter relationship between market needs, design, production, maintenance and the financial and human environments within which engineering activities operate.

(c) *Environment* : to develop an understanding of the interaction between engineering and natural environment.

(d) *Awareness of Skill* : to develop an awareness of the skills involved in transferring an idea into a functional, efficient, economically viable and aesthetically satisfying artifact, system or operation.

(e) *Systems* : to develop a sense of appreciation of the totality in which engineering, industrial, social and environmental aspects are involved.

(f) *Management* : to develop skill in managing the work of both personal and of others, by effective communication.

(g) *Responsibility* : to become accustomed in accepting responsibility for any decision or action taken and the results thereof.

(h) *Team work* : to develop the ability to appreciate the limits of personal competence and discover sources of further knowledge and expertise.

(i) *Logical approach* : to develop a logical approach to all problems.

(j) *Manufacture* : to develop an appreciation of engineering manufacturing processes, their control and efficient operation.

COMPANY SPECIFIC TRAINING

In addition to the general training proposed and characterised above, company specific training is also required which shall serve towards the special needs of the industry where the learner bears an effective part in that business. However, this area of training should not restrict the future development of the learner but will prove itself as a means of enhancing the general training for a particular industry and provide an opportunity for the company and the individual to make judgements of aptitudes and suitability for future prospects. This should orient the learner towards better performance that increase the learner's responsibility and accountability.

MONITORED PROFESSIONAL DEVELOPMENT SCHEME

The Monitored Professional Development Scheme (MPDS) should be preferred by the professional society in continuing education for quality-assured route to its members. The scheme leads to career development where an engineer acts as a mentor to the learners throughout the duration of the scheme. This provides a structured and strongly focussed approach to both technical and personal development, usually leading to corporate membership and chartered status at or near the respective minimum age prescribed.

CURRICULUM DEVELOPMENT

The Ministry of Human Resource Development, Government of India established curriculum development cells in some institutions in the country with the objective of framing and developing model syllabi and curricula for the core courses and various engineering courses. So the professional societies in continuing education may have to take active role to bring their own curricula at par with equivalent regular courses.

This exercise has gone a long way in bringing uniformity in the various programmes. It would be an interesting study to find out the deviations/variations in the various course structures throughout the country and find out the basis of such variations in each case. In a vast country like India, the relative merit of these modifications arising out of personal/institutional/locational factors would serve as a useful feedback to the design and improvement of the curricula in future.

DEVEPLOMENT OF INSTRUCTIONAL MATERIALS

The responsibility of any professional society should not cease after conducting examination. They can offer helping hands to their students by providing study materials at appropriate levels. Statistically speaking, the students of these societies are mostly unemployed, with poor financial background and are unable to pursue formal education due to lack of merit and/or fund. Therefore, the study materials developed and to be distributed should be cheap in price and written in a lucid manner.

CONCLUSION

Professional societies in continuing education are taking active part to make the slogan "*Education for all*" a reality. It provides wide ranging scope for learning which is open ended.

At this juncture, it is the responsibility of the Government of India to identify such professional bodies which offer courses leading to no where and the number of these societies are plenty in our country. Very often the students are misguided by the attractive advertisements in the news media and after spending a lot of time, energy and money they end with nothing. Commercialisation of technical education is a fact that can not be denied.

There is a long felt need for proper study materials. The professional societies are warranted to strengthen the activities of its state and local chapters, so that the gap between the institution and the students community gets shortened. The whole aim and objectives of continuing education managed by professional societies should not be diluted at any cost, otherwise technical education may reduce itself to a costly commodity for sale.

REFERENCES

1. "New Letters", Indian Society for Technical Education, New Delhi.
2. "Quest for Learning", Indira Gandhi Open University, New Delhi.
3. "On the Service of Education", Regal College, Agra.
4. "Engineering Opportunities", The British Institutes, Bombay July 1984.
5. "Information brochures", The Institution of Mechanical Engineers, London, June 1992.
6. "Engineering Project Management". Lancester University, U.K., August 1993.

10

Vocational Education for Better Employment Opportunities

Role of Government, Institute and Industry

H R Patel[*]

Nimish Shah[**]

ABSTRACT

Dr. Manmohan Singh, Former Finance Minister of India had implemented the policy of Liberalization, Privatization and Globalization in 1991. This policy has developed environment for free flow of information and technology through various means in efficient manner. This has lead to the technological change in very fast manner. Because of globalization Indian market is opening for the world. Lots of multinational industries are entering in Indian market and increasing demand of technically qualified manpower and quality product. Indian industries are facing lots of problem in the era of globalization, one of the problems

* **Chemical Engineering Department, Institute of Diploma Studies, Nirma University of Science & Technology, Sarkhej-Gandhinagar Highway, P.O. Chandlodia, Ahmedabad- 382 481, Email: harshadpinki@yahoo.com**

** **Chemical Engineering Department, Institute of Diploma Studies, Nirma University of Science & Technology, Sarkhej-Gandhinagar Highway, P.O. Chandlodia, Ahmedabad- 382 481 Email: nimish_nirma@yahoo.com**

is the quality of product and non availability of suitable qualified manpower. The Industry- Institute and Government have to work in isolation for the development of vocational skills in the technical stuff available in India and to provide quality education and quality training should be in tune with the emerging field[1]*. This chapter deals with the role of Government, Institute and Industry to upgrade vocational education to develop knowledge and employability in context to India and foreign country.*

Key Words: Vocational Technical Education (VTE), Industry Institute Interaction (III), Globalization.

INTRODUCTION

The new challenge before the country at the beginning of the 21st century is to become a developed nation by the year 2020, which requires not only knowledge driven economy, but human values are also important. Moreover, challenges in higher education are no longer only nation centric. They have already attained global dimensions, particularly after trade in services has been brought under the purview of the WTO regime. With the explosive growth of knowledge in the past century and with the development of handy tools of information and communication technologies as well as of other scientific innovations, competition has become a hallmark of growth all over the World. As a result, knowledge is not only driving the Indian economy, but also, it is going to permeate into all the strata of Indian society for a better quality of life and living conditions. Therefore, India has to rise to the occasion urgently and reorient its higher education system to be vibrant, competitive, meaningful and purposeful. Besides, there is absolutely no substitute to quality of higher education, although the country has been faced for a long time with the serious problem of meeting the quantity needs of our society[1].

TECHNICAL EDUCATION STATUS IN INDIA

"Education is the process of the individual mind getting to its full possible development...It is a long school which lasts a life time"

—Dr. Zakir Hussain

Information technologies has great role on rapid movement of globalism process. This great development process of information technologies has brought significant productivity and automation in each and every field. Generally national firms have become smaller except some specific sectors. Globalization has posed number of challenges to Technical Education. The biggest challenge ahead is to supply technically trained stuff to corporate world. Some of the challenges to technical education are listed below[2].

1. Inadequate instruction and academic facilities
2. Insufficient qualified and experienced faculty
3. Rigidity in curriculum
4. Poor curriculum design- less emphasis on training and practical
5. No proper implementation of programmes
6. Poor working environments
7. External factors such as lack of motivation
8. Inadequate interaction with customer industry and society
9. Policy and attitude of management
10. Changing mix of urban and non urban background of students without corresponding modification/ orientation of education methods
11. Non-selective admission of students
12. Lack of practical approach

Spending of Government of India on Education sector is 13.17 per cent of total budget. The quality of technical stuff is not as per need of industries. The graduating class of students are lacking in the practical knowledge and knowledge of emerging technologies and hence they found difficulties in employment in rapidly changing environment. One of the solutions to these problems is imparting vocational education with practical training oriented approach.

Table—10.1 Spending of Indian Government on Education Sector[3]

Year	Govt. expenditure on education in crores	Total Govt. expenditure on all sectors in crores	% of expenditure on Education to expenditure on all sectors
1	2	3	4
1965-66	432.61	4404.82	9.82
1966-67	487.83	5100.24	9.56
1967-68	593.14	5619.77	10.55
1968-69	649.13	6922.07	9.38
1969-70	760.23	7908.07	9.61
1970-71	892.36	8787.12	10.16
1971-72	1011.07	10610.89	9.53
1972-73	1150.43	11863.56	9.70
1973-74	1300.72	12884.48	10.10
1974-75	1570.67	14625.03	10.74
1975-76	1849.47	17958.99	10.30
1976-77	2039.09	20482.83	9.96
1977-78	2630.60	22666.31	11.61
1978-79	2994.69	26134.84	11.46
1979-80	3347.57	30915.39	10.83
1980-81	3884.20	36398.39	10.67

(Contd...)

1	2	3	4
1981-82	4435.29	33667.31	13.17
1982-83	5509.17	43996.18	12.52
1983-84	6229.53	61889.25	10.07
1984-85	7455.38	69025.45	10.80
1985-86	8713.02	67091.41	12.99
1986-87	9479.13	80454.66	11.78
1987-88	11798.35	92518.38	12.75
1988-89	14069.32	107543.75	13.08
1989-90	17192.50	126045.97	13.64
1990-91	19615.35	146711.53	13.37
1991-92	22393.69	170370.38	13.14
1992-93	25030.30	190327.45	13.15
1993-94	28279.69	218535.15	12.94
1994-95	32606.22	251691.92	12.95
1995-96	38178.09	286194.55	13.34
1996-97	43896.48	329389.92	13.33
1997-98	48552.14	380728.45	12.75
1998-99	61578.91	439768.11	14.00
1999-2000	74816.09	512519.33	14.60
2000-2001	82486.43	572160.14	14.42
2001-2002	84179.46	639048.06	13.17

VOCATIONAL EDUCATION STATUS IN INDIA

Day by day older technology becomes obsolete in terms of revenue generation because of explosion of newer technologies and hence it's hard reality that the technocrats are lacking in the required knowledge of emerging technology. Vocational Technical Education (VTE) is "Education and Training for Work and for Better Employment Opportunities". It is to develop skills and competencies of learners. It has traditionally been seen as post secondary, no university education and training, focusing on apprenticehips. But it reforms in the past decades now VTE programme offered with university education/after completing university education. VTE now-a-days should not be part of imparting the apprenticehips training in the secondary school students but it should be also implemented effectively for the higher studies after graduation or university study as the graduates are lacking in the required practical knowledge. To avoid this gap industries co-operation desirable in technical education for shaping of better tomorrow[4].

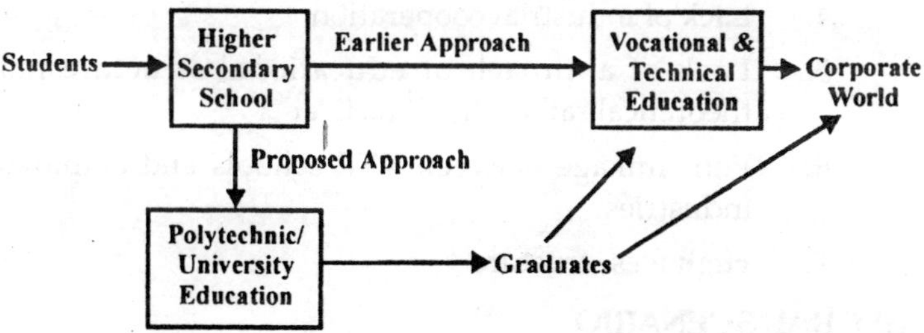

Fig. 10.1: Proposed New Approach for Vocational Technical Education

Results of studies on performance analysis of Asian countries is listed in Table—10.2, the results shows that VTE sector is ignored in India as there is less than 2 per cent enrollment of total enrolment in education sector.

Table—10.2 Per cent age enrolment in VTE sector (Asia Region)[4]

< 2%	2-5%	5-10%	10-15%	> 15%
Myanmar				
Bangladesh				
Oman	Malaysia	Brunei		Thailand
Kuwait	Hong Kong	Mongolia	Papua New Guinea	Korea
UAE	Vietnam	Cyprus	Indonesia	Israel
India	Lao	Iraq	Japan	Jordan
Pakistan	Singapore	Syria	China	Turkey
Cambodia	Iran			
Saudi Arabia				
Qatar				

VTE Sector ignored in India due to following reasons:

1. Education turn to business
2. Lack of experience in faculties
3. Lack of required infrastructure
4. Lack of industrial cooperation
5. Lack of approach of educational structure more theoretical rather than practical
6. Poor linkage between VTE schools and employing industries
7. High fees structure

GLOBAL SCENARIO

Globally the numbers of Governments have supported VTE and benefited out of it. The Australian Government had set the vocational education priorities as follows[5]

1. Proper funding to VTE by Government and Industries
2. Improve quality and consistency of VTE
3. Meet industry skill needs, responding to the evolving needs, reducing skill shortage
4. Support an open, flexible, competitive and high quality training

5. Foster adult skilling
6. Improve VTE opportunities through better linking of Institute and Industries.

MODERNIZATION OF VTE SYSTEM: CASE STUDY OF CHINA[6]

Internationalization has become a common trend for the reform and development of modern education in the world. Along with the reform and opening to the outside world, China has been actively engaged in the international cooperation and exchanges in the field of vocational education.

1. During the past 20 years, the government has sent many delegations to over 20 countries where vocational education is well developed to learn successful foreign experience and to implement it.
2. At the same time, China has received many foreign vocational education delegations, invited foreign experts to give lectures in China, and jointly provided education with foreign vocational education institutions to promote the development of Chinese vocational education. China has also made more and more contact with the UNESCO, UNDP, world Labour Organization, UNPF, APEC and other international organizations while the bilateral cooperation and exchanges between China and other countries has been increasingly expanded.
3. In order to improve the level of vocational education teachers, since 1987 China has sent thousands of administrators and teachers to America, the United Kingdom, Germany, Italy, Australia, Canada and Japan for study, which has received good results.
4. In 1990, the Chinese government signed the "Agreement on the Loan for Vocational Education Project in China" with World Bank. The two session project altogether will use US $ 80 million from world Bank and $ 100 million from the Chinese government.

5. In 1990, German government agreed to provide the fund to establish the Central Vocational Education Research Institute and two local research institutes in Shanghai and Liaoning. Since early 1980's, China and Germany have jointly set up over 30 cooperative projects in the field of vocational education and carried out the pilot reform which drew experience and form the German "Dual-track System" with wide and deep cooperation and research. In Addition, cooperating with Canada and Australia, China imported their educational and training models based on ability to reform the traditional teaching patterns. The Ministry of Labour and Social Welfare cooperated with the World Labour Organization to carry out the pilot work in skill worker schools and in-service training.
6. China undertook the International Seminar on Vocational and Technical Education organized by the UNESCO during 13th -18th September 1993,. In April 1997, the International Seminar on Rural Vocational Education was held in China and representatives from foreign countries, World Bank and World Labour Organization discussed and summarized the international development of vocational education, providing valuable experience for developing vocational education in China.

The Achievements of Vocational Education in China

1. The Rapid Expansion of the Scale of Vocational Education
2. The Big Stride Made in the Construction of Vocational Education Teachers
3. The Increase of the Quality and Level of Vocational Education
4. The Primary Fruits of the Teaching Reform of Vocational Education
5. Rapid Development of Vocational Education in Rural Areas

WHY CO-OPERATATION IS REQUIRED?

The universal agreement for strengthening cooperation between vocational educational institutions and industries is a very significant strategy for tackling the current pitfalls of VTE. Efficient co-operation is necessary between industry and institute to develop better employment opportunities in the corporate world. The co-operation effort should be initiated by institute as they are beneficiary, such co-operations have quadruple benefits as shown below[7].

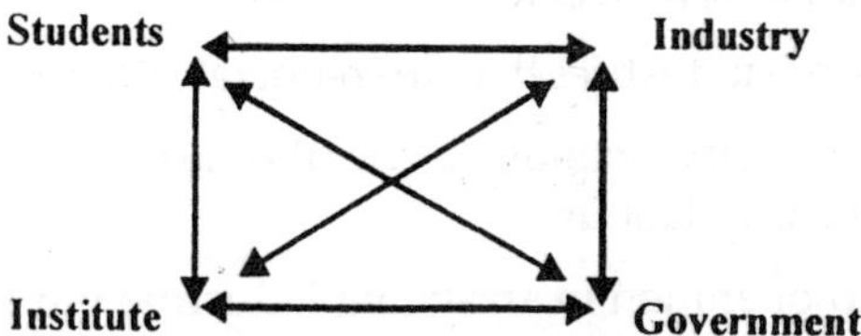

Fig. 10.2: Quadruple benefit through industry—Institute Co-operation

1. *Students* benefit from an introduction to the real world of work, their prospects in corporate world rise as a result of practical work experiences. As industries require personals having exposure and experience of their work. There is a gap between institute products (Students) and Industries requirements. The students having VTE background can narrow this gap are more acceptable to industries.

2. *Educational Institutions* need the advice of the world of work to frame their curricula as per industrial needs and to have access to the latest technology.

3. *Industry* can profit directly from co-operation at different levels and thus, secure the provision of a well skilled technical stuff. They can identify students at an early stage with the greatest potential for a future long term contract. The exchange of knowledge and know-how the joint undertaking of research and development projects have potential for lifting productivity. The experience by students and teachers of life within an industry and the participation in the renewal and adaptation of teaching and training programmes to suit productive work are of considerable value.

4. *Society and Government* benefit from the indirect effects of co-operation. In democratic market it is evident that by the effective designing of VTE improvement in employment situations and which in turn strengthening economies and healthy society will be formed.

ROLE OF INDUSTRY AND INSTITUTE

Current Status of Co-operation

1. Rather low/weak
2. Those industries that do co-operate do so half-heartedly
3. Many other exploit co-operation arrangement as means of cheap labour
4. Co-operation in arranging industrial visits
5. Students placement for training
6. Review by both parties to drawn up curricula in light of realities/challenges facing industries
7. Arrangement of expert lectures of industries personnel for the benefit of students

Areas of Possible Co-operation

1. Attachment of technical education students to industries for practical work experience
2. Making available special equipment & machinery to technical education institutions at agreed period for training purpose
3. Interaction between Teachers and relevant industries officers to draw up result oriented programmes and to jointly closely monitor the implementation of the same for maximum benefit of the students
4. Consultancy services (R & D Activities), industries should come forward with their problems
5. Upgradation of laboratory facilities by donating equipments/models to institute
6. Collaborating workshops, seminars on emerging technologies

7. Co-operation in arranging visiting faculties of international repute
8. Continuing education of industry personnel
9. Exchange of faculty
10. Project allotment to students based on burning industrial problems
11. Adoption of institute by industry

Hindrance of Co-operation

1. Lack of interest on both side
2. Inadequate follow-up/motivation by Government agencies to encourage/forge co-operation
3. Non availability of sufficient finance
4. Industry didn't come forward to discuss their problems when they are in monopoly business
5. Lack of practical knowledge at graduation level
6. Obsolete laboratory facilities do not attract industries to interact with institute

Role Of Government[8]

1. It is the primary responsibility of the government to provide the good quality higher education at reasonable cost
2. Government should setup every district level cell to promote Industry Institute Interaction process and provide appropriate funding facilities to carry out joint R & D projects
3. Industries may be encouraged to be partners with educational institutions
4. Government should promote the industries to establish the state of the art research and training centers to develop the necessary specialized manpower
5. Institute should have freedom to prepare tailor made specialized courses at institute level for industries
6. Industries and individuals may be encouraged to channel a percentage of their profits to the higher

education sector, with no strings attached to such contributions. Viable incentives may be offered for attracting such investments from the private resources

7. Strong quality control measures to assure performance above an acceptable benchmark is essential for the institutions. A Total Quality Management for courses offered, monitoring the achievement of the students at all stages of the course, shall be introduced at all higher education institutions
8. Accreditation system for individuals in various disciplines may be thought of
9. After completion of technical education in classrooms the inplant training should be made mandatory as a part of curriculum
10. Tax benefit should be introduce to induce industry to promote engineering education and collaborative R & D efforts
11. Private Universities are a reality now and, as such, strong regulatory mechanisms are to be put in place immediately to monitor and control their activities with the objective of ensuring quality and social accountability
12. According autonomous status to all performing institutions will facilitate rapid development of efficient and state of the art higher education institutions.

IMPLEMENTATION OF VTE AT UNIVERSITY: A CASE STUDY OF FOUNDRY TECHNOLOGY COURSE AT NIRMA UNIVERSITY, AHMEDABAD, INDIA[10]

Mechanical Engineering Department, Institute of Diploma Studies, Nirma University of Science and Technology had recently introduced Advanced Diploma Programme (ADP) on Foundry Technology. As the industries located near Ahmedabad region presented following problems:

1. The graduates entering the foundry industries are having Mechanical/Production/Fabrication Engineering/Science background;

2. Lack of practical knowledge;
3. To promote R & D in frontier areas pertaining to foundry technology.

With these views the institute had started ADP on Foundry Technology to enrich the graduates entering foundry industries. Board of Studies (BOS) was called on this occasion, Eminent Industrialist and Educationists and Government Representatives shared their views in framing the curriculum and designing structure of ADP. Table—10.3 shows list of members of BOS & Table 10.4 shows teaching scheme. Only one technical institute in India is offering this course on Foundation Technology by National Institute of Foundry and Forge Technology, Ranchi[9].

Table—10.3 Members of Board of Studies (BOS)

Members BOS	No. of Persons
Industrialists	14
Educationists	09
Government Representative	02

Eligibility Criteria for Admission

1. Diploma in Mechanical/Production/Metallurgy Engineering/Fabrication Technology
2. Degree in Mechanical/Production/Metallurgy Engineering/Fabrication Technology
3. Bachelor of Science in Physics/Chemistry

Table—10.4 Teaching Scheme of Advanced Diploma Programme (ADP)

Trimester	Teaching scheme (hours/week)				Total Credits
	Lectures*	Tutorials	Laboratories**	Total	
1	16	02	12	30	24
2	16	01	10	27	22
3	Project work at Industries				08

* Lectures by Institute Faculty and Industries Eminent Personalities

** Laboratory work is to be carried out in Industry

CONCLUSION

The unemployment ratio in India has acquired dangerous proportions. This has made us realize that it will be a futile exercise to spend time and energy on academic courses. Academic courses do not equip our children for a job. As a result, today, there is a tendency among students to join some technical educational institutions rather than joining some academic courses. They have begun to acknowledge the importance of technical education to secure a decent job. Students find it much safer and better to choose a technical course instead of some simple academic courses. They also find that the acquisition of a technical qualification coupled with a little bit of experience in a particular vocation would fetch them a lucrative job either in India or abroad.

Government has also introduced vocational education both at the school and college levels. The aims and objectives are to provide for the diversification of educational opportunities, enhance individual employment ability, reduce the gap between demand and supply of skilled manpower and provide an alternative for those pursuing higher education.

There are also hundreds of polytechnics and other similar institutions all over the country offering a wide range of vocational and skill-based career development courses such as gems and jewellery, footwear technology, plastics, food processing and construction management. There are hundreds of certificate and diploma courses available today which will suit any student and there are hundreds of institutions every where conducting short and long term courses.

REFERENCE

1. Ghodasara K. D., Patel H. R. & Bandyopadhyay K, "The Importance of Vocational and Technical Education in Global Economy", Proceedings of National Seminar on National Technical Manpower Information System, NIT-Rourkella,2004, p. 10.

2. Meirios Moechtar, " The Role of Engineering Education in Knowledge Based Economy," Proceedings of the 6th AEESEAP Triennial Conference, Bali, Indonesia, August 23-25, 2000.

3. "Public Expenditure In Education", www.thecommonwealth.org

4. Tilak J.B., "Vocational Education in Asia", www.norrage.org, p. 9.

5. "Vocational Education and Training Resolution", Australian Council for Trade Union Congress, 1997.

6. "Vocational Education in China : VTE Development", www.edu.cn

7. Aware H.V., Warkad U.G., Ghormade T.K., " A Role of Industry-Institute and Government to Develop Employment Oriented Vocational Education and Training", Proceedings of 33rd Annual Convention, KCT-Coimbatore, December-2003, pp. 625-632.

8 "Technical Education, National Institute of Foundry and Forge Technology—Ranchi", http://shikshanic.nic.in

11

Strategic Planning of Manpower at Institutes to Meet the Challenges for Changing Scenario of the Modern Industries Requirements

*Mamta Mainak Saiyad**

ABSTRACT

The challenges of present century will be enormous and exorbitant. The developments of human activities in all spheres of life are highly important and indispensable. The industries in the country, have flourished mainly by the Technocrats. They have been educated and trained by the technical institutions. Industrial organization in the country can come forward to expose the students as well as faculties to the real problem and developments of industry. On the other hand, the curriculums for various courses of the technical institutes should be developed in view of changing scenario of modern industries requirements, by adapting man who is capable of living in a technological society and of transferring it to meet the material and spiritual needs of the age.

Key Words: enormous, exorbitant, Technocrats, curriculums, changing scenario, spiritual needs

* **Lecturer, Plastic Engineering Department, Nirma Institute of Diploma Studies, Sarkhej-Gandhinagar Highway, Post Chandalodia, Via Gota, Ahmedabad-382 481, Email: ma2sa@yahoo.com**

INTRODUCTION

The challenges of the present century will be enormous and exorbitant. The developments of human activities in all spheres of life are highly important and indispensable.

The industries in the country, have flourished mainly by the Engineers and Technicians working there. These technical personnel have been educated and trained by the technical institutions.

Technological development is taking place at a fast rate. No one can ignore this fact and get them trained in these new fields. Industries should sponsor the Engineers and Technicians to undertake continuing education programmes run by technical institutions.

Industrial organization in the country can come forward to provide scholarships to bright students and shop floor training/ experience for students as well as faculties to expose them to the real problem and developments of industry.

On the other hand, the curriculums for various courses of the technical institutes need to be developed in view of changing scenario of the modern industries requirements.

The global technological advancement has forced the industries and technical institute to realize that they can no longer live in isolation from each other. Recent developments both in education and in industry have made this forward projection of education of far greater moment than previously.

The present day system of education is designed mainly to know things orally and locally perceived without giving scope for deep study for acquiring thorough knowledge. The ways and means of removing these difficulties; not by adapting man to the technological society, but rather by considering how education can form the "whole man" – that is, the man who is capable of living in a technological society and of transferring it to meet the material and spiritual needs of the age.

These suggestions are only a few of many by which manpower may be planned in proper manner and which in turn; institute can provide expertise and technocrats to serve the needs of industries.

ROLE OF INDUSTRY

There are many industries in the country, which have flourished mainly by the Engineers and Technicians working there. These technical personnel have been educated and trained by the technical institutions, but nowadays these institutions are finding it difficult to run due to scarcity of fund. They are finding difficult to come up to meet the growing demand of technical education and consequently industries have started finding following difficulties:

1. The technical knowledge at present given is wholly inadequate for industry needs;
2. Technical education including apprenticeship and other forms of in-industry training is liable to be too narrow in a world of rapid technological change;
3. The cultural content of technical education is inadequate.

The ways and means of removing these difficulties; the industries management should realize that for the better working of their establishment, they have to help the technical institutions. The various methods by which they can help are instituting scholarships, sponsoring projects, providing training for the students, involving technical institutions in the R & D programmes, involving the curriculum development work of the technical institutions, honouring best students and teachers, sponsoring faculties for participating in the continuing education programme of the technical institutions to update knowledge, running special courses in the industry itself.

Even industrial giants in the country can come forward and institute scholarship for students to pursue their studies and to undertake research work in the field of their requirements, so that the bright students may not deprived of the type of education they want to study. Many organizations in other countries are doing these effectively.

The government in turn should permit technical institutions to take these sponsored students over and above the sanctioned strength. After graduation these students can either be employed in the organization sponsoring them or serve the country for at least five years.

To provide the much-needed shop floor experience for the students and expose the students to real problem of industries, industries may come forward in providing industrial training. By these not only the students but also the industries gain. This scheme is beneficial to the industries as they get help not only from the students but also through the expertise of the technical institution.

For better industry – institution relation which is the much-needed aspect of technical education, faculties from industries and technical institutions must be freely exchanged for short periods. This will help in sharing the expertise of each other.

The best work done by students and the faculty are going unnoticed by society. Only when due recognition is given to the talents, will people come forward for displaying their best. Industries can come forward in instituting awards and cash prizes for the best student and best teachers.

ROLE OF INSTITUTES

The challenges of the present century will be enormous and exorbitant. The developments of human activities in all spheres of life are highly important and indispensable.

But the world today is in agitation. Problems between nations, within nation and among human beings are very large. In this situation, preparation of good curriculum for development of overall personality of the student is very much necessary to face the problems and challenges of the situation.

A curriculum is the planned programme of the activities to achieve the objectives of education. According to academicians, curriculum does not mean only the technological subjects, but includes totality of all experiences that a student should know through the manifold activities that go on in the institute, in the classroom, library, laboratory, workshop, playground and numerous informal activities.

For curriculum reforms there must be closer relationship between men and environment, greater identification of the subject should be made, job oriented and employment opportunities can be created, socio-economic conditions should be developed, co-ordination between subjects should be made, creative skill should be improved, ability of problem solving should be developed, right values should be increased and thus up-dating the knowledge of information is required.

In this sense the whole life of the college becomes the curriculum, which can touch the life of the students at all points and help, in attaining balance personality.

The present day system of education is designed mainly to know things orally and locally perceived without giving scope for deep study for acquiring thorough knowledge. The general education given is lacking in the realistic, contemporary knowledge necessary for life in a technological society and inclines towards bookish "know about" rather than a practical "know how".

Students are taught to repeat words precisely and to operate as mechanical and mathematical process without giving opportunity for logical thinking and reasoning. The present system of curriculum and syllabus can be reformed to develop the creativity factors, analytical power, problem solving ability etc.

Present structure of curriculum have neglected the student thinking and learning process that would assist them greatly to develop visualization, imagination and sensory perceptual abilities. The models so often presented to the students in their textbooks emphasis linear thought processes, ignoring intuitive, analogical and metaphorical thinking.

This does not mean that subject matter will not be used, or that it becomes unimportant. Things cannot teach without teaching something, and students cannot learn without learning something. Only the question is that what is the subject matter is for?

While framing the curriculum stress could be laid upon the proper teaching of fundamental subjects and as upon comprehensive knowledge as calculations and general science. Students can also be introduced to such subjects as business administration, economics and management, which are relevant to the immediate requirements of the chosen field.

The theoretical appreciation of fundamental principles could be constantly tested against practical application in the shape of workshop activity.

Neurological studies indicate that education as it is now structured develops only one part of the human brain and leaves the other part untouched, which has a high level, potential. Different teaching techniques and methodologies can be adopted to influence and activate the other part to be functioned of the brain.

The experiments throw new light on the visual process and its importance for behavior. It is the major tie that binds us to the outside world. We also gain some knowledge of what lies outside us by experimental process. This concept of vision leading to an experimental way of managing the life as well.

In general, the teaching should aim at developing the personality of the student, together with such a spirit of inquiring and independence of thought as would stand one in good stead not only in his work but in his free time activities as well.

Subject matter alone cannot educate and build a "whole man". The students should experience all kinds of things and not the fragmentation of knowledge.

The curriculum continues to be fashioned on the concept of preparing students for acquiring degrees and diplomas without practical content and thus the students become useless to be positioned in jobs immediately after college studies.

Curriculum for various courses of the technical institutes have been developed purely by teachers of the institutes. Now it has been realized that the industries and other research organization have to be involved in the curriculum development in view of the changing scenario the industries hold participate in the curriculum development work of various technical institutions. Sponsoring projects has become a reality nowadays. Many industries are now sponsoring projects as they find it useful for their own growth. The financial burden of the technical institutions is less, and students are able to acquire the real shop-floor experience in the development and execution work of the project in industries.

There are many reputed Industries and Research organizations contributing immensely in certain fields of specialization. Using this experience, they can come forward in framing proper curriculum for specialized courses, in consultation with technical institutions and university authorities, which can be offered by them at their place itself.

These types of steps can be encouraged by the universities and industries, before starting such practice; there are some following suggestions:

1. Regular statistical estimates are needed of a country's requirements in trained personnel for the major types of work at all levels. These estimates should be local and regional as well as national in their scope.
2. Moreover, as present education is not for the present but for future need of society, occupational trends should be continuously forecast as far as practicable.

These suggestions are only a few of the many aspects by which the industries and other organizations in India can come forward in lessoning the financial burden of the suffering of technical institutions.

Recent developments both in education and in industry have made this forward projection of education of far greater moment than previously. The technological advancement taking place in the world has forced the industries and technical institutes to realize that they can no longer live in isolation from one another. They need the help of the other. This has to be viewed as a good but only a starting point. In the years ahead, it can be said; there will be positive and encouraging cooperation between industries and technical institutions.

REFERENCES

1. John W Hanson and Cole S. Brembeck *Education and the Development of Nations* London Holt, Rinehart & Winston 1966.
2. OESER A O Teacher, Pupil and Task London. Tavistock. 1971; Trade p/b. Reprint. 196 pp.

3. Oppenheim *Questionnaire Design and Attitude Measurement*.

4. *The Hindu* speaks on Education.

5. Altbach, Philip G. *Scientific Development and Higher Education: The Case of Newly Industrialising Nations* Westport, CT, U.S.A.: Greenwood Publishing Group, Incorporated, 1989.

6. W. Cummings, *International Handbook of Education and Development Preparing Schools, Students and Nations for the Twenty-First Century* Elsevier Snience Ltd. North-Holland 1997.

12

Effective Approaches and Models in Manpower Planning

*A.C. Dhaneshwar**

ABSTRACT

Bowey—one of the known manpower planner in1977 has defined manpower planning as a "strategy for matching future manpower numbers and skills with organizational activities". Many researchers have published work in this area. Gregory presented a manpower-planning model based on the idea of career development and job assignment according to skills attained. Thomson's work was notable for its application of linear programming to manpower planning problems. The ATMR reviews are based on the data collected under the NTMIS project. The reviews deal with the existing facilities for technical education and engineering labour market. A pre-designed questionnaire has mailed to all the degree and diploma holders who passed out two years after they completed their courses. Now in this traditional approach, we are just in considering only two years after passing, but very important and serious thing, which has subsequent effect, should be addressed is the status about after two years to at present. As if one considers about that status then

* **Project Officer, NTMIS Nodal Centre for Gujarat, Directorate of Technical Education, 1st Floor, Block No. 4, Dr. Jivraj Mehta Bhavan, Gandhinagar–382010 (Gujarat), Ph. No. (079) 23253615, Fax No.: 23232048, E-Mail:acdhaneshwar @ hotmail.com**

the shape of the manpower planning and the size of unemployment might be dramatically change. The way to overcome of this traditional approach and model is to repetitive interaction with pass out students to have continuity. The second and more applicable to the problem at hand are aggregate planning models. Traditionally, aggregate planning principles have been more widely applied in the manufacturing industry than in the service industry.

Key Words: Introduction, Researches, Models, Linear programming, Forecasting model, the occupational model.

INTRODUCTION

The State of Gujarat follows the national pattern in data collection under the NTMIS project of All India Council for Technical Education. The review deals with the analysis of various aspects such as the existing facilities for professional education and labour market in terms of supply and demand of such qualified manpower. Besides it also provides detailed analysis of employment data by discipline and level, sector of employment, economic activities and main duties. The analysis further includes the time taken by fresh graduates for getting first employment, the emoluments drawn, and functions performed and most important of all, the Absorption Pattern into the economy.

Every year by 30th June a pre-designed questionnaire is sent to all the degree and diploma pass outs who have completed two years after their courses. Generally three reminders are to be sent periodically for collecting the response as a follow-up. The survey is concluded for each discipline where response exceeded 50 per cent. As migration affects the employment in the state, the relation between supply and demand can be worked out only after consideration of in and out for education, for working out the net outturn available in the state. The information of students, who have gone outside the state, for education is obtained from the Nodal Centers based in the nineteen other states. Both the data are then compiled together to get the net outturn in the state for education.

In the traditional approach only data of pass outs after two years are dealt with, which in turn leads to confused data as the time taken for reporting and further goes on. At present we allow parents to respond on behalf of absent student. The experience has shown that parents' literacy and sincerity results in erroneous data. In view of these it is likely that shape of the manpower planning and the size of unemployment might be dramatically change. The one of the approach to tackle such challenges is repetitive interaction either personal or by mail with pass out students to have continuity.

RESEARCH SO FAR

[1]*Bowey*, a well-known researcher has defined manpower planning as a "strategy for matching future manpower numbers and skills with organizational activities". Many researchers have published work in this area. American manpower planner [2]*Gregory* presented a manpower-planning model based on the idea of career development and job assignment according to skills attained. This followed along the same lines as [3]*Thomson* introduced a transportation linear programming model to be used for studying the design of a manpower system for planning. Golver introduced a model whereby jobs are assigned to individuals based on the costs associated with each individual doing a particular job. Although these models are useful for manpower planning, they are more concerned with matching employee's skills with different jobs.

The comparison between several manpower on the basis of transitions between various stages of employees' careers shows that *Markov process* is used as an underlying theoretical mode. *Verbeek* presents a DSS for strategic manpower planning of airline pilots. Unlike of a *Markov model*, this DSS uses a number of optimization models to accomplish various tasks in decision-making. The system permits representation, manipulation, evaluation, and generation of manpower plans. Many authors have worked on the shorter-term problem of restoring and scheduling of personnel. [4]*Gopalakrishnan*, a well-known Asian researcher report on a DSS developed to support planning and scheduling part-time workers at a newspaper company. Here used a rule base to generate the requirements of workers, and then a heuristic to find a near-optimal allocation of the workers over weekly periods. The aggregate service plan is a general plan on how an organization expects to respond to forecasted demand. *Linear programming* can be used to solve deterministic aggregate planning problems. *Dutch* researcher [5]*Dijkstra* that developed a DSS for the aircraft maintenance department of the Dutch national airline presents the deterministic planning model. The uniqueness of this *Dijkstra's* DSS is in handling various combinations of engineers. [6]*Fait* bridges the gap between aggregate planning models and restoring models by using a multistage approach where in the first stage an aggregate plan of personnel capacity is prepared. In the following section, overview of several important manpower planning models are described.

MODELLING PERSPECTIVES

In this section we offer some alternative modelling perspectives on manpower planning. Though the detailed description and solution for that is beyond the scope of this chapter. According to me, the simplest model to tackle this decision effectively would be a linear programming formulation.

Linear Programming

Linear Programming–Formulation

Some of the major application areas to which LP can be applied are:

- Manpower planning;
- Production planning;
- Oil refinery management;
- Distribution;
- Financial and economic planning.

The basic assumptions for a mathematical model to be solved as a linear programme (LP) are:

All variables must continuous (i.e. can take fractional values), It has single objective (minimize or maximize) and the objective and constraints are linear i.e. any term is either a constant or a constant multiplied by an unknown.

Important of Linear programming:

- Many practical problems can be formulated as LP's;

- There exists an algorithm (called the *simplex* algorithm), which enables us to solve LP's numerically relatively easily.

[7,8]*Example case study for Linear Programming:*

Two Mines Company

The Two Mines Company own two different mines that produce an ore which, after being crushed, is graded into three classes: high, medium and low-grade. The company has contracted to provide a smelting plant with 12 tons of high-grade, 8 tons of medium-grade and 24 tons of low-grade ore per week. The two mines have different operating characteristics as detailed below.

Mine	Cost per day	Production (tons/day)		
		High	Medium	Low
X	180	6	3	4
Y	160	1	1	6

How many days per week should each mine be operated to fulfill the smelting plant contract?

We guess here work 4 days a week on X, 3 days a week on Y. We say that such a solution is *feasible*. However it is quite expensive (costly). Rather than continue guessing we can approach the problem in a structured logical fashion as below. Reflect for a moment though that really we would like a solution, which supplies what is necessary under the contract at minimum cost. Logically such a minimum cost solution to this decision problem must exist. However even if we keep guessing we can never be sure whether we have found this minimum cost solution or not. Fortunately our structured approach will enable us to find the minimum cost solution.

Solution

What we have is a verbal description of the Two Mines problem. What we need to do is to translate that verbal description into an *equivalent* mathematical description. In dealing with problems of this kind we often do best to consider them in the order:

1. Variables;
2. Constraints;
3. Objective.

We do this below and note that this process is often called *formulating* the problem.

1. Variables

These represent the "decisions that have to be made" or the "unknowns".

Let

x = number of days per week mine X is operated & y = number of days per week mine Y is operated

Note here that x >= 0 and y >= 0.

2. Constraints

It is best to describe each constraint into a mathematical form.

High 6x + 1y >= 12,Medium 3x + 1y >= 8 & Low 4x + 6y >= 24

Note we have an inequality here rather than equality. This implies that we may produce more than we need. In fact we have the general rule: *given a choice between equality and an inequality choose the inequality.*

The reason for this general rule is that choosing an inequality rather than equality gives us more flexibility in optimizing (maximizing or minimizing) the objective (deciding values for the decision variables that optimize the objective).

- Days per week constraint—we cannot work more than say e.g. for a 5 day week.

x <= 5 & y <= 5

3. Objective

Again our objective is to minimize cost which is given by 180x + 160y. Hence we have the complete mathematical representation of the problem as:

Minimize

$180x + 160y$

Subject to

$6x + y \geq 12$, $3x + y \geq 8$ & $4x + 6y \geq 24$. Where constraints are $x \leq 5$ & $y \leq 5$, $x, y \geq 0$

This development is evident in the completely changed role of manpower forecasting.

Forecasting Model

The forecasts of expansion demand are based on the employment level forecasts for economic sectors. The predicted growth in the various occupational classes is determined. The expansion demand per type of education refers to the number of people with a particular educational background that employers would like to be able to employ. Demand on the labour market consists of expansion demand, replacement demand or switch to another occupation etc. A worker undertakes part-time study for a higher-level qualification, when he or she completes that qualification it means in fact an outflow of one worker to another educational category (level of education). In that case a replacement demand does arise in the educational category under which this worker's previous education was counted.

An indication of the future labour market prospects for newcomers to the labour market is derived, for each type of education, by confronting the expected flows of demand and supply with each other. This indicator shows what discrepancy may be expected between the demand and supply for each type of education. But excess supply does not imply that the group in question will as a matter of course become unemployed, and a supply shortfall does not automatically mean that there will be unfilled vacancies.

For those with educational backgrounds, which are in short supply, there will be extra job openings. These passive substitution effects are thus important determinants of the labour market prospects of types of education. The confrontation between demand and supply also gives an indication of the future risk of labour recruitment problems for each type of education. If employment for a particular type of education is declining, this recruitment requirement is calculated in a somewhat different manner than the number of job openings for newcomers to the labour market, because from the employers' point of view it is possible to achieve part of the retrenchment by limiting their recruitment. Employers will be especially likely to use this option when they face a tight labour market for a particular type of education.

Expansion and Substitution Demand Forecasts

The expansion demand forecasts are probably the most difficult element of information system on education and the labour market. In contrast to the traditional manpower-requirements approach, no fixed relations between occupations and types of education are assumed. As in some earlier studies a somewhat more flexible relationship is assumed based on explanatory variables for the changes in both the occupational and educational structures of employment.

The employment projections by sector are the starting point for the forecasts. This means that the more detailed forecasts, which distinguish the prospects of particular types of education and occupations, are consistent with the broadly accepted macro-economic and economic sector forecasts.

The Occupational Model

Starting from the forecasts of employment by sector, a two-step model is estimated to explain the occupational structure of the sectors. The changes in employment levels per economic sector are first translated into employment changes per occupational segment. Then occupational classes further disaggregate the forecast of expansion demand. The assumption in the design of the occupational models is that the occupational structure of a sector is entirely determined by the demand side of the labour market.

Borghans and Heike provides a detailed description of this model. Separate occupations, a random coefficients model have been used. In this random coefficient model each parameter value is a weighted average of the average parameter value over all the pooled occupations on the one hand and estimates for each separate occupation on the other hand. The weighting is determined by the accuracy of the two components. If there is a great deal of variation between the various occupations, a pooled estimate is relatively inaccurate and more weight is placed on the separate estimates.

There have been changes not only in the estimation techniques, as compared to the approach used in earlier versions of the information system. A specification which forecast employment levels has now been replaced with one which forecasts growth. Each parameter is thus specific for each occupation (o) in each economic sector (s). Because the method described above led in some instances to implausible results, some ad hoc modifications have been made to this general structure. *The first modification* is for the sector 'Other commercial services', which includes both the banks and insurance companies and other commercial services. In order to prevent implausible results for the economic sector 'Other commercial services', the constant term here is replaced, as a trend variable, by the growth and forecast growth for the banking and insurance sector. *A second modification* to the general method described above relates to the occupational segment 'Government, police, defence and education'. If the employment prospects in a particular occupational group are less favourable then it will relatively easy to switch to occupation levels i.e. more favourable. Moreover those who have chosen these types of education also have more flexibility in the labour market, which may perhaps mean that career prospects, which originally appeared attractive, become less appealing.

Supply forecasts the previously used measure of future prospects. Not all the errors in the forecasts by occupational class have an effect on the forecasts by type of education. Also, both the labour market inflow and the replacement demand are components with a high degree of reliability.

MATCHING EDUCATION AND THE LABOUR MARKET: SOME POLICY APPROACHES

The allocation process on the labour market is characterized by serious imperfections. Due to the heterogeneous character of the market and a range of inflexibilities of both supplies and demand, the labour market could suffer serious mismatch phenomena. While some workers face unemployment, firms may have recruitment problems for other skill categories. For this reason public policies continuously pay attention to the coordination between the educational system on the one hand, which provides skills supplied and, on the other hand, the demand in the labour market for the various skill categories. In particular the 'manpower requirement approach' was considered to be an important tool in educational planning. In this approach the planning begins with the determination of the target growth in the Gross National Product over a period of several years. From this, after a number of steps, the labour requirements in the various occupations and the educational qualifications are determined. The labour requirements are then compared with forecasts of the working population and the flow of graduates from the various types of training onto the labour market. The graduate-flow forecasts are compiled with the aid of a student-flow model that describes the flows of students within the educational system.

Various methodological and fundamental objections have been made to the manpower requirements approach. The methodological objections focus particularly on the fixed coefficients, which are used in the forecasting models to translate economic development into changes in employment differentiated by training and occupation, and on its mechanical concept of labour market functioning, in which there is no place for the working of substitution and other adjustment processes. The fundamental objections are that future developments are not in fact sufficiently predictable, and that an exclusive relationship between job requirements and training is assumed without adequate justification.

PERCEPTION

This chapter has discussed few manpower-forecasting models, which goes several steps beyond the scope of the traditional manpower requirements approach. We have dealt particularly with the objectives, the basic principles, the theoretical foundations and the general structure of labour market information system approach and the central labour market indicators. To illustrate the capacity of the forecasting model to distinguish the various components of expansion demand, the employment forecasts by type of education have been presented. Moreover, an impression is also given for the evaluation of the traditional approaches.

The steps now been suggested to transcend the traditional manpower requirements approach can be summarized as follows:

- A change from a planning tool to a transparency approach;
- A better theoretical foundation;
- An extension of the manpower forecasts into a 'labour market information system';
- Improved data input;
- The use of occupational and educational classifications, which distinguishes homogeneous groups of workers;
- The use of more sophisticated econometric models.

Although progress has been made on several points and the methodology, which has been developed, further improvements in both the quality and the utility of the information system approach will remain an important goal.

The Conclusion and Future Scope

To increase the explanatory power of the forecasting models, particularly of expansion demand and the inflow of newcomers on the labour market because so far, the forecasting model for the inflow of newcomers lacks any explanatory variables. A first step in the development of an explanatory model would probably be the introduction of a 'discouraged workers effect' with respect to the choice between further full-time education and labour market entrance. The educational model of expansion demand should be more explicitly based on the theoretical foundations—To improve the consistency between the models for expansion and replacement demand for types of education, which face declining employment levels. Moreover, it is the intention to develop the sectored approach of the information system further in the coming years. The usefulness of the labour market information for the human resource management of firms will also be increased by incorporating the expected adjustment processes of firms in case of a gap between supply and demand in a similar way as estimated in Attention will also be paid to the regional imbalances of the labour market information broken down by economic sector, occupation and education. Recently a major step in this direction has been made in the Regional Labour Market Information system (RAIS) project. Finally, attention will be given to the international context relevant to the supply and demand, which will probably become more important due to the integration process of the national labour market in the Asian domain, especially in Indian region.

REFERENCES

Printed

1. Bowey, A. M. (1977). Corporate Manpower Planning. *Management Decisions*, 15, 421-469.
2. Gregory, G. (1983). *Mathematical Methods in Management*. Bath, Avon: John Wiley & Sons.
3. Thomson, G. L. (1979). *A Network Transshipment Model for Manpower Planning and Design*.
4. M. Gopalakrishnan, *A Decision Support System for Scheduling Personnel*.
5. Dijkstra, M. C., Kroon, L. G., van Nuen, J. A. E. E., and Salomon, M. (1991). A DSS for Capacity Planning of Aircraft Maintenance Personnel. *International Journal of Production Economics*, 23, 69-78.
6. Fait, J., Schneewei, C., and Wolf, F. (1991). A Hierarchically Structured Decision-support-system for Demand Oriented Shift Planning. *International Journal of Production Economics*, 23, 89-98.

Web Based

7. http://www.wipro.co.in/casestudies/index.htm
8. http://www.wipro.co.in/enterprisesolutions/ebusinesssolutions/casestudies/gskfinal.pdf

13

Effective Models and Approaches in Manpower Planning

A Case Study at JSS Polytechnic, Nanjangud

*T.H.Udayashankara**

*M.P.Kiran***

ABSTRACT

Progress in technology was never as fast as it is now, which is making yesterday's product obsolete today. Globalization calls for producing quality products using the latest technology. Industries can quickly adopt the new technology but it is not the same for educational institutions. Unless technical institutions make quick changes in adopting latest to suit the requirements, the technicians may not be well accepted by the employment sector. Classroom training alone is not sufficient to make them competitive. Exposure to the latest technology and hands on training is a must. Industry institution interaction is the best solution. Automation in every field is providing opportunities for R & D and other activities. Hence, multidisciplinary approach is being accepted widely for providing engineering solutions. Water quality and safe sanitation is the basic infrastructure to be provided for the people. No trained manpower

* **Principal, JSS Polytechnic, Nanjangud – 571 302, Phone: 08221 – 226491, Email: hugs_th@rediffmail.com**

** **HOD of Mechatronics Engg., JSS Polytechnic, Nanjangud – 571 302, Phone: 08221 – 226491, Email: kiran_mss@rediffmail.com**

is available for the same at present. A few models have been suggested and approaches through case study of our polytechnic where all of them are already in practice, have been presented in this chapter.

Key Words: Industry Institution Interaction, Automation, Multidisciplinary Engineering, Trained Manpower

INTRODUCTION

"Industrialize or Perish"—addressed to the young engineers of this nation more than half a century ago, came from none other than one of the greatest engineers this country has ever seen—Sir M.Vishweshwaraiah. Ever since, India excelled in almost all the fields. Though we have achieved a lot in these years there is a huge gap to be filled in the global scenario and hence those golden words are more relevant to the present situation. This is an era of ever changing/improving technology. Globalization has increased competitiveness and every one of us must accept the fact and become more competitive. Growth of the nation lies in producing quality products. Resources are plenty, opportunities are countless but end result is not appreciating. What do we really need to do to bridge this gap? The answer is human resource with better technical skills. The future of the nation depends on how well their human resources are developed and equipped with latest knowledge and skills. Technical development of the people is important because technology plays a major role in every aspect of our lives.

Technical education plays a vital role. Industry Institution Interaction programme is a key to the success. Time has come and all technical educational institutions in the country must look into their practices and procedures. This chapter gives an idea to the technical educational institutions to think creatively and take up a key role in the rapid growth of the nation. Industry Institution Interaction in technical education serves the purpose in developing the required manpower to build the nation. In addition to this new courses have to be offered to meet the requirements of the latest developments in technology (courses on specific engineering applications). A few models for the development of required technical manpower along with approaches and case study are listed below.

MODELS

(a) Industry institution interaction programmes;

(b) Developing curriculum in interdisciplinary engineering;

(c) Offering courses in the emerging field and thrust areas;

(d) Additional training on latest developments in the relevant field.

Model (a): Industry Institution Interaction Programme

Need for Industry Institution Interaction

Training inside the four walls of the classroom provides the most required theoretical inputs for the student. That alone cannot contribute to the overall development of the technical skills. We all know that "An ounce of practice is better than ten ounces of theory". Hence, more emphasis has to be given to the practical training. Curriculum does have practical subjects but not sufficient to train the student such that they will be absorbed soon after the completion of the course in to the user system. There is a wide gap between the technology used in industry and syllabus taught in institutions.

It is known that this gap can never be closed, if institutions do not think creatively. Institution cannot adopt itself to the latest changes in technology but industries can. Industries have to play an important role in producing technical manpower, which in turn is beneficial to them. Industries are putting their efforts in this by training the students under apprenticeship training scheme and many other schemes through which they can. Time is an important factor, and training given after the completion of the course requires one year of extra time to develop the student's technical skills.

The most significant factor, which decides the quality of education, is the quality of teacher. He is not only the most effective audio visual aid but also the guide and philosopher of the pupils. Hence the teacher should get a periodical exposure to industry to gauge the applications of the changes in technology. Hence exposure for short spells to industrial situation will help in generating a sense of professionalism in the technical teacher. This boosts his/her confidence to face the challenges in teaching to the requirements, which ends in great success. Any technician worthy of his name should have had a feel of the real floor situation or an exposure to Industrial cultures during the diploma course. The Industry often raises an accusing finger against the educational system, which produces half-baked technician little realizing the complimentary roles of education and industry.

This is where the innovative thinking makes a big difference. Industrial training along with regular theory inputs from institution makes the students acquire more skills. The students must be exposed to the latest equipments/machineries used in various departments, manufacturing processes, maintenance of machines, designing, scheduling etc.. Hence, total Industry Institution Interaction is a must to produce quality technicians. Active participation from the industries during the curriculum development takes the education system a long way in achieving the desired goals.

The technical courses would lose their relevance unless they are sensitive to the rapid changes in technology. Further the curriculum of the courses should be so modified as to meet the real needs of industry. Sizeable effort is called for continuously monitoring the changing trends in technology as well as the varying moods of the Industry.

The above factors indicate that there must be a continuing interaction between Industry and Institute has to be ensured, if necessary through the process of the legislation. Industry may have to sacrifice its immediate connivance to a certain extent in order to safeguard the long-range interest in manpower development. Involvement of industry in technician education right from the time of designing of courses and framing of curricula will certainly help to strengthen the bonds which are essential for ensuring the relevance of courses and enhancing the employability of the technicians turned out from the Polytechnics.

Industry participation in designing the curriculum, consultancy, project work and guest lectures/technical talk sessions are essential to achieve the professional goals of the academic programmes in technician education. The curriculum has to be updated at regular intervals, keeping in view the needs of industry, particularly in this rapidly changing technological scenario. Industry can utilize the expertise from the teachers for their consultancy work and this will also give the much-needed exposure for the teachers in return.

Approach/Case Study

JSS Polytechnic, Nanjangud has made a sincere attempt in bridging the gap through industry institution interaction programme and is running the three diploma courses successfully for the past 12 years.

Nanjangud is located on the banks of river Kapila, on the NH 212 connecting Mysore, a city of palaces and Ooty, a hill station. It is a pilgrimage town. Nanjangud is 24 kms south of Mysore.

His Holiness Jagadguru Sri Shivarathri Rajendra Mahaswamigalavaru, the founder President of J.S.S. Mahavidyapeetha had a clear vision of the fact that nation would be strengthened if the rural people were strengthened with education in professional courses. J.S.S. Polytechnic at Nanjangud is a result of the great vision of his holiness. The present pontiff His Holiness Jagadguru Sri Sri Shivarathri Deshikendra Mahaswamigalavaru has been blessing us in all our activities, which has contributed to the overall development of the Polytechnic.

JSS Mahavidyapeetha, Mysore, started this polytechnic during 1984 with Electronics and Communication branch. Later, in the next year two more branches were introduced viz. Mechanical Engineering and Civil Engineering. This polytechnic is also catering the needs of rural people in technical education.

Change in industry and market needs has made the polytechnic to offer a need-based education with on the job practical training in industry. Since 1992 we are offering Co-operative scheme of education, which is an Industry Institution Participation Programme. JSS Polytechnic has made collaborations with many leading industries of the country. This is the only polytechnic in the entire state of Karnataka to offer Diploma education under Co-op scheme.

Polytechnic has started Diploma in Mechatronics Engineering under Co-op scheme from the academic year 2000-01. This is the only polytechnic to offer this diploma in the entire state of Karnataka under Co-op scheme.

During the year 2001, this polytechnic was admitted under Grant-in-Aid rules of Govt. of Karnataka.

Polytechnic has started Diploma in Computer Science Engineering from the academic year 2001-2002, under general scheme and Diploma in Water Technology and Health Sciences from the academic year 2004-05.

Other than its regular academic work, the polytechnic has been conducting various non-formal programmes like short-term courses in various disciplines, training the rural youths under TRYSEM scheme, training the rural people under community polytechnic scheme (an extension of Community polytechnic, JSS polytechnic for women), etc.

The polytechnic works by anticipating the needs and expectations of the Society. Hence, it does not believe in stagnation, but in progression.

ABOUT CO-OP. SCHEME OF DIPLOMA (INDUSTRY INSTITUTION INTERACTION COURSES)

This is the only polytechnic in the entire state of Karnataka to offer Diploma under this scheme. It is a semester scheme of diploma education, consisting of 06 semesters, of which students will be trained in institution for 04 Semesters and will be deputed to undergo one year (02 semesters) of industrial training in two phases.

OBJECTIVES OF INDUSTRIAL TRAINING

The objectives of the industrial training is to develop the students contextual ability, bring self-confidence in the student, bring an awareness about the accuracy and schedule thereby bringing an awareness about quality, give hands on training for the students thereby exposing them to the latest technology in the field, develop an entrepreneurship attitude of the student, develop the student in terms of leadership qualities and take up challenging projects in the field of interest of the student.

ABOUT INDUSTRIAL TRAINING

Industrial Training–I

During the first phase of industrial training (during the III semester of their course), the students will be given induction training soon after reporting and will be made to practice industry culture i.e. punctuality and discipline. Later they are exposed to modern measuring instruments and sophisticated machines used in manufacturing process.

Industrial Training– II

During the second phase of industrial training (during the VI semester of their course), the students will be deputed for job training in different sections/departments. They are made to practice planning, scheduling, quality, dispatching. During this period they have to carry out a project work which involves all the process of the industry and should be helpful to the industry.

Note: In addition to the industrial training, the students have to study theory subjects prescribed, which will be taught by the experts from industry and faculty of polytechnic. The students have to appear for the End examination at the polytechnic, which will be conducted by the Board of Technical Examinations.

Examination for the practical subjects "Industrial training" and "Project work" will be conducted by the concerned industries.

Industries Participating

M/S BEML, KGF, M/S HMT Ltd., B'lore, M/S BEL, B'lore, M/S BHEL, B'lore, M/S ITI Ltd., B'lore, M/S AT&S INDIA Ltd., N'gud, M/S Rane (Madras) Ltd., Mysore.

Polytechnic offers the following three years Diploma programmes under Co-op scheme:

1. Diploma in Mechanical Engineering [DME (Co-op)];
2. Diploma in Electronics and Communication Engineering [DECE (Co-op)];
3. Diploma in Mechatronics Engineering [DMT (Co-op)];

These courses are recognized by *All India Council of Technical Education (AICTE), New Delhi,* approved by the *Directorate of Technical Education, Govt. of Karnataka,* and the industrial training is recognized by the *Board of Apprenticeship Training, Chennai.*

The Board of Apprenticeship Training, Govt. of India, is extending its cooperation by approving the training of students in Industries. These students are considered as *Sandwich Apprentices.* Presently these trainees are entitled for a *stipend of Rs. 1,140 per month.*

MERITS OF CO-OP. SCHEME OF EDUCATION

This scheme results in significant savings in time, money and effort in recruitment and training for the Industry. The Training Scheme becomes more user friendly and user oriented. It provides valuable feed back from Industry to keep improving and modifying curricular structure. Industrial training helps in developing contextual ability in student, aiding them to do well functionally in the world of work. Exposure of teachers regularly to Industrial Culture updates his knowledge.

Industry Institution Interaction programme is a tool that helps institution to produce quality technicians who are readily accepted by the industries and in turn industries can come out with quality products that are readily accepted by the society. Thereby there will be a rapid growth of the nation.

Model (b): Developing Curriculum in Interdisciplinary Engineering

Need for Interdisciplinary Approach

It is known that any human working on a machine continuously, would lose concentration, however experienced he/she may be, which would result in the variation in quality of the product. Some times it calls for rework or even rejected. Therefore, Automation is the new 'mantra' in every part of life. Automation itself is branching out into home, office, factory, medical in many and other ways. No single engineering concept alone is sufficient to achieve automation. It calls for perfect integration or blending of two or more engineering skills. Building systems like washing machines, auto focus digital cameras, microwave ovens, automatic brightness and volume control television sets for home automation, computers, printers, fax, xerox machines, scanners, automatic telephone exchange (small purpose) for office automation, CNC machines, robots for factory automation, CT scanners, bed side monitors, Ultrasound scanners, MR imaging for medical automation was possible due to the integration of different engineering skills. A lot of manpower is required in designing, manufacturing of such products and their maintenance.

Approach/Case Study

Diploma in Mechatronics Engineering was introduced in the academic year 2000-2001, under Co-op scheme. This programme is our creative response to the need to provide education and training for a new breed of engineers who are proficient in the combined application of systems design as well as mechanical, electronic and computer-based control to managing sophisticated manufacturing processes and technology-intensive operations; producing high value-added products, be they consumer goods or otherwise; and providing quality multi-disciplinary engineering services.

Model (c): Offering Courses in Emerging Field and Thrust Areas

Nearly three quarters of the worlds poor, live in rural areas and a large parts of this population does not have access to clean water and safe sanitation facilities. Even more shocking is the number of deaths, mostly of children, that are largely preventable, through water/hygiene related measures and water related borne diseases, which result in millions of deaths every year.

Despite the importance of water resources in our lives and well being, we are increasingly disrespectful to them. We abuse them. We waste them. We pollute them forgetting how essential they are to our very survival. Perhaps more than any other sector, water supply and sanitation has become the themes of the development agenda.

The challenge ahead of us is enormous. Proper management of water is not only simple but also a cost effective way to save the society from diseases and deaths. Improper human resource management is a hurdle to be crossed to overcome difficulties in management of water. Those trained can be employed in industries (Treatment plants), Govt. organizations (Water supply and sanitation, rural development), NGO's who are working for the infrastructure development of the nation.

Approach/Case Study

New courses have to be designed to cater the demand. JSS Mahavidyapeetha, has started a separate institute for this purpose, viz. JSS Institute of Water Technology and Health Sciences. JSS considered the fact that, in order to enable better systems and management practices there is a need for number of basic trained people to manage the water quality at the operation level, followed by supervisory staff and have already started following courses:

1. *Technician in Water Technology and Health Sciences at JSS Industrial Training Centre, Nanjangud:* Duration of the course is Two years and is approved by State Council for Vocational Training, Karnataka;
2. *Diploma in Water Technology and Health Sciences at JSS Polytechnic, Nanjangud:* Duration of the course is Three years and is recognized by All India Council for Technical Education, New Delhi and approved by Directorate of Technical Education, Govt. of Karnataka.

It is proposed to start Bachelor of Engineering in Water Technology and Health Sciences and also Post-graduate and Ph.D. programmes under this institute.

Model (d): Additional Training on Latest Developments in the Relevant Field

Need for Additional Training

As discussed earlier, the change in trends in technology and varying moods of the industry calls for quick adjustment in training methodology. If there is academic autonomy, then there will be flexibility in revising the curricula. Many a times the students have to study the out-dated technology since the designing/revision of curricula is done once in five/six years. Now, the question is how to cope up with the change in technology?

Approach

The best way is to arrange short term training programmes. Training programmes should be arranged for both students as well as faculty members. Training programmes on Advancements in Design of Integrated Circuits (ADIC), Operation and maintenance of medical equipments, Computer Aided Design, Embedded system development, CNC programming, operation and maintenance of CNC machines, operation and maintenance of water and waste water treatment plants, etc. will take a long way in developing required manpower.

This polytechnic is arranging short term training programmes for students on CNC programming, and maintenance of equipments, arranging industrial visits, arranging technical talks/ guest lectures from experts from both industries and other institutions (Professors of Engineering colleges). These programmes are being conducted in addition to one year industrial training as per the Co-op scheme.

CONCLUSION

We have made a modest attempt to present a few innovative ideas in developing and managing the required manpower to take this country towards the list of developed nations. We are proud to be the first to introduce many new kinds of education system and at the same time take this opportunity to extend support to those interested in starting such courses for building a better society and make this country a developed nation.

14

Training Based Teaching-learning Process

An Approach Towards Quality Technical Manpower Development

*Tanmoy Maity**

ABSTRACT

There is a belief that people cannot be developed, they can develop themselves through their own desires and actions. Learning is a continuous process throughout the lifetime and it brings relatively a permanent change to a people's mind. Conventional learning is teacher-centered rather than learner-centered. Here learning is a function of capacity of the participant to learn and ability of the teacher to teach. In most of the cases the role of the learner is passive and there is little scope of immediate feedback. The training based teaching learning process, suggested in this chapter, encourages learners to see themselves even as a source of information and knowledge about the real world as it is participatory in nature. Here the involvement gives a sense of improvement through their own experience. Learners actively share the collective responsibility for seeking new knowledge. It provides an

* **Assistant Professor, Department of Electrical Engineering, College of Engineering and Management, Kolaghat, West Bengal – 721171, E-mail: tanmoy_maity@yahco.com**

opportunity to practice and to become adoptable to specific problems. With this teaching-learning process there is a challenging role of the teachers and this role can be divided into broad categories which are analysed in this chapter. Also based on this methodology a whole classroom based lecture model is proposed in this chapter.

Key Words: Teaching-learning, Training-based, quality technical manpower.

INTRODUCTION

"Active learning involves students in doing things and thinking about the things they are doing"

—Charles Bonwell

Learning is a continuous process throughout the lifetime and it brings relatively a permanent change to a people's mind. Learning is self initiated and autonomous, it involves feelings and cognitive aspects of the learner. Learning depends on the learner's motivation and it becomes effective in safe, accepting, challenging, supporting environment. But, it is true that different learners learn differently from the same environment.

According the Carroll's model of the teaching/learning process[1].

Learning (Output) = f(Context, Input and Process).

Output includes the specific measurement or measurements of learning (e.g., student achievement, social skills, cognitive development, etc.). *Context* includes the environmental or situational factors such as home environment and changing global conditions that influence the definition and measurement of important educational outcomes as well as levels of important input and process variables. *Input* includes the characteristics of teachers and students that they bring to the teaching/learning process. *Process* includes the thinking, feelings, commitments, and actions of teachers and students within the classroom or learning situation as well as the interaction patterns and descriptions of the learning environment that result from those interactions.

CONVENTIONAL LEARNING OR PEDAGOGY

Conventional learning is teacher or trainer centered rather than learner centered. Here learning is a function of capacity of the participant to learn and ability of the trainer to teach. In this system learning is the responsibility of the teacher and the teaching institution. Pedagogy is derived from the greek words 'Paid' and 'agogus' meaning 'child' and 'leader of'. It is assumed that a learner is an empty bottle and to be filled by the teacher. Here a teacher defines what to teach and how to teach without considering the current prevailing situation. In most of the cases the role of the learner is passive and there is little scope of immediate feedback. Ashton reviewed research[2] that shows there are two components to teacher expectations:

- the teacher believes that, in general, students can learn the material;
- the teacher believes that these particular students can learn under his or her direction.

Frudden and Stow[3] identified some steps in the planning of teaching process:

- Establish goals and objectives;
- Establish allocated time;
- Identify strategies and models of teaching;
- Determine methods of evaluating of student outcomes;
- Select instructional methods and techniques;
- Design student activities;
- Provide for variety and individual differences.

They also concluded that, it is necessary to properly implement the plan and to properly evaluate results in order to determine if the plan was a success.

PARTICIPATORY TEACHING-LEARNING

There is a belief that people cannot be developed, they can develop themselves through their own desires and actions. Participatory Teaching Learning process encourages participants to see themselves as a source of information and knowledge about the real world. Here they are encouraged to participate in their own learning and their involvement gives a sense of improvement through their own experience. Participant actively shares the collective responsibility for seeking new knowledge. Here the learner feels the real need to learn through active participation and they feel a sense of progress towards their learning goal. Any learning environment, in which the problem drives the learning, motivates students. The necessity for implementing the method is to simplify the teaching-learning process and improve the quality of education.

CHALLENGES TO THE FACULTY

Responsibility

There are definitely some responsibilities of the classroom faculty to introduce the participatory teaching-learning process. Those can be selected as:

- Identification of students' needs and attitude, mood with analytical sensitivity;
- Designing of the proper teaching programme – framework of defining the objectives of the topics, content sequencing;
- Teacher preparation based on content knowledge. It also depends on his self-strengths and weakness as a person;
- Administration – based on students' management, creating learning environment, proper use of facilities in the classroom;
- Monitoring and evaluation—adopting different methods; collecting, recording and feedback of data;
- Follow-up—use of proper framework of methods, identify the support needed by the individual or group.

Expected Characteristics of Teacher

- High self-image with proper dress code, voice quality and smile;
- Good instructional communication skills;
- Active listening skills;

- Adequate level of sympathy and sensitivity towards the students;
- Initiative and commitment to assigned task;
- Good administrative skills;
- Good facilitation skills;
- Managing odd/errant behaviour;
- Hands on experience of the teaching aids;
- Proper time management skills.

Teachers must demonstrate that they possess these skills during student teaching, and then should be evaluated each year to determine if they have maintained these skills. However, one teacher characteristic that has been consistently related to student achievement, but which is not systematically measured is teacher efficacy. Teacher efficacy relates to a teacher's belief that students in his or her classroom can learn and that he or she can teach them.

There are many teacher characteristics that have been shown to be related to student achievement. Many of these should be assessed prior to or during the teacher training process. For example, at Valdosta State University (VSU) students must pass a particular course in both reading and writing and must complete a two English courses with a "C" or better before being allowed to enroll in teacher education.[4] With this the communication skills is ensured as an important teacher characteristic.

A sound knowledge base is also thought to be an important teacher characteristic. Again, in the state of Georgia, students must complete the required lower division curriculum with a CGPA of 2.5 before being allowed to enter the education programme. Students must then take a certain number of courses in the subjects they expect to teach and must maintain the 2.5 CGPA in order to enroll in student teaching. They then must pass a specific test covering content they will teach and principles of human development and the teaching/learning process before they are certified to teach. All of this is based on the belief that teacher knowledge is an important teacher characteristic.[4]

Teaching Requirements

- Present the process in a structured manner. At start outline of talk is important and cover the topic in steps and conclude with a recap. Involving the students during the lecture. Eye-contact with participants, proper use of hands, proper use of words make lectures attractive. Selection of methodology according to the subject. Encouraging of students responding with answers using appropriate word:
- Following things should be avoided during the teaching:
  - Looking down while talking;
  - Showing back to the audience frequently;
  - Talking fast to cover many points in a specified time;
  - Not to stick on to any one or two student;
  - Not to put hands inside the pockets. To avoid unnecessary body movements.

TTAINING BASED LECTURE

Advantages of Training Based Lecture

- It provides an active participation by the learners. The learning objective becomes clear to them.
- It provides an opportunity to practice and to become adoptable to specific problems.
- It motivate in general to all the students to improve their performance, not to some specific ones.
- It provides a timely feedback on their performance. The teacher as well as students can evaluate their achievements more specifically.

Proposed Lecture Model

- *Student profile:* To consider the knowledge level, their listening level, their ability of understanding the language of lecture. Start with some general information of the subject and gain acceptance for the new points.

- *Time management:* Total time available, time taken for formalities , time for interaction.
- *Subject matter:* Knowledge and confidence of the subject, not only the topic covered. Not covering 4-5 critical points in a single lecture.
- *Lecture Frame:*
  - I. Introduction– very brief and to the point.
  - II. Body of main talks: well structured.
  - III. Conclusion brief capitulation of main points.
- *Lecture Delivery:* Maintaining of proper posture, appearance, , sincerity, courteous, poised manner, gesture. Use of simple vocabulary and voice modulation. Ask short questions related to the lecture topics. Give real life examples as much as possible. Gain their interests with some sort of small group discussion.

CONCLUSION

With the transition from resource based economy to knowledge based economy, the great challenge in front of India is how to cope with local needs in an increasingly globalised environment. India has to restructure its total education system specially considering the role of technical education. There is a burning need of re-examination of the role of the faculties in universities and institutions in technical fields. There is not only the need of upgradation of the quality of teachers but also the need of restructuring the teaching-learning process. The methodology described in this chapter can be used as a possible solution for that. But this definitely requires careful analysis before implementation to a particular technical institute.

REFERENCES

1. Carroll, J., A Model of School Learning. *Teachers College Record,* 1963 64, 723-733.
2. Ashton, P., Teacher Efficacy: A Motivational Paradigm for Effective Teacher Education. *Journal of Teacher Education,* 1984, 35(5), 28-32.
3. Frudden, S., & Stow, S., Eight Elements of Effective Preinstructional Planning. Education, 1986, 106(2), 218-222.
4. http://chiron.valdosta.edu/whuitt/ccl/teacher/tchchar.html

15

Engineering Manpower Scenario for Certain Selected Industries in West Bengal

*J. Paul Choudhury**

ABSTRACT

It is very much essential to know the demand of a particular engineering discipline. The stock of engineering manpower (number of engineering personnel) working in a particular industrial unit or for a group of industries can be used to ascertain the demand. Here an effort in this chapter has been made to show the trend of engineering manpower for a number of industrial units and from those available figures certain analysis can be drawn in those areas.

Key Words: Manpower, Trend, Demand, Stock, Forecasting.

INTRODUCTION

After independence the number of engineering colleges and engineering institutions were few, but now-a-days quite a number of engineering colleges and engineering institutions are set up. Now the question comes, whether the number of engineers passed out are getting jobs or not, whether there is a shortage of

* **Project Officer, NTMIS, Board of Practical Training (ER), Block EA, Sector 1, Salt Lake City, Kolkata- 700 064, email: ntmiskol@yahoo.com**

engineering manpower belonging to a particular discipline or not, whether there is a surplus of engineering manpower belonging to a particular discipline. In order to get a clear picture of engineering manpower NTMIS Technical Manpower Profile[1] may be consulted.

NTMIS Technical Manpower Profile[1] are published in almost every five years. Apart from that state wise manpower information are available in Annual Technical Manpower Review.[2,4,11,12] In order to get the demand of technical manpower, an effort has been made to see the trend of engineering manpower based on stock of manpower for an organization. Here an effort has been made to see the trend of technical manpower using the number of employed engineers working in a particular organization belonging to a particular industry group. To see the trend of manpower certain analysis may be carried regarding the manpower prediction.

IMPLEMENTATION

Step-I

The manpower data belonging to mechanical engineering working in two organizations both of which is the producer of electrical items, the manpower data belonging to mechanical engineering working in one steel manufacturing industry, the manpower data belonging to dairy technology working in two organization which are producing milk and other related products, the manpower data belonging to jute technology working in one mill, the manpower data belonging to electrical engineering working in one electricity generation organization, the manpower data belonging to aeronautical engineering working in an airline are taken. All these organizations are located in West Bengal, India.

Step-2

The data gathered are furnished below:

BEPB (Producer of Electrical Products Private Limited Co.)

Year	Mechanical Engineer
1989-90	2
1990-91	2
1991-92	3
1992-93	8
1993-94	11
1994-95	13
1995-96	11
1996-97	11
1997-98	11
1998-99	21
1999-2000	32
2000-01	33
2001-02	33
2002-03	34

ALSTA (Producer of Electrical Products Public Limited Co.)

Year	Mechanical Engineer
1989-90	48
1990-91	47
1991-92	46
1992-93	44
1993-94	44
1994-95	43
1995-96	43
1996-97	34
1997-98	22
1998-99	20
1999-2000	19
2000-01	18
2001-02	16
2002-03	16

ASA (Steel Manufacturing Organization Govt.of India Undertaking)

Year	Mechanical Engineering
1989-90	350
1990-91	370
1991-92	425
1992-93	422
1993-94	420
1994-95	418
1995-96	403
1996-97	393
1997-98	389
1998-99	103
1999-2000	103
2000-01	103
2001-02	86
2002-03	75

MDM (Producer of Milk and Related Products State Govt. Undertaking)

Year	Dairy Technology
1989-90	31
1990-91	41
1991-92	50
1992-93	50
1993-94	50
1994-95	50
1995-96	50
1996-97	51
1997-98	51
1998-99	51
1999-2000	51
2000-01	51
2001-02	51
2002-03	51

CDC (Producer of Milk and related Products State Govt. Department)

Year	Dairy Technology
1989-90	45
1990-91	46
1991-92	41
1992-93	40
1993-94	35
1994-95	35
1995-96	34
1996-97	34
1997-98	33
1998-99	36
1999-2000	38
2000-01	38
2001-02	36
2002-03	34

BJP (Producer of Jute and Related Products Private Limited Co.)

Year	Jute Technology
1989-90	53
1990-91	53
1991-92	53
1992-93	49
1993-94	49
1994-95	50
1995-96	55
1996-97	48
1997-98	40
1998-99	40
1999-2000	36
2000-01	36
2001-02	25
2002-03	20

DPD (Electricity Generation Organization Govt. of India Undertaking)

Year	Electrical Engineering
1989-90	27
1990-91	30
1991-92	33
1992-93	36
1993-94	38
1994-95	38
1995-96	46
1996-97	47
1997-98	49
1998-99	49
1999-2000	39
2000-01	41
2001-02	41
2002-03	38

IAI (Airline Govt. of India Undertaking)

Year	Aeronautical Engineering
1989-90	74
1990-91	103
1991-92	107
1992-93	108
1993-94	107
1994-95	99
1995-96	105
1996-97	108
1997-98	110
1998-99	111
1999-2000	116
2000-01	113
2001-02	116
2002-03	148

OBSERVATION

The organization whose activity was huge in quantity and engaged a number of technical personnel previously, is now engaging less number of personnel. This has been observed in ASA, ALSTA, BJB. The organization whose activity was not huge, rather started with few activity and engaged less number of personnel, is now engaging more number of personnel. This has been observed in BEPB, MDM, CDC. The organization IAI is an all India based company and their demand is totally based on national demand. Therefore unit-wise demand can not be ascertained from the available figure. The organization, whose activity was not huge initially, is enhancing its activity and the demand of technical manpower becomes more in that type of organization. The same concept is applicable for a Govt. organization or a private or public organization. The economic factors and Govt. policies and rules are not much affecting the time series stock of data.

CONCLUSION

The futuristic requirement of technical manpower can be ascertained by applying statistical models (least square techniques based on linear, exponential or parabolic equation or based on certain polynomial). If the data is disturbed that can be smoothened through application of exponential smoothing or ARIMA models. Now-a-days fuzzy technique is used. In the field of soft computing models like neural network and genetic algorithm can be applied. In various fields of forecasting (in the field of economy and marketing) neural network based models have shown excellent result.[5-9] Using NTMIS manpower data J. Paul Choudhury[10] has shown that neural network based model has given excellent result in the field of forecasting.

REFERENCES

1. Prof. Ashok Chandra, K. Raghavan, Bal Krishna, A.K. Mathur, A. Kamala Devi and Santosh Vij, Technical Manpower Profile 1995 India and the States, *Institute of Applied Manpower Research, New Delhi*, 1998.
2. Prof. H. Ramachandran, Annual Technical Manpower Review, West Bengal 2001. *Institute of Applied Manpower Research, New Delhi*, 2002.
3. Prof. Ashoka Chandra, Annual Technical Manpower Review, West Bengal 1999. *Institute of Applied Manpower Research, New Delhi*, 2000.

4. Prof. H. Ramachandran, Annual Technical Manpower Review, West Bengal 2000. *Institute of Applied Manpower Research, New Delhi*, 2001.

5. G.A. Tagliarini, J.F. Christ, E.W. Page, Optimisation Using Neural Networks, *IEEE Transactions on Computers*, Vol. 40, No. 12, December 91, 1347-1358.

6. F.G. Donaldson and M. Kamstra, Forecast Combining with Neural Networks, *Journal of Forecasting* 15 (1996) 49-61.

7. J.V. Hansen and Ray D. Nelson, Neural Networks and Traditional Time Series Methods: A Synergistic Combination in State Economic Forecasts, *IEEE Transactions on Neural Networks* Vol. 8, No. 4, July 1997.

8. S.F. Brown, A.J. Branford, W. Moran, On the Use of Artificial Neural for the Analysis of Survival Data, *IEEE Transactions on Neural Networks*, Vol. 8, No. 5, Sept. 1997.

9. S. Ghosh and D. Lien, Forecasting with Preliminary Data, *Journal of Forecasting*, Vol 16, 463-477 (1997).

10. J. Paul Choudhury, Trend of Engineering Manpower for Certain Number of Industries Under a Particular Industry Group, Proceedings of National Seminar on Technical Manpower Development and Utilisation, Rourkela, April 15-16, 2004.

11. Prof. H. Ramachandran, Annual Technical Manpower Review, West Bengal 2000. *Institute of Applied Manpower Research, New Delhi*, 2003.

12. Prof. H. Ramachandran, Annual Technical Manpower Review, West Bengal 2000. *Institute of Applied Manpower Research, New Delhi*, 2004.

16

Manpower Planning in Health Centres of Andhra Pradesh

*N.Kiran Kumar**

ABSTRACT

In today's day-to-day life, lots of works are done in very short span of time. This causes a severe stress in one's body. The only ray of hope for all these people is health centers. The quality of treatment includes both usage of effective equipment and also services of effective and efficient staff. number of employees a health center can prefer to employ in Andhra Pradesh, period within which employee is evaluated in health centers, source where health centers prefer to approach for potential employees, training methods health centers adopt for manpower they recruit, ratio between nurses to patients and doctors to patients. Survey shows that there is a huge requirement for doctors, nurses and other staff.

Key Words: Allopathy, Attenders, Ayurveda, Casuality Medical Officer, Doctors, Experience, Health, Health Centers, Homoeopathy, In-patient, Job Evaluation, Lab Technicians, Manpower, Nurses, Out patients, Quality, Questionnaire, Radiographers, Responsibility, Staff , Survey, Training, Weighted Average Ranking Method.

* **Department Of Management Studies, J.B.Institute of P.G.Courses, Tirupati–517501 (Andhra Pradesh), Email: kirsir_in@yahoo.co.in**

MANUSCRIPT

"When health is absent, wisdom cannot reveal itself, art cannot manifest, strength cannot fight, wealth becomes useless, and intelligence cannot be applied". This saying clearly indicates the importance of health. It may be for poor or rich, educated or uneducated, from rural area or from urban area for every one, health is of prime importance. In today's day-to-day life, lots of works are done in very short span of time. This causes a severe stress in one's body. The only ray of hope for all these people is health centers. Let it be a health center practising Ayurveda or Homoeopathy or Allopathy, the only criteria to be considered is the quality of treatment given to both in-patients as well as out-patients. The quality of treatment includes both usage of effective equipment and also services of effective and efficient staff. Even when one of these two is not up to its mark, quality naturally comes down. The health centers should take utmost care while appointing Doctors, Nurses, Radiographers, Lab technicians etc. for giving the best treatment to the patients. Training improves an individual so that he can accomplish his industrial task efficiently and effectively[1]. Training is an ever-continuing process in all organizations and it is employed as a technique of control as well as of imparting information and developing new skills[1]. Job evaluation is a systematic process of evaluating different jobs of an organization. Depending upon the characteristics and requirements of a job, job evaluation determines its relative worth and attaches a value to it[1]. The Marketing Research process includes defining research objectives, developing the Research Plan, collect the information, Analyze the information and present the findings[2].

RESEARCH OBJECTIVES OF THIS STUDY

The chapter attempts to study two main objectives 1) To find out number of employees a health center can prefer to employ in Andhra Pradesh. 2) To study the importance of various criteria like age, experience, educational qualifications, patience etc. in planning manpower in health centers of Andhra Pradesh. 3) The chapter also attempts to study period within which employee is evaluated in health centers. 4) This chapter also deals with source where health centers prefer to approach for potential employees. 5) It also attempts to study training methods health centers adopt for manpower they recruit. 6) To find out ratio between nurses to patients and doctors to patients. 7) To give suggestions to improve health centers.

HYPOTHESIS

H 1: All factors like age, experience, educational qualification, patience, local availability of staff are equally rated by health centers while appointing staff.

H 2: All sources like within organization, advertising in newspapers, advertising in electronic media, word of mouth, consultancy services are equally approached by health centers in process of their recruiting potential employees.

H 3: All factors like skill, mental effort, responsibility, physical conditions, dependability, physical effort, character and loyalty are equally rated by health centers for carrying out job evaluation of employees.

DATA COLLECTION

Survey method was adopted for collection of data and the instrument used for the purpose was pre-tested structured questionnaire on the objectives under study. Health centers were approached with the questionnaire and data was collected personally by getting appointments from doctors. In total health centers were approached for study and finally 39 usable responses were available for the analysis. Data is collected from Chittoor, Madanapalli, Srikalahasti, and Tirupati.

Questionnaire consists of close ended, Dichotomous, multiple choice questions and open ended question. Convenience-sampling method was adopted. Statistical technique adopted in the present study is weighted average ranking method.

In health centers approached 36 health centers are practising allopathy alone, one health center is practicing ayurvedic alone. One is practising ayurvedic and allopathy. And one is practising ayurvedic and homoeopathy.

In health centers approached 17 health centers are exisisting for a period more than 10 years, eight are exisisting for about 10 years, Twelve are exisisting for about 5 years and 2 are exisisting for a period less than one year.

DATA ANALYSIS

To realize the objectives of the study, primary data was collected from the sample units.

Table—16.1 Present staff and future increase of staff in health centres

Sl. No	Staff	Present Strength	Future Increase in Strength	Total Strength
1.	Doctors	99	19	118
2.	Nurses	162	41	203
3.	Radiographers	13	6	19
4.	Lab Technicians	29	10	39
5.	Attenders	124	20	144
6.	Security Guards	19	4	23
7.	Clerks	30	8	38
8.	Receptionists	20	10	30

Fig. 16.1 clearly shows present strength of doctors are 20 per cent and nurses is 32 per cent Attenders strength is 25 per cent. Lab technicians and clerks are at 6 per cent each. Receptionist and security guards are at 4 per cent each. Radiographers are at 3 per cent.

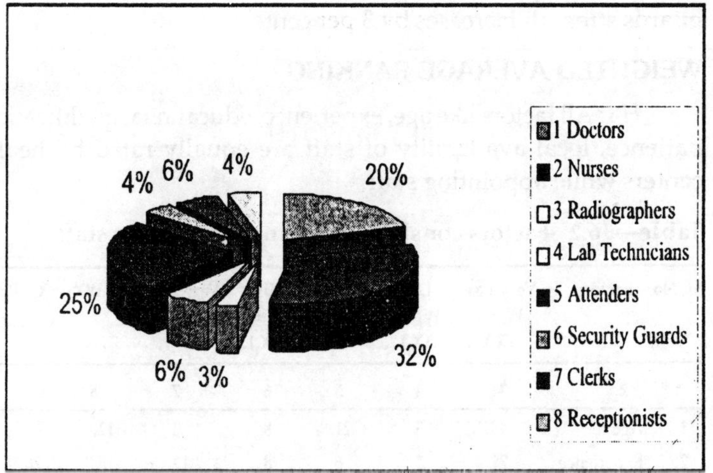

Fig. 16.1: Present staff in the health centres

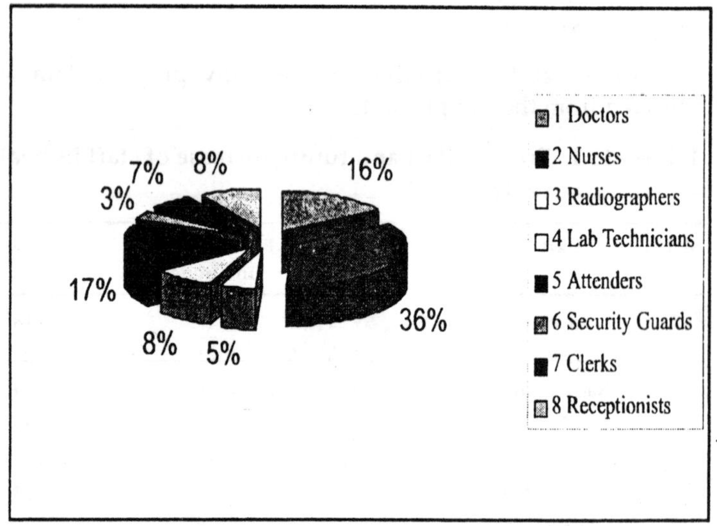

Fig. 16.2: Future increase in staff of the health centres

Fig. 16.2 clearly shows that there is increase in strength of doctors by 16 per cent and nurses by 36 per cent attenders strength increase by 17 per cent. Lab technicians and receptionist strength increases by 8 per cent each. Clerks strength increases by 7 per cent. Radiographer's strength increases by 5 per cent. and security guards strength increases by 3 per cent.

WEIGHTED AVERAGE RANKING

H 1: All factors like age, experience, educational qualification, patience, local availability of staff are equally rated by health centers while appointing staff.

Table—16.2 Factors considered during appointing staff

Sl. No.	Factors	Very Low $W_1 = 1$ (X_1)	Low $W_2 = 2$ (X_2)	Medium $W_3 = 3$ (X_3)	High $W_4 = 4$ (X_4)	Very High $W_5 = 5$ (X_5)	E WX	X	Rank
1	2	3	4	5	6	7	8	9	10
1.	Age	4	3	21	8	3	120	8	V
2.	Experience	2	1	6	18	12	154	10.26	I

(Contd...)

1	2	3	4	5	6	7	8	9	10
3.	Educational Qualification	1	0	14	12	12	151	10.06	II
4.	Patience	1	2	12	12	12	149	10	III
5.	Local Availability of Staff	9	0	7	11	12	134	8.9	IV

Note: 5 points are assigned to very high, 4 points to high, 3 points to medium, 2 points to low, 1 point to very low. Here what health centers prefers is given high importance. Health centers rated experience as first at 10.26, followed by educational qualification, patience, local availability of staff. Health centers rated age as last at 8.

X = (E WX)/(E W)

X = Variables (X_1, X_2, X_3, X_4, X_5)

W = Weight attached to the variable.

Here

E W = $W_1 + W_2 + W_3 + W_4 + W_5$

= 1+2+3+4+5

= 15

H 2: All sources like within organization, advertising in news papers, advertising in electronic media, word of mouth, consultancy services are equally approached by health centers in process of their recruiting potential employees.

Table—16.3 Sources approached by health centres for potential employees

Sl. No.	Factors	Very low $W_1=1$ (X_1)	Low $W_2 = 2$ (X_2)	Medium $W_3 = 3$ (X_3)	High $W_4 = 4$ (X_4)	Very High $W_5 = 5$ (X_5)	E WX	X	Rank
1	2	3	4	5	6	7	8	9	10
1.	Within Organization	22	5	6	1	5	79	5.26	III
2.	Advertising in Newspapers	19	5	6	7	2	85	5.66	II

(Contd...)

1	2	3	4	5	6	7	8	9	10
3.	Advertising in Electronic Media	22	3	9	4	1	76	5.06	IV
4.	Word of Mouth	11	2	9	7	10	120	8	I
5.	Consultancy Services	27	6	2	2	2	63	4.2	V

Note: 5 points are assigned to very high, 4 points to high, 3 points to medium, 2 points to low, 1 point to very low. Here what health centers prefer is given high importance. Health centers rated word of mouth as first at 8, followed by advertising in newspapers, within organization, advertising in electronic media. Health centers rated consultancy services as last at 4.2.

H 3: All factors like skill, mental effort, responsibility, physical conditions, dependability, physical effort, character and loyalty are equally rated by health centers for carrying out job evaluation of employees.

Table—16.4 Factors considered by health centres for job evaluation of employees

Sl. No.	Factors	Very Low $W_1=1$ (X_1)	Low $W_2 = 2$ (X_2)	Medium $W_3 = 3$ (X_3)	High $W_4 = 4$ (X_4)	Very High $W_5 = 5$ (X_5)	E WX	X	Rank
1.	Skill	6	1	3	19	10	143	9.5	II
2.	Mental Effort	7	1	7	18	6	132	8.8	IV
3.	Responsibility	4	0	4	12	19	149	10	I
4.	Physical Conditions	10	3	11	8	7	116	7.7	VII
5.	Dependability	8	2	9	11	9	130	8.66	V
6.	Physical Effort	11	3	7	14	4	114	7.6	VIII
7.	Character	7	1	4	18	9	138	9.2	III
8.	Loyalty	11	1	4	13	10	127	8.46	VI

Note: 5 points are assigned to very high, 4 points to high, 3 points to medium, 2 points to low, 1 point to very low. Here what health centers prefer is given high importance. Health centers rated responsibility as first at 10, followed by skill, character, mental effort, dependability, loyalty, physical conditions. Health centers rated physical effort as last at 7.6.

5 health centers expressed the view that they will be evaluating employees every day. 2 health centers are doing job evaluation once in three months. 14 health centers are doing job evaluation once in six months. 9 health centers are doing job evaluation once in a year. 2 health centers are doing job evaluation once in two years. Others are doing it once in more than 2 years.

32 health centers are carrying out training and 7 health centers are not doing it. As many as 9 health centers preferred individual method. Individual method and oral instruction combined was preferred by 4 health centers. Group instruction was preferred by 3 respondents. Oral instruction and demonstration method combined was preferred by 3 respondents. Demonstration method was preferred by 2 health centers. Individual method, oral instruction and demonstration method combined was preferred by 2 health centers. Conferences and written instructional method was not at all preferred.

Total number of in-patients are 767 and number of out-patients are 1565. Number of beds are 513. There are 1.5 patients per bed. Total number of doctors in health centers presently is 99. Patient to doctor ratio is 23.5: 1. Total number of nurses in health centers presently is 162. Patient to nurse ratio is 14.4:1.

FINDINGS

Present strength of doctors is 20 per cent and nurses are 32 per cent attenders strength is 25 per cent. Lab technicians and clerks are at 6 per cent each. Receptionists and security guards are at 4 per cent each. Radiographers are at 3 per cent. There is increase in strength of doctors by 16 per cent and nurses by 36 per cent. Attenders strength increases by 17 per cent. Lab technicians and Receptionist strength increases by 8 per cent each. Clerk's strength increases by 7 per cent. Radiographer's strength increases by 5 per cent. And security guards strength increases by 3 per cent.

For the hypothesis that all factors like age, experience, educational qualification, patience, local availability of staff are equally rated by health centers while appointing staff , the results show that health centers rated responsibility as first at 10, followed by skill, character, mental effort, dependability, loyalty, physical conditions. Health centers rated physical effort as last at 7.6.

For the hypothesis that all sources like within organization, advertising in newspapers, advertising in electronic media, word of mouth, consultancy services are equally approached by health centers in process of their recruiting potential employees, the results show health centers rated word of mouth as first at 8, followed by advertising in newspapers, within organization, advertising in electronic media. Health centers rated consultancy services as last at 4.2.

For the hypothesis all factors like skill, mental effort, responsibility, physical conditions, dependability, physical effort, character and loyalty are equally rated by health centers for carrying out job evaluation of employees, the results show health centers rated responsibility as first at 10, followed by skill, character, mental effort, dependability, loyalty, physical conditions. Health centers rated physical effort as last at 7.6.

5 health centers expressed the view that they will be evaluating employees every day. 2 health centers are doing job evaluation once in three months. 14 health centers are doing job evaluation once in six months. 9 health centers are doing job evaluation once in a year. 32 health centers are carrying out training and 7 health centers are not doing it. As many as 9 health centers preferred individual method. Individual method and oral instruction combined was preferred by 4 health centers. Group instruction was preferred by 3 respondents. Oral instruction and demonstration method combined was preferred by 3 respondents. Patient to doctor ratio is 23.5: 1. Patient to nurse ratio is 14.4:1.

SUGGESTIONS

A request for training in communication and social skills, financial and time management skills to doctors and staff may be arranged so that they can bring into reality service motto of the health centers.

A request is made that every patient in emergency should be attended by senior doctor not junior doctor. It is prayed to see that each health center have a separate Casuality Medical Officer. A request regarding availability of investigative requirements is needed in Srikalahasti. A request for free camps (as conducted by Desai hospital in Madanapalli on 26-7-2004 in Madanapalli) is made.

CONCLUSION

There is a huge requirement of doctors and nurses and the other staffs. The patient to doctor ratio and patient to nurse ratio also support this.

Appendix

Questionnaire on Manpower Planning in Health Centers of Andhra Pradesh

Name of Organization: Name of Respondent:

Address of Organization (With Phone No, Fax etc.): Designation of Respondent:

1. Type of treatment followed in your organization
   (a) Ayurveda
   (b) Homoeopathy
   (c) Allopathy
   (d) Others specify________

2. Since how many years your organization is serving the patients.
   (a) Less than 1 year
   (b) 1 year-5 years
   (c) 5 years-10 years
   (d) more than 10 years

3. How many staff are there in your organization (presently and staff required).

Sl No.	Staff	Present Strength	Future Strength	Total
1.	Doctors			
2.	Nurses			
3.	Radiographers			
4.	Lab Technicians			
5.	Attenders			

6. Security Guards
7. Clerks
8. Receptionists

4. Specify degree to which you consider various factors in appointing staff in your organization.

	Very Low	Low	Medium	High	Very High
(a) Age					
(b) Experience					
(c) Educational Qualification					
(d) Patience					
(e) Local availability of staff					

5. Degree to which your preference of source for potential employees.

	Very Low	Low	Medium	High	Very High
(a) Within Organization					
(b) Advertising in Newspaper					
(c) Advertising in Electronic Media					
(d) Word of Mouth					
(e) Consultancy Services.					

6. Specify degree to which you consider various key factors for job evaluation.

	Very Low	Low	Medium	High	Very High
(a) Skill					
(b) Mental Effort					

(c) Responsibility

(d) Physical Conditions

(e) Dependability

(f) Physical Effort

(g) Character

(h) Loyalty

7. You evaluáte your employees once in

(a) 6 months

(b) One year

(c) 2 years

(d) 3 years

(e) Others specify __________

8. Do you give training to your staff

(a) Yes

(b) No

9. Which method of training you adopt, if yes to 'question no 8'

(a) Individual instruction

(b) Group instruction

(c) Lecture Method

(d) Oral instruction

(e) Demonstration method

(f) Written instructional method

(g) Conferences

(h) Meetings

(i) Others specify_______

10. Number of in-patients_______

Number of out patients_______

Number of Beds______

11. Suggestions if any______________________________

Signature of the Respondent

REFERENCES

1. O.P. Khanna, A.Sarap, *Industrial Engineering and Management,* Dhanapat Rai Publications (P) Ltd, New Delhi, 1999.
2. Philip Kotler, *Marketing Management,* Prentice-Hall of India Private Limited, New Delhi, 1997.

17

Manpower Planning in IT Sector

Challenges, Constraints and Solutions

C. Padmavathi[*]

ABSTRACT

Manpower planning is the part of strategic planning process. In the past, manpower tended to be a reactive process because business needs usually defined human resources needs. But today, major changes in business, economic and social environments are forcing organizations to integrate business planning with manpower and to adopt a long-term proactive perspective. The pace of change is accelerating. It is essential to adjust the skills of manpower according to changes in environment. These skills are technical oriented. In order to improve the technical skills there should be proper linkage between manpower and education. Technical manpower planning concentrates on developing and controlling people with specified technical skills, so that no plan or programme suffers from lack of trained manpower and education. It improves overall competencies of people and leads for adding value to products and services for contributing to national economy.

Key Words: IT sector, manpower, short and long term demand, solutions.

* Asst. Professor, M.B.A.-Dept., Sreenivasa Institute of Technology and Management Studies, 74, Bangalore-Tirupathi Bye-pass Road, Chittoor. (A.P.) – 517 127, E-mail: vathi_padma@rediffmail.com

INTRODUCTION

In the manpower survey, it is revealed that there is a geometric rise in the demand of IT professionals in National and International wise. Keeping the International manpower demand in view the National demand as per the survey report given by NASSCOM and MIT, the estimated figure goes up to 16 lakhs in the direct employment and 32 lakhs by the year 2008 in the indirect employment as shown in the *Annexure-I*. In order to meet the demand of IT professionals, the present system has to go for serious manpower planning.

To achieve this objective, the All India Council for Technical Education should ensure the coordinated development of facilities and proper maintenance of standards on an all-India level. For this purpose, there should be up-to-date and meaningful manpower information available in the AICTE to help planning facilities in the conventional engineering disciplines.

OBJECTIVES

- To ensure proper linkage of economic planning with manpower and education;
- No programme or plan suffers from lack of trained IT professionals;
- To estimate short-term and long-term demand of IT professionals;
- To provide data for reviewing the matching of the job requirements with education and training;
- Identifying the latest teaching methods to improve the quality of education.

IMPORTANCE OF MANPOWER PLANNING IN IT SECTOR

The main objective of manpower planning in Information Technology is the estimation of short-term and long-term requirements of IT professionals. Day-by-day the number of IT jobs is increasing and the people with more technical skills are required to meet the demand in the dynamic market place. This can be possible by introducing the number of IT courses and IT related courses in the education system, shown in *Annexure-II* and IT enabled services are shown in *Annexure-III*.

The abundant availability of trained manpower in technical and managerial fields is one of the strong factors, which has helped India's development and which is one of the main attractions to foreign investors looking for opportunities for profitable investment.

A reliable information system is a prerequisite to planning, specially in the field of IT education and training. In the absence of up-to-date and meaningful manpower information, it will neither be possible to anticipate areas of growth in the field of science and technology nor plan for technical manpower development. Such a system is at present not available; the necessary data are not even collected, much less updated, systematised and stored suitably for retrieval as and when necessary. From the available data it is not possible to undertake studies relating to productivity of the educational programmes or absorption patterns of the educated in the software companies. A number of personnel with the background of IT education is also deployed in Industry. It is necessary for any Survey of Technical Manpower to take cognizance of this factor. It is, therefore, necessary, to establish a National Manpower Information System. In order to make such a system operational, it is necessary to establish effective coordination of efforts among the data generating and collecting agencies through a well-knit country-wide organization. The Regional Engineering Colleges and other selected technical institutions could assist as nodal points in the operations of the information system and thereby benefit from the system. Manpower information can also be used usefully for purpose of placement through agencies such as the Boards of Apprenticeship Training.

It is considered to be necessary to lay special emphasis on consolidation, diversification and improvement of quality rather than on further expansion.

It is necessary to the National Manpower Information System to store, update, retrieval and analysis of manpower information to assist technical education planning in IT sector.

CHALLENGES

To meet the gap between the demand and supply for the long term planning, capacity expansion in the engineering colleges and schools have been encouraged both in Govt. and private sectors.

Courses/Programmes-Modification

- — Integration of relevant Information Technology courses in technical courses at all levels;
- — Flexibility in programmes through credit system and multi-point entry;
- — Advanced courses should teach to students with Central assistance;
- — Continuous review of curricula to cope with technical changes and manpower needs;
- — Application oriented research projects and consultancy centres, turned to needs of national development.

Staff Selection and Appraisal

- — Appointment of permanent senior teaching positions;
- — Personnel promotions to motivate deserving staff;
- — Encouraging the staff to update knowledge in the changing environment;
- — Adjunct professorship for engineers from the industry and industrial residency for teachers.

Students

- — Selecting the students based on aptitude and ability;
- — Remedial programmes to help weak students;
- — Improving the skills of the students, through encouraging them to participating in various activities seminars, paper presentations etc.

Institutional Support Services

- — Improvement in library services through competent library staff and reprographic facility;
- — Establishment of learning resources centres;

— Modernisation of laboratories considering equipment obsolence and curricula changes.

CONSTRAINTS

Lack of effective coordination of efforts among the data generating and collecting agencies through a decentralised organization structure. Depending on the demand of IT jobs only it is possible to estimate the supply of IT professional and thereby increasing the number of seats in education system.

Since IT sector is in its infancy stage, changes are frequent and the failures are quite common. It is very difficult to predict the future requirements.

The quality of IT education is a very important aspect as, at present, market competency plays a very important role for employment. To ensure the quality steps have been taken to induct skilled people in teaching of the subject. But at present number of IT professionals are attracted towards the software jobs and number of skilled people in teaching are limited.

SOLUTIONS AND IMPROVEMENTS

— Involvement in consultancy work, and testing/service activities on selection basis will promote interaction between the institution and industry, which will be mutually beneficial. It will build up expertise and confidence of the staff and students and the image of the institution. To undertake and promote such activities, a consultancy centre should be established in each institution. A separate development fund should be created from out of the earnings through consultancy, which could be used for further development of the consultancy centre;

— Steps must be taken to induct skilled people in teaching the subject. Introducing the modern teaching methods i.e., Computer Based Training (CBT) from expert lecturers, video conferencing, collaborations with foreign universities for mutual exchange of technology etc.;

— Number of the IT courses and IT related courses are introduced in the education stream and regular revision to ensure its suitability for the market environment;

— Expenditure by the industry on IT education to be exempted totally for income tax purposes and Central share of assistance to be given direct to institutions earmarking funds for IT education;

— A reliable information system is a pre-requisite to planning, specialy in the field of technical education and training. A national manpower information system should be established with a lead centre in the Institute of Applied Manpower Research for the storage, updating, retrival and analysis of manpower information to assist technical education planning. The institute of applied manpower research should be suitably strengthened for this purpose with provision of requisite facilities;

— To ensure effective implementation of policies and programmes of the AICTE measures rather than making its statutory.

CONCLUSION

The main aim of the Technical Manpower Planning in IT sector is "The development of world-class, technically skilled and educated IT professionals with positive work values, acting as the vital force in building a prosperous Philippines where citizens enjoy a life of greater economic security, social well-being and personal dignity.

ANNEXURES

Annexure—I

	NASSCOM	MIT
Software Products & IT Services	11.00	7.77
IT enabled services	11.00	15.90
Teachers for Tertiary Education	-	0.20
Teachers for Secondary Education	-	1.00
Professionals for hardware industries	16 lakhs direct employment 32 lakhs indirect employment	

Source: Prospective IT Manpower Planning for the State of Orissa, Prepared by —DTE & T, Orissa and STPI, Bhubaneswar.

Annexure—II

IT Courses

— Bachelor of Computer Application (BCA);
— Bachelor of Information Technology and Management (BITM);
— Computer Science Hons. (B.Sc.);
— Computer & Management Information System (C & MIS);
— Information Technology (IT);
— Master in Business Administration & Informational Technology (MBA & IT);
— Master in Computer Application (MCA);
— Computer Programming and Application (CPA);
— Diploma in Computer Application (PDCA/PGDCA/DCA);
— O/A/B/C/level.

IT Related Courses

— Applied ETC and Instrumentation (AE & I);
— Electronic and Telecommunication (ETC);
— Bachelor of Business Administration (BBA);
— Electrical and Electronics (EL & ETC);
— Electronics and Instrumentation (ETC & I);
— Communication Engineering (CE—PG Course);
— Master of Business Administration (MBA).

Annexure—III

IT Enabled Services having Potential in India

- Transcription;
- Translation;
- Data entry;
- Design services;

- Finaicial and accounts services;
- Network management;
- Data search and analysis;
- Website services;
- Remote education;
- Monitoring services;
- Secretarial services;
- Help deck;
- Call centres;
- Insurance claim processing.
- Back office operation like:
  - Medical;
  - Security;
  - Human resource services;
  - Sales and marketing;
  - Banking.
- Creation of animations for television and movies;
- Geographical information system which include digital maps of buildings, roads and underground utilities;
- E-mail management;
- Internet patrol and security;
- Management of Internet commerce—acting as an exchange of data, payment and clearance;
- Supply chain management;
- Creation of portals and content.

Internet Connections in India

1997	0.04 million connections
1999	0.65 million connections
2000	1.50 million connections
2002	5.50 million connections

REFERENCES

1. Wayne F. Cascio, *Managing Human Resources*, Sixth Edition, Tata McGraw Hill Publishing Co., Ltd., 2003.
2. Edwin S. Flippo, *Personnel Management*, Sixth Edition, McGraw Hill Publishing Co., Ltd., 2003.
3. Gray D.H., *Manpower Planning: An Approach to the Problem*, London: Institute of Personnel Management, 1966.
4. Arun Monappa and Mirza Saiyadain, *Personnel Management*, Second Edition, Tata McGraw Hill Publishing Co., Ltd., 1998.
5. Gantz & John, To Keep Your Best IT People, Keep Them Learning, *Computer World*, Vol. 34, 7-3-2000, Issue 27.
6. Mathungwa P.D. & Schmitt. N., Work Motivation in Developing Country, *Journal of Applied Psychology Resources*, 68 (1), pp. 34-42.
7. Robberts K., Kossek E.E., & Ozeki. C., Managing the Global Workforce: Challenges and Strategies, *Academy of Management Executive*, 12 (4), 93-106.

18

Planning for Middle Level Paramedical Personnel in the Health Care System

*Bani Baral**

ABSTRACT

Health care system of every country requires services of competent and dedicated paramedical manpower who plays a pivotal role in the diagnosis and treatment of diseases.

With the introduction of computerized diagnostic and life supporting machines, the spectrum of the paramedical personnel has widened enormously. Besides the nurses, pharmacists and Lab Technicians taking care of routine work of the health care systems, a large number of technicians specializing in handling and maintaining these highly sensitive and sophisticated machines are also required. Increased health consciousness and a need for studying the pattern of diseases have led to the requirement of another group of health care personnel for keeping the record of patients. Skilled manpower is also required to handle the cases arising out of emergent situations e.g. accident, drowning, child birth, fire, riot etc. and for rehabilitation for persons with orthopaedic, neural and muscular disorders.

* **Government of Delhi, Department of Training and Technical Education, Muni Maya Ram Marg, Near TV Tower, Pitam Pura, Delhi– 110088, Email: banibaral2000@ yahoo.com**

In this chapter, the spectrum of middle level health care professionals required to cater to various needs has been mentioned. Details regarding existing availability of training facility and their proposed future growth have also been narrated in respect of Delhi State. A comparison has been made with the courses available in the USA, where these courses have been standardized and mechanisms of registry, licensure etc. exist for ensuring the credibility of these professionals.

Key Words: Health Care, Paramedical Personnel, Training Facility.

INTRODUCTION

Health care system is one of the social indices indicating the stage of development of a country and health care is a core element of the Governments' attempt to improve and promote health of their citizens. Dedicated and competent paramedical personnel are the lifeline for providing the health care of desired level. In this present era of globalization, automation, fast changing technology, population explosion and challenges of modern living, there is an urgent need to plan for the skilled manpower capable of handling specified jobs in the area of health care. Widely acclaimed doctors and huge network of super speciality hospitals has made the India a potential destination for medical tourism to get 'First World Treatment at Third World Prices'[1]. Middle level health care personnel are essential for all activities related to the patient care—from diagnosis to record keeping.

Currently, approved training facilities are available mostly in the limited areas of Nursing, Clinical Laboratory Technology and Pharmacy both at Delhi State Level and at the National Level. The Annual Technical Manpower review, 2003 of 24 states refer to the areas of Medical Lab Technology Diploma in four states (Punjab, Delhi, Maharashtra and Madhya Pradesh) with a total intake of 685 students, Pharmacy Diploma in 7 states (North Eastern states, West Bengal, Delhi, Andhra Pradesh, Gujarat, Maharashtra, Madhya Pradesh) with annual intake of 7231 students and Optometry in two states (Maharashtra, Madhya Pradesh) with 110 intake[2].

In Delhi State, AICTE approved paramedical courses are Diploma and Degree level courses in Pharmacy, Diploma in Medical Lab Tech., the interdisciplinary areas like Public Health and Environmental Engg. and Medical Electronics. Besides, there are a few Institutes offering Bachelors' level programmes in Medical Lab Technology and Physiotherapy. Delhi being the capital has to gear up for generation of competent paramedical manpower for catering to the current and future need of Delhi as well as the country as a whole.

This report gives the current availability of health care at Delhi State, aims at identification of the spectrum of paramedical personnel vis-à-vis the training facilities currently available and justification for having specialized personnel in relation to the requirement envisaged for Delhi State.

A fully developed health care system requires manpower with proven competence. As a guideline, mention has been made regarding the concept of Licensure, Registration etc. that is mandatory in the USA[3] along with some suggestions for a competency based curricula and expected role of the AICTE in governing quality in this area.

OVERVIEW OF THE HEALTH CARE FACILITY AVAILABLE IN DELHI

The ever-growing metropolis of Delhi State caters to more than 138 lakhs of Delhi population as well as the floating population from neighbouring states that constitute 33 per cent of the total intake at major hospitals run by Govt. of Delhi[4].

The facilities available in Delhi recognized by the Department of Health and Family Welfare, Government of Delhi are summarized in following table[4].

Table—18.1 Health facilities in Delhi: An overview

Sl. No.	Health Facilities	Nos.	BEDS
1	2	3	4
A.	HOSPITALS		
1.	Delhi Govt.	32	6551
2.	MCD (Hospitals 13. T.B. Clinics-10. Ayur Hospitals-02)	25	3625
3.	NDMC (1-General, 1 Maternity)	02	200

(Contd...)

1	2	3	4
4.	Delhi Cantt. Board	03	1855
5.	Central Govt. (CGHS-5, DGHS-4)	09	3821
6.	Railways	02	466
7.	Stat. Bodies (ESI-4, Autonomous-5)	09	3994
8.	Private (Regd. N. Homes-559. Vol. Org.-5)	564	12429
	TOTAL	**646**	**32941**
B.	**DISPENSARIES**	**No.**	**BEDS**
1.	DELHI GOVT. (HOMOEO-57, AYUR-17, UNANI-07, ALLOP-175,SHS-77, MHS-70	403	
2.	MCD (M&CW-115, ALLOP-40, HOMOEO-23, AYUR-106, UNANI-17, IIPVIII-06)	307	
3.	NDMC (M&CW-14, ALLOP-13, HOMOEO-11, AYUR-10)	48	
4.	Central Govt. (ALLOP-84, HOMOEO-11, AYUR-03, UNANI-1)	106	
5.	Railways	12	
6.	Statutory Bodies (including ESI-34, SBI-9, RBI-8, DJB-12) DVB-24, DTC-27 etc.	117	
	TOTAL	**993**	
C.	Primary Health Centres	07	79
D.	Sub-Centres attached to PHCs per PHC)	48*	
E.	Maternity Homes (MCD-23, NDMC-2)	25	321
F.	Polyclinics	05	
G.	Special Clinics (TB/STD/Leprosy)	44	
H.	Family Welfare Centres	125#	
	TOTAL	**224**	**400**
	GRAND TOTAL	**1863**	**33341**

Population of Delhi as per Census 2000—13,782.976

Total Beds in Delhi—33.341

* Projected as per norms.

\# 69 Urban Family Welfare Centres. 8 Rural Welfare Centres. 28 Health Posts, 20PP Units List does not include School Health Scheme of MCD

Population of Delhi as per Census 2001-13.782.976

Total Beds in Delhi 33.341

Bed Population Ratio in Delhi: 2.2 per 1000 Population

National Average 0.7 beds per 1000 Population.

WHO Recommendation 5.0 beds per 1000 Population.

Future plan of Govt. of Delhi in the Health sector emphasizes on strengthening the existing facilities and also establishment of two super speciality hospitals in East Delhi and West Delhi to achieve expected target of 2.5 beds per 1000 population by 2007 and 3.5 beds per 1000 population by 2020.

To cater to the need of these hospitals/ primary health care centers and also to those unrecognized nursing homes and clinics, there are limited facilities for training the persons with appropriate skill. The existing facilities range from in-house training of in-service persons to the formal training in recognized training institutes.

The existing training facilities are far from satisfactory even in the AICTE approved institutes. The training imparted is not at all competency oriented. Relatively better employment potential of these paramedical personnel and lack of approved norms has resulted in the mushrooming of institutions (both recognized and unrecognized) with least concern for the quality.

CLASSIFICATION OF PARAMEDICAL PERSONNEL, JOB PROFILE AND EMPLOYABILITY

With the vast network of health care facilities, population they cater to and the emergence of specialized methodologies in all diagnostic and therapeutic services, the profile of paramedical personnel has also become specialty oriented. Various groups of these paramedical manpower, their role, responsibility, employment profile and existing training facilities available at Delhi State is summarized in the following table:

Table—18.2 Classification of health technicians

Sl. No.	Classification of Health Technician	Job Profile	Employability	Current status on Training Facility in Delhi State
1	2	3	4	5
1.	Anaesthesia Technologist/ Technician	To assist doctors in operation theatre	All places equipped with operation theatre	In-service in some hospitals. Not recognized outside.
2.	Audiometry & speech pathology Technicians	To assist ENT Specialist. Rehabilitation of deaf & dumb.	Large hospitals & clinics of ENT specialists	In service training in some hospitals Not recognized outside
3.	Cardio vascular Technicians	To assist the cardiologist in conducting different diagnostic procedure e.g. ECG, stress test, angiography, angioplasty etc.	Large hospitals heart stations private & Govt. hospitals & research centres	In service training in some hospitals Not recognized outside.
4.	Clinical Laboratory Technicians	To check body fluids/samples for absence, presence, extent & cause of disease	All places dealing with patients, research labs, pharmaceutical companies etc.	Recognised DMLT-4 Institutes BMLT-2, Institutes
5.	Dental Hygienist/ Dental Assistant	To assist dental surgeon	Large hospitals, dental clinics	In service training in some hospitals Not recognized outside
6.	Dialysis Technician	To assist the kidney specialists in the gustative units	Specialized hospitals	In service training in some hospitals Not recognized outside

(Contd...)

1	2	3	4	5
7.	Dispensing opticians	To assist ophthalmologists	Hospitals & eye clinics	In service training in some hospitals Not recognized outside
8.	EEG Technicnans	To assist neuro surgeons, neurologists	Large hospitals, Tertiary Health Care centres	In service training Not recognized out side
9.	Emergency Medical Technician	These paramedics are trained in diagnostic, therapeutic and communication skills to take care of emergent situations like automobile accident, drowning heart attack gunshot etc.	Casualty & Trauma centres	No facility
10.	Medical Record Technician	To organise & evaluate the records of patients e.g. History, result of laboratory tests, diagnosis & treatment plan. To analysis the results for improved patient care	In all places dealing with health including Law Farms Insurance Companies etc.	No facility
11.	Nuclear Medicine Technician	To administrator radio pharmaceuticals to patient, & then the monitor the characteristics & functions of the tissues in which abnormal areas show higher or lower concentration of radioactivity than normal. To operate gamma scintillation cameras.	Tertiary Hospitals, Cancer Hospitals, Research labs	In service Training

(Contd...)

1	2	3	4	5
12.	Pharmacist	Dispenses medicine	All hospitals, Research labs, pharmacy companies	D. Pharm-7 B. Pharm-7
13.	Physiotherapist	Works in orthopaedics & rehabilitation Departments. They also have important role in the treatment of patients with muscular & cerebral problems.	All hopitals & Rehabilitation Centres	B. Physiotherapy-3 Institutions (Private)-2 Govt.-1 (RCI)
14.	Radiological Technician	Operation & maintenance of machines working on principles of radiation/sound wave eg. X-Ray, CT Scan, MRI, Ultrasound etc.	Hospitals	In service Training.
15.	Surgical Technicians	To assist doctors in all surgical procedure		In service training
16.	Sanitation & Public Health	To check & air pollution	Municipality	In service training; Certificate course under SCVT

ASSESSMENT OF FUTURE REQUIREMENT & PLANNING FOR EXCELLENCE: ROLE OF AICTE

As seen in the chart at previous section there is need to have trained manpower in all areas where training facilities are not available and also to strengthen the facilities in existing areas. Out of the areas listed above, there are only a few AICTE approved Institutes in Delhi State imparting training in limited areas as detailed below:

Table—18.3 AICTE approved paramedical diploma courses: Delhi State

Course	No. of Institutes			Annual Intake		
	Govt.	Private	Total	Govt.	Private	Total
DMLT	1	3	4	45	180	225
D.Pharm	1+1	5	7	110	300	410
PHEE	1	–	1	30	–	30

In the developed countries, due attention is given to the quality of the personnel entrusted to assist in the health care. Required level of training is ensured by prescribing the pre-requisites and the credibility of both the Institutes offering the courses and the training hospitals linked with these Institutes. The Institutes are accredited by the professional societies. The persons seeking job are required to be registered by taking examinations conducted by the professional societies at the national level. In USA, this is done by the Professional societies like American Society of Clinical Pathologists, American Health Information Management Association, and National Accrediting Agency for Clinical Laboratory Sciences (NAACIS) etc. through their respective Boards of Registry. Besides that, there is procedure of licensure[3, 6, 9].

In our country, conduct of these service oriented courses are taken only as a business proposition by the privately managed Institutes taking advantage of absence of any specific norms prescribed by the AICTE and absence of any professional society in these areas.

AICTE as an apex body for Technical Education may consider prescribing certain conditions while issuing Letter of Intent for establishment of the training Institutions for the paramedical professionals in view of the fact that unlike other profession, a lapse on the part of these middle level workers of the health care system may be irreversible and fatal to the patients.

Following are some of the suggestions in this regard:

- Entry qualification for the courses should be minimum 10+2;
- Prerequisite subjects for the entry level must be specified;
- AICTE must insist on giving a detailed project report by the societies indicating the Institutional and Hospital components, the strength at the Institution level and the linkage hospital level indicating the number. of indoor/out door patients and monthly turnover of various specimens before issuing Letter of Intent;
- As far as possible, the approval for these courses be given only to the societies running reputed hospitals;
- National Board of Accreditation of AICTE may decide the norms for accreditation of paramedical course to establish the credibility of the Institutes offering these course;
- AICTE may also coordinate with Medical Council of India to have a branch with paramedical and medical professionals as members in order to take up issues related to quality education in paramedical courses;
- AICTE may introduce of certification and licensure at the national level to judge the competency level of these persons.

SOME SUGGESTIONS ON CONDUCT OF EFFECTIVE AND QUALITY PARAMEDICALCOURSES

Organizations

The programmes are envisaged to be cooperative educational programmes developed and supervised by an educational Institution in collaboration with selected hospitals/clinical laboratories with academic and clinical rotation terms suitably sequenced to achieve curricular objectives.

Partner Institutions offering the programme must be able to provide all supporting resources.

Resources

(a) *Human Resources:* Faculty, supporting staff and administrative level staff should be as per AICTE norms. Faculty must demonstrate by education, certification and experience, the ability to teach and continue to strive for professional development. The Institute offering the course is required to have a fact sheet on all the faculty members including the clinical faculty documenting their bio-data.

(b) *Finance:* Finance to run the programme must be assured by an adequate budget for efficient conduct of the programmes.

(c) *Space:* Adequate class rooms, library, laboratories and computer centres be provided as per AICTE norms. There should be special provisions to safeguard the health and safety of the students, staff and patients associated with all educational activities associated with the programmes.

(d) *Instructional Materials:* All instructional materials eg. Reference materials, clinical materials, demonstration and other multi-media presentations be provided.

Curriculum

The curriculum should have two components:

(i) *General Education Component* (GEC) addressing to the contemporary issues on inter-disciplinary areas, communication skill, inter personal relationship, societal responsibilities and development of quantitative and logical skills.

(ii) *Professional curriculum* comprising classroom teaching and clinical rotations addressing to the cognitive, psychomotor and affective domains of the trainees.

The curriculum structure can be presented as:

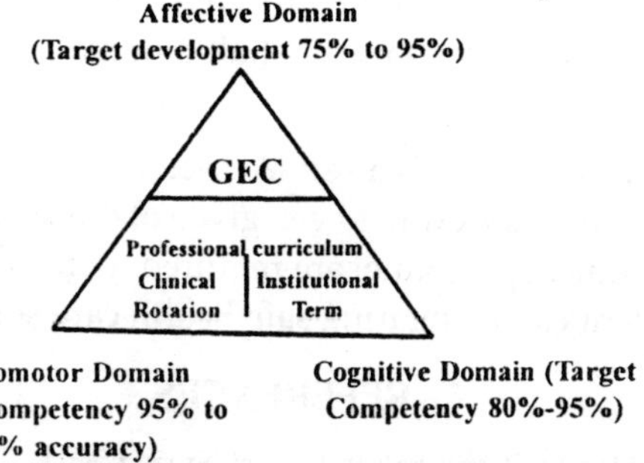

Fig. 18.1: Curriculum structures for health technician courses

Instructions shall follow a document with clearly written programme goals and course syllabi which include individual course objective and the expected degree of competency to be achieved.

Evaluation and Monitoring of the Programme

Suggested mechanisms for evaluating and monitoring of the health care programmes are:

- — Review of the functioning of the Institute by the accreditation board;
- — Review of the standard of passed out products by an external certifying/ licensing agency;
- — Students assessment by faculty;
- — Faculty and clinical rotation evaluation by the students;
- — Survey of the passed out products 3-6 months after completion of the programme;
- — Self study.

The programme evaluation and other elements of the programme be reflected in the future curricula.

CONCLUSION

TIFAC survey of the future scenario of India's health predicts that India will have the emerging diseases of the developing world, there shall be an increase in the non communicable diseases like cardiovascular diseases and an increased rate of suicide and homicide. Moreover, according to TIFAC, in another 5 - 10 years, safety, health and environment shall emerge as important areas for consultancy inputs[6].

Health care sector is a service sector. In the limited scope of this chapter, an overview has been given of the areas where middle level paramedical personnel are required to meet the present and future challenges for ensuring safe health care services to all.

REFERENCES

1. World Health Organization Report, Spring 2004.
2. *Annual Technical Manpower Reviews* 2003 for the States of North East, Bihar, West Bengal, Uttar Pradesh, Maharashtra, Madhya Pradesh, Andhra Pradesh, Tamil Nadu, Kerala, Karnataka, Gujarat, Rajasthan, Goa, Assam, Orissa, Punjab, Chandigarh, Himachal Pradesh, Jammu & Kashmir, Delhi, Haryana.
3. Web site of American Society of Clinical Pathologist.
4. *Health Facilities in Delhi 2004*, Department of Health and Family Welfare, Govt. of Delhi.
5. Norms and Standards, AICTE Publication 1999.
6. Sh. A.P.J. Abdul Kalam Azad India 2020. —A Vision for the New Millennium, Penguin Books India, 2002
7. National Bureau of Health Standard (1986) Published by the Directorate General of Health Services.
8. American Medical Association Allied Health Education Directory 2001-2002.
9. Joint Commissioner on Accreditation of Health Care Organizations Accreditation Manual for Hospitals—99-108 (1995).

19

Synergism Between Hospitality Education and Industry

Some Recommendations

Dalip K. Singha[*]

ABSTRACT

Education and industry need to combine in order to enrich and enhance inputs given to the "Generation Next". It is only then that the human resource in hotel and hospitality will be able to stand up to global competition. The Government has an equal investment in this and will need to share the responsibility in this direction. This chapter attempts to make recommendations in this regard.

Key Words: Anatomy of the Hotel Industry, Hotels need different training, Core Competencies, Synergy, Three Pronged Approach, Education/Industry combine, Generation Next, Government, Equal Investment.

INTRODUCTION

In my 33 years of work experience I have worked for approximately 14 years in Hotel Operations, as a Personnel/HR

* **Vice Principal, Welcomgroup Graduate School of Hotel Administration, Valley View International, Manipal - 576 104 (Karnataka), Email: dalipsingha@yahoo.com**

Manager. I have spent the last 8 years in a College offering a degree of "Bachelors in Hotel Management", of those 8 years, I have taught for 6 years.

My unique positions in the past have given me the opportunity to experience, both, the "Consumer" and "Producer" end of the supply and demand chain in r/o the human resource vis-à-vis Hotels.

I am therefore competent to comment on the present state of education in Hotel/Hospitality Management and the requirements of the Industry. My experience enables me to perceive and understand the chasm that exists between the educational initiative and industry requirements.

I believe that my presentation will have a novel and fresh approach to the subject, which would have optimum utility when received with an open mind.

AIMS AND OBJECTIVES

Most, if not all professions have a theoretical foundation. This theoretical base would enable the individual to optimise his contributions in the chosen field, thereby generating incremental value to the job and in the process enhancing ones' own advancement along the vertical axis of the organizational hierarchy. This advancement would naturally have the spin-off effect of creating better material prospects and gains for the individual while having consequent benefits for the organization.

The process envisaged above would bring into line, both, organizational and individual objectives, aims and aspirations.

As a consequence, all parties concerned benefit from the symbiotic advantages that accrue . The increased competition and complexity of tourism and hotel industry as well as the sophisticated demands for tomorrow's travellers, mean that tourism and hotel employees will need to be better educated. Both are changing industries and have gone through drastic transformation.

A hotel combines production and sale, under one roof. It is in close and intimate contact with its customers, who consume hotel products at the point of sale. Basically, it is a capital intensive business i.e. high capital to sales ratio. Being a service oriented industry, it places strong emphasis on the management of people taking into account different nationalities, their cultural tastes and all personal values, including education, standard of living etc.

Now, hotel management has become a profession which young boys and girls are proud to join, and get trained for various level positions. The hotel management education has proliferated into a series of courses across the length and breadth of the country, offering technical certificate courses of specialised nature, diploma, post-graduate and master degree programmes in hotel, catering and tourism. Herein lies the problem.

It is an unfortunate fact that "Education" per se has, in our country come to mean, by and large, an instrument for making the "quick buck". Education is the proverbial "money-spinner" which unscrupulous persons foist on a gullible public, with no thought for its consequences.

Misfortune, however, does not warp the truth that this fact has a derogatory effect on the innards and fiber of our social fabric and national character in general and the quality of the potential human resource, which resides in "Generation Next" , which is waiting in the wings, in particular.

Nowhere is the destructive effect of this trend more noticeable than in the discipline of Hotel Management, which happens to be one of its prime victims.

The proliferation of innumerable establishments supposedly teaching and imparting the knowledge and skills of Hotel and Hospitality Management is mind boggling.

These institutions neither have the mission nor the infrastructure and requisite manpower inventories to deliver. They are money making machines in disguise and the veneer of this disguise is very thin.

- The chapter aims to examine the current scenario with regard to the preparation of the nascent human resource (individually and collectively) and examine the process of preparation, its' results and as to whether the need of the ultimate consumer, i.e. the industry, are met or found wanting.

- If the latter, what would be the necessary steps, both, at the macro and micro levels to alleviate the situation in order that the student emerging from institutions providing "Hospitality Education" is well equipped to take on the role that he/she finds himself/herself with at entry level to the industry.
- The chapter also intends to suggest that the Hotel/ Hospitality Industry has a direct vested interest in the direction and quality of education which is turning out prospective Managers/Supervisors in the same discipline and industry.
- The chapter will recommend that on account of this vested interest the Hotel/Hospitality Industry has a responsibility in being involved with the mechanics of education as also policing the same.
- In other words, a synergy needs to be built and developed between educators of the human resource and the ultimate consumers.
- This synergy would need to be continuous, long term and inter-twined, one with the other.

It is hoped that recommendations made during the course of this chapter would have a 3-pronged effect viz: one at the individual level, two at the institutional level and three at the National level.

Improving the quality of human resource in the Hospitality Industry would directly impact Hotels, Airlines and other establishments immediately connected with "Hospitality", as also have ripple effects on the tourism industry, which is one of the largest foreign exchange earners.

India, with its rich and varied cultural heritage has a lot to offer, yet its infrastructural inferiority (including the Human Resource) is an impediment to attracting tourists (both foreign and domestic), thereby inhibiting the level of earnings through this all important channel.

The chapter will attempt to recommend basic / broad dimensions of improvement which, it is hoped, would considerably improve the translation of theoretical inputs into practical output at the shop-floor level.

It is also understood that the effort in this direction cannot be individual, partial, unilateral or one sided. It is to be tackled at a National level including the Ministries of Education and Tourism, Governing Bodies of Educational Institutions and regulating authorities such as the AICTE etc. Into its ambit would also fall the Government, both, at the centre and the State.

THE ANATOMY OF THE HOTEL INDUSTRY—SOME VIEWS

Earnesh Henderson Sr. of the Sheraton Hotel Corporation has very aptly explained the changes taking place in the hotel industry. As recently as two or three decades ago, the stature of a hotelman was often measured by his personal charm, his popularity and his social standing. Today the priorities are shifting.

May be we are sacrificing some of the industry's glamour on the altar of hard facts, know-how and a familiarity with the tools of scientific management. But it is the latter that pays off when the monthly statement or annual report is issued.

The field of hotel management is inter-disciplinary. Managing a hotel is a complex activity involving the application of a wide range of skills and a broad spectrum of knowledge to many types of business problems. It essentially deals with employees, guests, suppliers and other trade men who are the prime human relationship spectrum, through which the hotel functions.

Hotel management can be interpreted as "management is what management does". It is dynamic. It is result oriented. The success of a hotel lies in good management. Traditionally, all hotel managers spent their time in doing, instead of planning, organising, staffing, directing and controlling the actual tasks of management. They were involved with the routine jobs of production and service at the cost of other important managerial jobs.

Hotel managers in these establishments remain in touch with the needs of their guests which tempts management to participate in the minute details of service.

Men of outstanding technical competence sometimes fail when they assume the management of a department or business. A highly skilled cook may not be a capable Chef de Cuisine (Executive Chef) despite his outstanding culinary skill. Similarly, an outstanding Room Clerk may prove to be a failure as a house manager/resident manager despite his knowledge. Hotel management is a combination of professional and technical abilities. . The large number of graduates from hotel and catering institutions entering directly into management jobs, indicate the growing need for professionals.

Less technical skill is needed in this industry compared to some other professions but this does not mean that no technical competence at all is necessary.

It is only technical competence that can assure the successful implementation of managerial principles. All the managerial functions which include planning, organising, staffing, directing and controlling, are applied to the hotel trade. The levels of management depend on the technical knowledge of the hotel staff.

1. There is a singular uniqueness to the demands and requirements of the hotel industry.
2. The profile of the hotelier tends more to a well-rounded personality rather than a specialist in any one particular field.
3. He has to be of above average intelligence, an excellent diplomat, a durable door-mat, an instant fixer of problems, suave, sophisticated and skilled in the art of communication. The more languages he knows the better his proficiency.
4. He has to "do", "think", and "feel".

The Hotel Manager, in other words is almost a hybrid, ie: a cross between a professional manager and a magician. The preparatory ground for this rare breed must be one groomed with meticulous care and precision. Equal attention needs to be paid to the theoretical inputs as well as the practical aspects of the education and training.

My college is now rearranging its focus on these hitherto unattended aspects of hoteliering. The College curricula, both in its formal and informal sense addresses the unique needs of a Hotel Manager with due weightage being given to aspects over and above the technical knowledge and skills. While these may not be tackled at the class room level, inputs are given to the student through the media and means of Club activities, extra curricular functions and other similar platforms.

CORE COMPETENCIES FOR HOTEL MANAGEMENT

I quote below important extracts from an article contained in the cover story of the FHRAI magazine of December 2002:

1. It is generally recognised that hotel management institutes or educational institutions giving degree/ diploma courses in hotel management must prepare their students in the core competencies required by them, when they serve in a hotel;
2. This job can only be done right if the institutions know about the core competencies that are required to be learnt by the students;
3. Is it managing the operations of cooking, serving, making rooms, the front office or is it the management skills of finance, management strategies and marketing?
4. Is it providing good service and ambience to the customer;
5. Or is it a combination of all of these?
6. But it has to be recognised without doubt that teaching the portfolio of hotel management competencies that graduates are required to possess seems to be central to the success of hospitality management education;
7. In the recent Christou and Eaton study the most significant finding is that both the general managers and the graduates identifies as most essential

competencies those that are associated with soft skills (or interpersonal, human relations associated competencies);

8. It could thus be concluded that the soft skills are in great demand on both sides of the Atlantic and in both northern and southern Europe;
9. Therefore, it could be argued that the industry's most important expectation of education is the development of the students transferable skills;
10. This has to be taken very seriously into account by hospitality educators ; and should be seen as an indication for appropriate adjustments in the programmes of study and for the introduction of appropriate relevant teaching methods;
11. An important outcome of the survey was the identification of what is considered to be the single most important skill in the international hospitality industry;
12. It is therefore suggested that the hospitality educators in the future may have to consider ways for enhancing further the students abilities to manage guest problems with understanding and sensitivity. At present, these skills, if taught are incidental, specially in the context of India.

REDESIGN HOSPITALITY EDUCATION

1. Despite the fact that the accomplishment of more detailed research appears necessary, the outcomes of the research described here can be used as a starting point for the assessment and redesign of further and higher education courses in hospitality management.
2. The development of students' management competencies should receive special consideration during the revamping of hospitality management curricula.
3. Perhaps, the starting point to increase the breadth and quality of hotel management course could be based on the pursuit of the continuous improvement of the students soft skills.

4. This might be related with the six "major contents areas" for hospitality curricula that were described by Umbreit (1992) : Leadership, human resources management, services marketing, financial analysis, total quality management and communication skills.

5. The hospitality educators efforts towards improving the soft skills of the students could be assisted by redesigning the forms of teaching and learning.

6. More emphasis might need to be given on creative forms of learning like role-playing, case studies, simulations, business games, out of class assignments, internships (industrial training) and psychodrama. Paucity of time cannot be a factor allowed to raise its ugly head.

7. In addition, educators could consider the adoption of even more sophisticated forms of teaching. Such as for example, the "laboratory sessions" (Bell and Weitman, 1995), which allow students to study the connection between theoretical concepts and the real world and the "business group experience" (Fitzgerald and Cullen, 1991) which provides an external laboratory for implementing and experiencing the dynamics of management.

8. There has been much written in recent years on the importance of high quality teaching and learning in higher education. This was one of the issues addressed by the Dearing Committee Report "Higher Education in the Learning Society". One of these recommendations specifically highlighted the importance of developing and implementing teaching strategies which focus on the promotion of student learning. In specifically highlighting the importance of promoting learning rather than just the quality of teaching. Learning is not a by-product of teaching but is an active process in its own right, undertaken by students themselves, which results in a transformation of the individual through the acquisition of knowledge and understanding but

also involves the development of a range of intellectual, problem solving and communication skills.

HOTELS NEED DIFFERENT TRAINING

1. The training programmes being designed for hotel managers and supervisors should have more emphasis on the soft skill which is currently lacking.
2. The same problem will exist in teaching such soft skills in educational institutions in a country like India where the majority of faculty members have never served a customer or have never been exposed to experiencing the professional appearance and poise required from up market hotel manager.
3. Still it is a very significant study for both hotel managers and educators and points to major training needs which need to be followed to the extent possible. It may be a slow journey, but we shall at least be treading on the right road."

CERTAIN THOUGHTS AND OBSERVATIONS IN THIS REGARD

1. The emphasis is on what is called "soft skills" or "transferable skills".
2. This may be understood as a slant on soft skills as opposed to the earlier emphasis on hard core technical skills in operational areas.
3. What are the ingredients/features of these soft skills. Initial attempts to identify these would include the following:
   - Ability to understand human behaviour and all (or a large portion) of its complexities;
   - Ability to manage guest problems with understanding and sensitivity ; this would include the capacity to empathize with the guest and after appreciating the situation (from the guest's point of view) developing the ability to handle the situation with sensitivity, aplomb and creativity;

- Strong communication skills, both, in English and the vernacular where possible;
- Use of correct body language and other non verbal communicators (conscious/semi-conscious/ unconscious);
- Quick, result - oriented thinking;
- The ability not to get flustered and hyper in crisis situations;
- Ability to remain calm and also maintain the balance and equilibrium of the guest;
- A sound knowledge of the written and spoken language with all its nuances, including developing a sound vocabulary base;
- Ability to appreciate consequences of action/non-action taken, both, in human and in legal terms;
- *Capacity to endure:----* which, will require preparation at the college level, ensuring that the prospective hotel employee enters the industry with optimum awareness levels about the vagaries and demands of the industry in all its dimensions, physical, emotional and, at some levels even intellectual;
- Ability to anticipate guests needs and requirements.

4.

- From the above it becomes apparent that not only is the course (inclusive of syllabi), the institutional curricula and infrastructure important, but it needs to be realized that the persona of the teacher has its own unique importance and special requirements, where mere knowledge of a subject may not suffice.
- Obviously, a person who has not worked with a hotel guest cannot inform the students of their requirements, their preferences and ways and means to deal with them.

- Soft skills/people skills/social skills can only be transferred from the teacher to the student, if, in the first place, the teacher himself possesses these skills.
- In this regard industry and education become competitors for the same human resource.
- And this is where the crunch lies; compensation levels to a Hotel Manager and those to a teacher in a College are vastly different, with the Hotel Manager earning many times more compensation than does the Hospitality educator.
- With this scenario the market forces come into operation with "quality" going to the highest bidder.
- It is not surprising that "Education" gets the leftovers from this fray.
- If "Market forces" are going to create this great Divide, an agency such as the Government (or Government appointed body) needs to step in and bring about some form of checks and balances which may not equate one with the other but manage to at least reduce the disparity.

5.

- Keeping the above situation in mind it is important that "Industry" realises that its future in terms of Management Personnel lies in establishing a sound foundation. This foundation can only be laid in the educational curricula of the educational institutions in the Country. The approach will need to be holistic, keeping in mind all contributors to superior education, including the quality and compensation of the individual teacher.
- The concept of rotation comes to mind which would bring about this synergy between Education and Industry.

RECOMMENDATIONS WITH REGARD TO SYNERGY; THE TWO PRONGED STRATEGY

Micro Level

1. The basic premise would be that both Industry and Education understand that quality in the future would depend entirely on their mutual cooperation and working together.
2. Both entities would have their vested interests fulfilled through such a process:

   (a) Education:

   - With the opportunity to stay contemporary;
   - Opportunity for quality industrial exposure for both, students and faculty;
   - Improvements in infrastructural status;
   - Better opportunities for provision of jobs to their graduating students on account of this synergy and subsequent rapport that would build between the two entities;
   - Opportunity for research, hitherto unknown;
   - Opportunity for personnel, belonging to both disciplines, to relocate depending on requirements and the situation at hand.

   (b) Industry:

   - Opportunity to influence the moulding and development of fresh talent;
   - Opportunity to stake a claim on the best available talent, depending on capacity to pay.

3. Would encourage propagation of sound Educational Institutes, while automatically eliminating institutes not up to scratch or out to make the "quick-buck".

This is one discipline that is akin to "swimming"; all theoretical inputs are pointless until and unless the student enters the water and attempts to swim. Theoretical inputs are useless until practical, hands on training is included in the curriculum.

This hands-on training is aimed at inculcating not only technical skills in the individual but also giving him knowledge and a feel of handling the clientele/customer/guest.

The infrastructural requirements of such education cum training are tremendous and not all educational institutes have the wherewithal to provide the necessary training.

Obviously, hotels would be reluctant to absorb trainees with problems in communication (more specifically English), technical skills and job knowledge.

Educational institutes would require to have close contact and liaison with hotel chains in order to place their students as trainees. Further, the quality and content of training imparted would depend to a large extent on the hotel's felt need to train. There are no statutory obligations on the part of the employer to absorb such trainees, unlike apprentices under the Apprenticeship Act of 1961. Acquiescence on the part of the employer is entirely voluntarily, depending, directly or indirectly on the vested interests of the employer.

In the Indian context, a majority of educational institutions providing education in the disciplines of Hotels and Hospitality are unable to meet this demand on account of inadequacies in infrastructure and the wherewithal to deliver.

Macro Level

In today's world change is introducing new work and life cultures throughout the developed world. New and different demands are being made on workers and employers alike. Static function - based skills and traditional management models and techniques are becoming inadequate and inflexible in work places requiring the very opposite. The world is becoming a virtual global village. Consequently, the mobility of labour is also assuming global dimensions as human capital becomes the new currency in the dichotomy between the developed and undeveloped economics and as the imperatives of the market place take hold.

The volume diversity and rapidity of emerging new knowledge requires a concomitant effect on the capacity of people to respond and assimilate the veritable communications revolution which is ongoing.

The methods, forms and location of learning are also undergoing change. In particular the shift of emphasis from teaching to learning represents a new paradigm in which people are increasingly required to take much more responsibility for their own development. Formal learning in institutions is rapidly being supplemented and/or replaced by learning at work, in the home, in the community and in recreation. Further, the focal point of "learning" no longer remains trained on the students but brings into its ambit the "teacher", who, by necessity and not choice, will need to constantly keep his knowledge base and teaching techniques fresh and abreast with modern trends of today while anticipating the new requirements of tomorrow.

The UNESCO report Learning: The Treasure within, identifies the four pillar of education as:

(i) Learning to know

(ii) Learning to do

(iii) Learning to live together

(iv) Learning to be.

It is not yet clear whether the traditional learning institutes are responding appropriately to those changes or whether they can succeed in doing so in the future.

The development of a national qualifications framework provides a new and significant opportunity to address many of these issues. Establishing such a framework can provide the basis for identifying gaps and lacunae in the current certification arrangements and highlight barriers or obstacles in the pathways for learners within the framework.

The process of developing the framework will give effect to a very proactive role for all stake holders in ensuring the optimum structure and initiatives to meet the needs of the learners and the labour market, keeping in mind the "employability" factor of the product so turned out.

Practical Issues

"What is the difference between training and education"?

Charles Handy provided the basis of an answer when he opined that "---if you are well educated, you are easy to train."

Some of the practical issues that need to be addressed towards finding a more comprehensive answer:

(i) The recognition that the better educated the population, the better the people and the country as a whole will prosper (The sooner Industry comes to the realisation the better it will be for all the stake holders);

(ii) Links between schools, vocational, adult and higher education require better sign-posting;

(iii) Curricula require change and new pro-active approaches to their development to make such links more apparent and accessible;

(iv) Qualifications systems have to be reshaped to enable learning to be taken in chunks (modules, if you like). Individualised learning and records of competence are required throughout life to enable people to repeatedly enter and exit the formal qualification structure as required. This is quite unlike the Indian experience, where the link of learning is given as inputs at the initial stage and little or no top ups done subsequently;

(v) Learning has to become far more flexible. Irrespective of mode, there should be parity of esteem, and, particularly for adults, moving in and out of various modes of learning should be feasible and seamless;

(vi) Acceptance of the need to build on the constructivist skills of teachers is imperative;

(vii) An extensive retraining programme for teachers is required to produce independent learners, together with standards for the assessment of such independence;

Alternatively, where needed, constant interface of the teachers on a sustained basis so that their knowledge base and skills remain contemporary;

(viii) "Real" commitment and input of resources is required for both curriculum and staff development.

CONCLUSION

The Third Prong: All that has been suggested above could only operate against a background where strategies and implementations are employed against a National Qualifications Framework. This would be a mechanism through which all relevant learning achievements may be referenced to one or more of a generic set of coherently related qualifications for the purpose of national accreditation and/or recognition. The qualifications framework should become the single, nationally and internationally accepted entity, which relates uniformly to awards in respect of further and higher education and training. The underpinning principles of this framework would be :

Coherence: which is ensured through the use of a generic set of related qualifications as the basis of the framework. The selected classification of qualifications must have both national and international significance, and be based on sound principles and supported by clear definitions.

Relevance: which requires that the generic qualifications forming the main scaffolding of the framework be related to the needs of learners and industry, and to the social, cultural and educational needs of local, regional, national and international communities.

Inclusivity: which provides for the referencing, accreditation and/or recognition of all relevant achievements within the framework, thereby characterising such achievements with a sense of participation and parity of esteem. An inclusive framework assimilates the accreditation and recognition of inherent differences in achievement relating to the range of human abilities and intelligences.

Referentiality: which utilises properties such as distinctiveness, relatedness, equivalence and comparability of qualifications as evidenced by clear, relevant and differential standards.

Flexibility is a property which renders the framework capable of adaptation to different contexts and changing needs and of reflecting different emphases. Accreditation processes will require adaptation to take account of the different contexts in which learners learn and the different types of providers of education and training programmes seeking accreditation.

Transparency: which ensures that the framework is clearly presented and disseminated in such a variety of ways as to be easily understood by and accessible to all. Transparency is a principle that underpins the design of the framework and also informs its operation. In the operation of the framework, transparency relates to the achievement of a condition where all principles, processes and procedures are made explicit in order to ensure that they are easily understood by users of the system.

The task ahead is uphill and enormous in magnitude, but it is not beyond the realm of reality. It would need a determined and concerted effort to fructify, with distinct advantages to all the stake-holders. It can only be described as a Win/Win scenario.

REFERENCES

1. FHRAI Magazine - December 2002
2. UNESCO Report Learning: The Treasure within.
3. Peter Serge: "The Fifth Discipline"
4. Umbreit (1992): "Leadership, Human Resources Management, Services Marketing, Financial Analysis, TQM and Communication skills.
5. Bell and Weitman 1995, Laboratory Sessions
6. Dearing Committee Report: "Higher Education in the Learning Society."

Also, from the following web sites:

1. www.nqai.com/pospaper1.htm
2. www.business.itsn.ac.uk/events/best%2020003/Abstracts.htm

20

A Case Study on Selection and Evaluation Approach in Manpower Development for Farm Machinery and Comparative Study Before and After Adopting the Model

*S. B. Chattopadhyay**

ABSTRACT

In present national unemployment scenario rehabilitation on farm machineries plays an important role since utilization of surplus educated youth in mechanized farming is very essential to abolish urban and rural imbalance. Selections of manpower, training and evaluation are major criteria for rehabilitation. In view of this a model new approach was established. In this chapter a comparative statement before and after establishing the model was computed and presented. The study reveals that at the time of handling, manpower selection and evaluation plays a vital role in implementing the rural technology. Graphical representation is purported in this matter. A reasonable guideline for this purpose was established.

* **Chief Instructor-Workshop, Agricultural Training Centre, Ramakrishna Mission Ashram, Narendrapur, Kolkata-700103, Email: s5_ch@yahoo.co.in**

INTRODUCTION

In the present unemployment scenario manpower development in farm machineries and agro industries is essential. It will bridge between industrial economics and agriculture economics. Several institutions, universities and colleges are to put thrust on manpower development on farm machineries and agro Industries. Mushroom like institutions are growing without any selection criteria or evaluation character or E.D.P character development style. As a result training/is education looked at for their survival not for the trainee's rehabilitation institutions like Ramakrishna Mission having a sound faculty staff on farm machineries and for manpower development are the only agencies may be entrusted for this purpose. I have taken the opportunity to study a few characters in this regards.

MATERIAL METHOD

Three measure characteristics for selection were taken into consideration such as:

1. Age group with two grades;
2. Formal education with three grades;
3. Socio-economic area with three grades.

Details of evaluation system were as follows:

Grade both for theoretical and practical examination (i.e. learning and exposition with suitable multiple factors.)

Thus if a traniee gets the following grade point

Learning	Exposition
A = 7	B = 6

$$\text{His overall grade} = \frac{(7 \times 3) + (6 \times 8)}{(3 + 8)} = \frac{69}{11} = 6.27$$

As 6.27 is below 7 his overall grade has been stated as B evaluating the overall grade point in this fashion; this differences has in mean performance among the groups in each characteristic or dimension has been tested by using the test of significance.

- **Other Guidelines**

1. Selection of Trainees
   - (i) Potentiality of place—by survey and interview;
   - (ii) Potentiality of person;
   - (iii) Selection may be from sun of the soil to avoid uprooting problems and projects may be according to area need through Gram Unayan Samity.

   Problems of catching target group
   - (i) Educated surplus youth;
   - (ii) Running formal students due to future uncertainty;
   - (iii) Trade migration.
2. Neither knowledge nor skill is vital, man behind the project is vital—14 EDP characters may be developed.
   - (i) Risk bearing attitude;
   - (ii) Problems solving attitude;
   - (iii) Goal should be positive and clear etc.
3. Selection should be of homogeneous group, if not make it homogeneous by extra credit points.
4. Knowledge from successful entrepreneurs and failure entrepreneurs should be recorded.
5. Interaction between industry and training centre is essential:
   - Curriculum may be adjusted according to need;
   - Short in-plant training may be given to create confidence of the training;
   - Project may be in the zone of co-relation between agricultural and industrial economics.
6. Cooperative may be formed amongst the equal for larger exposition.
7.
   - (i) Financial institution may be tagged for financing the project;

(ii) Utilise the have group for the interest of have-nots;

(iii) Feeling for have-not is essential, crying may be avoided.

8. Regular follow-up mechanism may be established:
   - Refresher course may be conducted for making up technological gaps.
9. Search the opportunities of the trainees and convert into investment.
10. Cost Conscious input and idea of techno-economical viability given regular, intermediate and final evaluation may be recorded.

RESULTS

Mean Overall Grade Points Along With Respective C.D. Value of Different Groups in regard to Age Group for Four Years

Above age group above-20 years is Significant

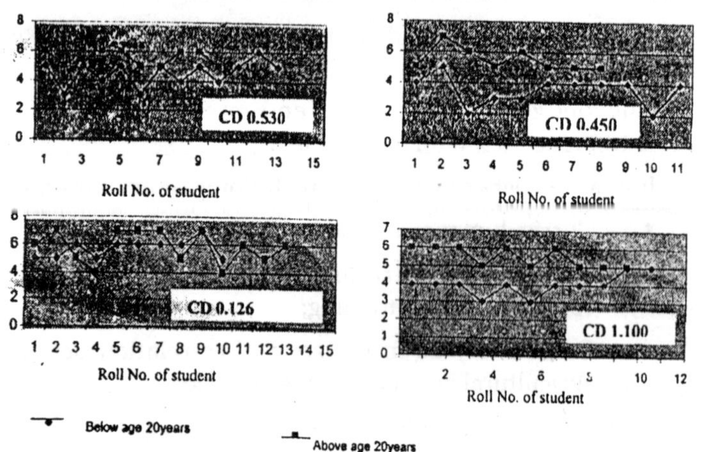

Mean overall grade point along with respective CD value of different groups in regard to educational background for four years

Read up to class IX is significant

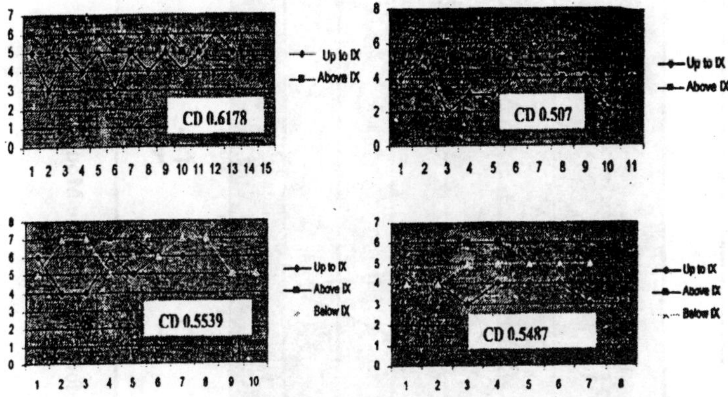

Mean Overall Grade Point Along with Respective CD Value of Different Groups in Regard to Socio-economic Areas for Four Years

Developing Multiple Crop Areas is Significant

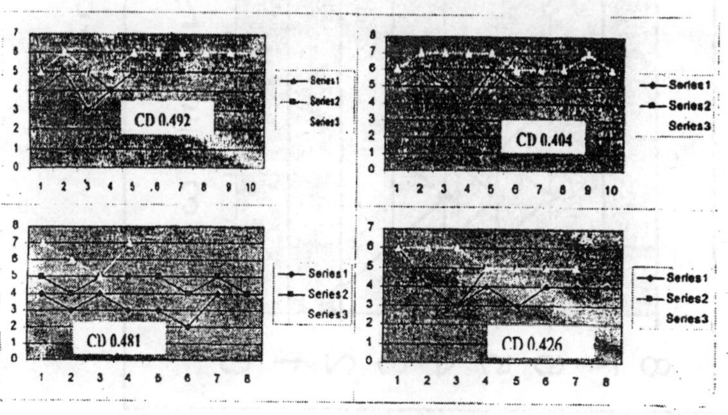

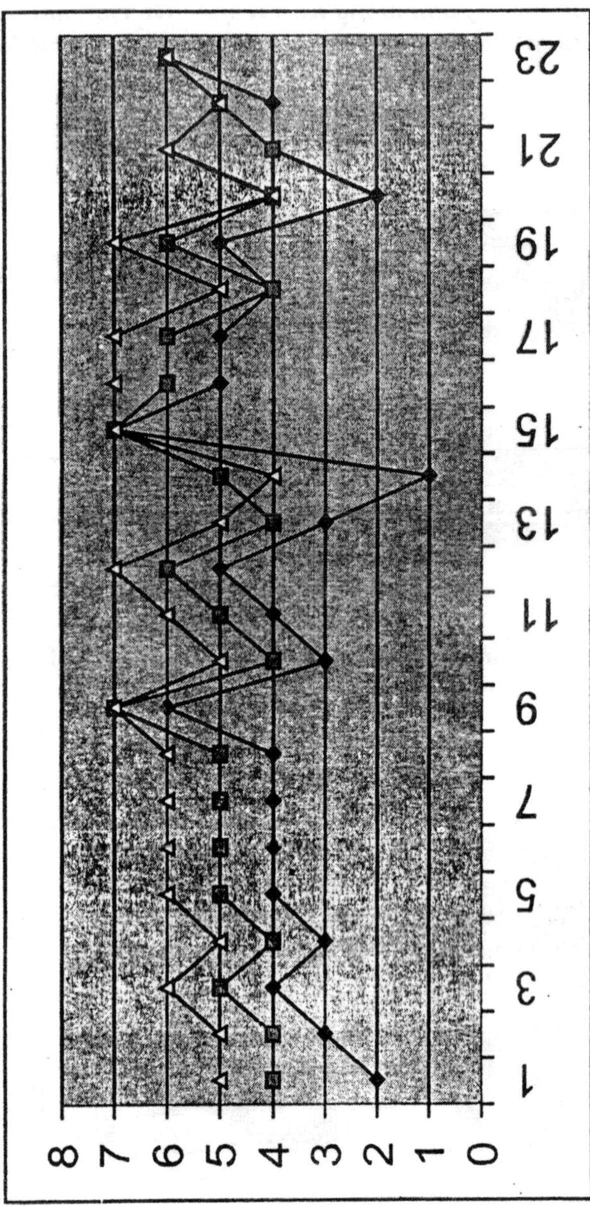

Fig. 20.1: For Comparative Study Before Adopting the Model

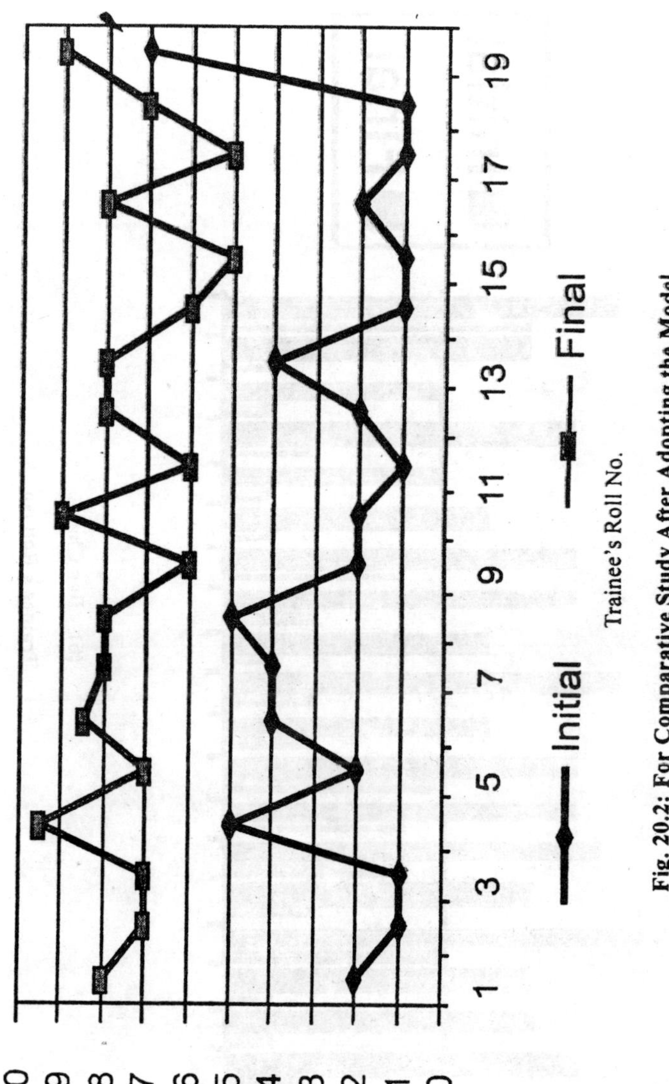

Trainee's Roll No.

Fig. 20.2: For Comparative Study After Adopting the Model

(a) Line Diagram

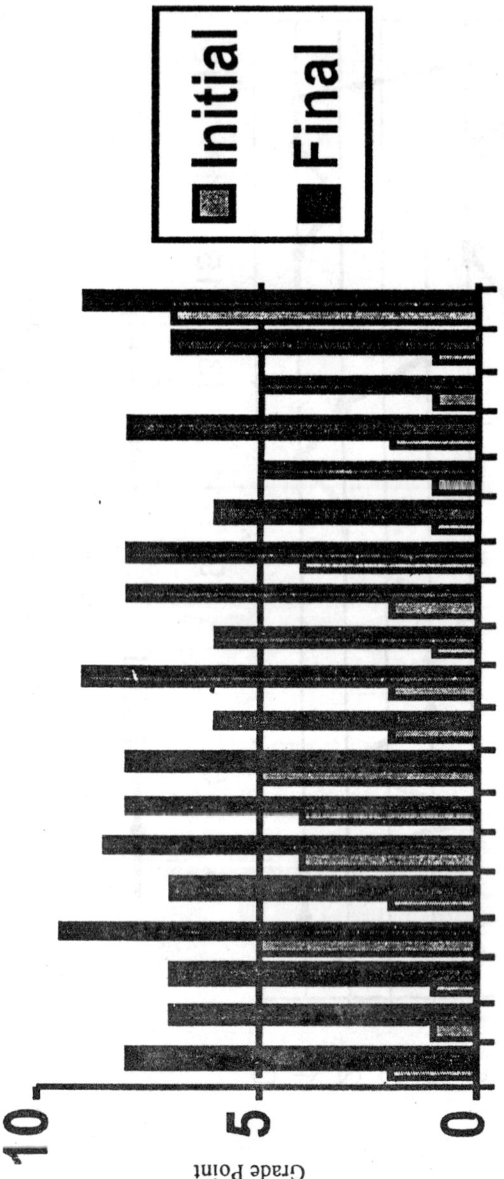

(b) Bar Chart

Trainee's Roll No.

DISCUSSION

In selection criteria it is obserbed for three months of farm-machinery programme i.e. operator mechanic of pump or power-tiller and tractor:

(i) Above age group 20years;

(ii) Read up to class IX; and

(iii) Developing Multiple Crop Areas are significant.

Regarding evaluation system overall grade point with learning and exposition criteria is appropriate.

For comparative analysis from Figure 20.1 (i.e. before adopting the model) starting point of training is Grade I in initial evaluation; in intermediate evaluation group displacement is only Grade Point II; although task was up to grade IX; overall achievement reached up to VII only; and in final evaluation it is observed that the management fault or training fault is only 2(from VII to IX)

For comparative analysis from Figure 20.2 (i.e. after adopting the model) it is revealed that the starting point of training was same as the initial (i.e. Grade I) but achievement was 9.5 although goal was IX. It indicates the appropriate training management was in the model.

We are searching another opportunity for study learning and exposition criteria 60 per cent to 75 per cent when fund is available.

REFERENCES

1. Bajpai, J.N. *Hand Book on Socially Useful Productive Work in School Instructional Material (Agriculture VIII)*, National Council of Education Research and Training; 1978, p. 105.

2. Chakraborty, S.S. *Vocational Training for the Rural Poor* (Paper Represented at the Workshop on *Training for Rural Development* Held in Peshawar, Pakistan); 1979

3. Chattopadhyay S.B., *Rehabilitation with Agro-machineries—A Study on its Character and Employability.* (Paper Presented at the *XVII Annual Convention of ISAE* held at IARI, New Delhi); 1980.

21

Manpower Planning in the Field of Pharmacy Education

*Baljeet S. Kapoor**

*Sunita Sharma***

*Sukhwinder Singh****

ABSTRACT

Pharmaceutical education is busting now-a-days due to privatization of education and lots of new colleges are coming up every year which offer courses that are recognized by All India Council for Technical Education, New Delhi. In the last two decades pharmacy education has become one of the top choices of students both of girls and boys.

The growth in Pharmacy education could however be justified only when it is accompanied by corresponding increase in employment opportunities. The analysis of the available data has clearly brought out the fact that the significant proportions of fresh pharmacy degree and

* NTMIS Nodal Centre, Punjab Engineering College, Sector 12, Chandigarh-160012

** NTMIS Nodal Centre, Punjab Engineering College, Sector 12, Chandigarh-160012

*** NTMIS Nodal Centre, Punjab Engineering College, Sector 12, Chandigarh-160012, E-mail: sukhi25@sify.com

diploma holders are not absorbed fully in the pharmaceutical industry. An attempt has also been made to analyse some of the crucial parameters like estimates of size of unemployment at the end of 2005 and the average emoluments offered to fresh Pharmacy degree and diploma holders at the time of their first paid employment.

The scope of the study is limited to degree and diploma holders in Pharmacy from engineering colleges and polytechnics for the States of Punjab, Himachal Pradesh and U.T. Chandigarh for the analysis of data. This implies that the post-graduates have been kept outside the purview of the study for want of requisite information.

INTRODUCTION

"Health is Wealth" is the common saying which we are listening from the time immemorial and maintenance of good health remained the main concern of all the welfare states during the ancient times. Even during the modern age of machines the sound health of people of our country is the major thrust of government policies. It may be recalled that on the occasion of birthday of Ex Prime Minister Sh. Atal Bihari Vajpayee ji on 25th December 2002 we pledged "Better Health to Every Indian", further stating that "Health of the Nation is the Wealth of the Nation". For keeping people fit and healthy, medical services are essential which are useless without proper medication. So medical and pharmacy are sister professions and both are equal partners in public health education. For proper health care system, pharmaceuticals play a vital role and these persons are pharmacists who come out of various universities and academic institutions recognized by the AICTE, New Delhi. India has already proved its technical competence and capabilities by producing basic drugs in every therapeutic segment including preventive medicines for both domestic and global market. By 2005, Indian drug manufacturers are expected to become major exporters to European countries.

In view of the above discussion, analysis of job prospects, earning differentials, waiting period for getting employment becomes important.

GROWTH OF PHARMACY EDUCATION SYSTEM

On independence the country inherited the profession of Pharmacy practice which was unorganized and in a very poor state. The need of the education facilities for the licentiate pharmacist, graduate pharmacists and pharmaceutical technologist was felt during the British rule. The University of London started B. Pharma course at the School of Pharmacy in 1925. The Banaras Hindu University was not too far behind where the B. Pharma degree course began in1937 and again in 1942, the post matriculation two years course in Pharmacy was started but it had to be abandoned after the first batch was out as the government did not come forth with the promised financial support. A beginning for correcting the situation was made on promulgation of the Pharmacy Act 1948 and in 1954 an institution imparting diploma in pharmacy was started in Birla College in Pilani. The Pharmacy Council of India continued to revise the course contents of the two years diploma. There are now about 318 institutions providing diploma in Pharmacy with total intake capacity of nearly 19000 per annum. The work force of the diploma holders is the mainstay of Pharmacy practice. At degree level, there are more than 358 institutions with intake capacity reaching close to 17000.

In this chapter, analysis is restricted to D. Pharma and B. Pharma only while the post-graduate Pharma is kept outside the purview of this chapter. This chapter analyzes certain issues relating to employment such as activity status, waiting period for getting employment, absorption pattern, average monthly emoluments and estimates of size of unemployment etc. for the states of Punjab, Himachal Pradesh and U.T. Chandigarh for the students who have passed out during the year 2001.

The number of institutions (2001-2003) in the states of Punjab, Himachal Pradesh and U.T. Chandigarh for degree and diploma level is shown in Table 21.1. It shows that there are 4 degree level and 18 diploma level institutions imparting pharmacy education in the state of Punjab during the year 2001. In the year 2002, six diploma level institutions were upgraded to degree institutions in pharmacy. In the state of Himachal Pradesh, there is no degree level institutions and 2 institutions offering diploma in pharmacy. In Union Territory of Chandigarh there is one degree level and two diploma level pharmacy institutions.

Table—21.1 Growth of number of institutions in the states of Punjab, Himachal Pradesh and U.T. Chandigarh (2001-2003)

State	Number of Institutions					
	Degree			Diploma		
	2001	2002	2003	2001	2002	2003
Punjab	4	10	10	18	11	11
Himachal Pradesh	–	–	–	2	2	2
Chandigarh	1	1	1	2	2	2

EMPLOYMENT SCENARIO OF PHARMACY EDUCATION

This chapter discusses the manpower planning of pharmacy education in the State of Punjab, Himachal Pradesh and U.T. Chandigarh which is based on the data collected by our Nodal Centre. A pre-designed 'Graduate Follow-up Questionnaire' is mailed to all the graduates after two years of passing out the examination at degree and diploma levels. Those reporting employed are further asked to indicate the time taken for getting the first paid employment. This information is used to work out the percentage rate at which the fresh graduates get absorbed each year after graduation.

The analysis presented here is based on the Graduate Follow-up Survey of 2001 pass-outs degree and diploma holders from the States of Punjab, Himachal Pradesh and U.T. Chandigarh. The follow up survey of 2001 batch means that the survey was started in July 2003 i.e. two years of passing out, and concluded in the year 2004.

Activity Status

The activity status of Pharmacy degree and Diploma holders of 2001 batch of the three states are given in Table 21.2 and Table 21.3 respectively. Among degree holders in the state of Punjab, out of 31 degree holders, 16 (52%) are employed in India, 7 (22%) are enrolled for higher education in India and 8 (26%) are unemployed and looking for paid job. There is no degree course of Pharmacy in the state of Himachal Pradesh. In Union Territory of Chandigarh out of 32 degree holders, 25 (78%) are employed in India, 2 (6%) are self-employed and 5 (16%) are unemployed during the batch year 2001.

Among diploma holders in the state of Punjab, out of 503 diploma holders, 84 (17%) are employed in India, 28(5%) are self-employed, 75 (15%)are enrolled for higher education in India and 316(63%) are unemployed and looking for paid job. In the state of Himachal Pradesh, out of 56 diploma holders, 21 (38%) are employed in India, 3(5%) are enrolled for higher education and 32(57%) are unemployed during the batch year 2001. In Union Territory of Chandigarh out of 83 diploma holders, 22 (27%) are employed in India, 2 (2 %) are employed abroad and self employed each, 17(20%) are enrolled for higher education and 40(49%) are unemployed during the batch year 2001.

Table—21.2 Activity status for degree holders of pharmacy education based on graduate follow-up survey of 2001 batch

Activity Status	Punjab	Himachal Pradesh	Chandigarh
Having a paid job in India	16	–	25
Having a paid job Abroad	–	–	–
Self Employed	–	–	2
Enrolled for higher education	7	–	–
Unemployed	8	–	5
Total	**31**	–	**32**

Table—21.3 Activity status for diploma holders of pharmacy education based on graduate follow-up survey of 2001 batch

Activity Status	Punjab	Himachal Pradesh	Chandigarh
Having a paid job in India	84	21	22
Having a paid job Abroad	-	-	2
Self Employed	28	-	2
Enrolled for higher education	75	3	17
Unemployed	316	32	40
Total	**503**	**56**	**83**

Pattern of Absorption

The estimated absorption of degree and diploma holders of pharmacy education is shown in Table 21.4 and Table 21.5 respectively. It can be seen from Table 21.4 that in Punjab and Chandigarh, for full absorption, the degree holders have to wait for more than three years. In the state of Punjab, more than 50 per cent degree holders are absorbed in the first year. In case of diploma holders, the absorption rate is very poor in all the three states. For full absorption, the diploma holders of all the three states have to wait for more than four years.

Table—21.4 Estimated absorption (in %) for degree holders of pharmacy education based on graduate follow-up survey of 2001 batch

State	1st Year	2nd Year	3rd Year	4th Year	Beyond 4-years
Punjab	51.98	17.46	16.26	14.30	-
Himachal Pradesh	-	-	-	-	-
Chandigarh	18.41	30.37	28.35	22.88	-

Table—21.5 Estimated absorption (in %) for diploma holders of pharmacy education based on graduate follow-up survey of 2001 batch

State	1st Year	2nd Year	3rd Year	4th Year	Beyond 4-years
Punjab	9.33	13.08	11.90	09.25	56.43
Himachal Pradesh	15.16	25.88	24.50	22.38	12.09
Chandigarh	14.86	14.98	14.22	13.90	42.05

Sector of Employment

Table 21.6 shows the distribution of employed graduates and diploma holders by sector of employment. Analysis reveals that out of 16 employed degree holders, 8 (50 per cent) of the degree holders are employed in Public and Private Sector Undertakings each in the State of Punjab. In case of diploma holders in Punjab, Public sector (43 per cent) absorbed more than private sector (27 per cent) and government department (Central and State) employed only 10 per cent of the degree holders. In case of diploma holders in the State of Himachal Pradesh, the employment opportunities in the State Govt. Organizations are higher as compared to other sectors as this sector absorbed 76 per cent of the diploma holders. About (3) 14.28 per cent of the employed diploma holders are absorbed in Private Sector Undertakings. In the Union Territory of Chandigarh, pharmaceuticals are absorbed in Public and Private Sector as compared to the government departments.

Table—21.6 Distribution of employed degree/diploma holders in pharmacy by sector of employment

	Punjab		Himachal Pradesh		Chandigarh	
	Degree	Diploma	Degree	Diploma	Degree	Diploma
1	2	3	4	5	6	7
Central Government	-	3	-	-	3	2
State Government	-	5	-	16		

(Contd...)

1	2	3	4	5	6	7
Public Sector	8	36	–	–	5	10
Private Sector	8	23	–	3	17	8
Others		17	–	2	–	2
Total	16	84		21	25	22

Emoluments

It can be seen form the Table 21.7 that the degree holders pharmacists from U.T. Chandigarh got the maximum emoluments (Rs. 10379/-) followed by Punjab (Rs. 6875). In case of diploma holders the average monthly emoluments earned by them is the highest in the state of Himachal Pradesh (Rs. 4912/-).

Table—21.7 Emoulments (in rupees) earned by fresh degree/ diploma holders in pharmacy

State	Degree Holders	Diploma Holders
Punjab	6875	3010
Himachal Pradesh	–	4912
Chandigarh	10379	3909

EMPLOYMENT PLANNING

Pharmaceutical education is fast exploding and has become the main choice of the students as many fields are available for them after doing diploma and degree in Pharmacy. It is very important that the students should be made well aware about the different options after pharmaceutical graduation. They should choose their careers which suit to their personality so that greater success could be achieved with less effort.

Options Available After Diploma

1. Hospital Pharmacist/Clinical Pharmacist/Community pharmacist.
2. Employment opportunities in medical stores, wholesale dealers and manufacturing units.
3. As an entrepreneur for repacking of drugs and chemicals.

4. Sales/Medical representatives.
5. Analysts in chemical drug analysis laboratories.
6. Technicians in biochemistry and pathology lab.
7. Research/biotechnological research and development in the private national/multination firms such as RanBaxy has expanded the sphere of business activity of this field.
8. Teaching.
9. May start their own chemist shops for which pharmacy diploma is a must to obtain the licence.

Options Available After B. Pharma

1. Higher Education–M. Pharma., Ph.D
2. Pharmaceutical Production
3. Pharmaceutical Research and Development
4. Pharmaceutical Marketing
5. Government Services
6. Jobs Abroad
7. Own Business

CONCLUSION

The analysis in this chapter gives the clear picture of degree and diploma holders of Pharmacy in the State of Punjab, Himachal Pradesh and U.T. Chandigarh that the degree holder pharmacists are getting job in Private and Public sector as compared to the government sector. The position of diploma holders is quite different as most of the diploma holders are getting jobs in the government sector in the State of Himachal Pradesh. Pharmacy professionals can choose suitable job as mentioned in this chapter as per their strengths and weaknesses to have maximum job satisfaction.

REFERENCES

1. Chandel, H.S., Career Planning After Graduation in Pharmacy Vis-à-vis Individual Personality, *Indian Journal of Technical Education*, Vol. 27, No. 2, April-June, 2004.

2. Chotai, N.P., V.A. Patel, B.G. Patel and H.V. Patel, Growth of Pharmacy Education in the Gujarat as Compared to Other Selected States, *Indian Journal of Technical Education*, Vol. 27, No. 1, January-March, 2004.

3. Singh, Harkishan, History of Pharmacy in India—Pharmacy Practice, Vallabh Prakashan, Vol. 3, 2002, p. 226.

22

Manpower Planning in Computer Applications

*K. Sadasivan**

*P. Vanitha***

INTRODUCTION

Despite the availability of training manpower, a demand supply gap still exists in the IT manpower market. If India's IT software and services sector wants to climb the success ladder, it will have to educate at least two million additional knowledge workers over the next eight years. After a great depression in 1999, now it is the right setback were there is a boon in IT industry which created ways to more manpower requirements in India. Recently, many leading IT companies such as TCS, Infosys, CTS, Wipro etc. spreading their wings by way of BPO's, Call centers, Back operations etc. and thereby manpower planning became the need of an hour in order to place right people at work. TCS has planned to expand their manpower to 8000 in forthcoming year. This is

* Senior Lecturer, SRM School of Management Studies, SRM Institute of Science and Technology (Deemed University) SRM Nagar, Kattankulathur–603 203.

** Lecturer, SRM School of Management Studies, SRM Institute of Science and Technology (Deemed University) SRM Nagar, Kattankulathur– 603 203.

one such company there are many more on the line. All these issues gives rise to HR planning were demand and supply should go hand on hand to fulfill the IT Manpower requirements. Though the quantity of workers is important, it is the quality of this knowledge base that will ultimately play a crucial role in deciding the fate of the IT industry in India.

A comprehensive Human Resource Strategy plays a vital role in the achievement of an organization's overall strategic objectives and visibly illustrates that the human resources function fully understands and supports the direction in which the organization is moving. A comprehensive HR strategy will also support other specific strategic objectives undertaken by the marketing, financial, operational and technology departments.

An HR strategy should aim to capture "the people element" of what an organization is hoping to achieve in the medium to long term, ensuring that:

- It has the right people in place;
- It has the right mix of skills;
- Employees display the right attitudes and behaviours; and
- Employees are developed in the right way.

The HR strategy will need to show that careful planning of the people issues will make it substantially easier for the organization to achieve its wider strategic and operational goals. The achievement of the goals depends on the following issues:

- Workforce planning issues;
- Succession planning;
- Workforce skills plans;
- Employment equity plans;
- Black economic empowerment initiatives;
- Motivation and fair treatment issues;
- Pay levels designed to recruit, retain and motivate people;

- The co-ordination of approaches to pay and grading across the organization to create alignment and potential unequal pay claims;
- Career development frameworks which look at development within the organization at equipping employees with "employability" so that they can cope with increasingly frequent changes in employer and employment patterns.

The external environment also plays a vital role in formulating HR planning strategies. They likely to have a major impact on the organization, such as:

- Changes in the overall employment market—demographic or remuneration levels;
- Cultural changes which will impact on future employment patterns;
- Changes in the employee relations climate;
- Changes in the legal framework surrounding employment;
- HR and employment practice being developed in other organizations, such as new flexible work practices.

Giving a strong practical slant to the proposed strategy may help gain acceptance for the idea, such as focusing on good management practice. It is also important to build "early or quick wins" into any new strategy.

OUTSOURCING IT TO INDIA—INCREASED MANPOWER REQUIREMENTS

India's abundant, high quality and cost effective services and its vast resource of skilled software human power have made it an attractive location for global software clients. There has been a healthy growth in the number of India's IT professionals over the last decade.

Today, MNCs are rushing into India to stake a claim to the IT outsourcing market looking at the changing E-commerce scenario in India. While a large number of companies are outsourcing their software development to Indian companies, others are establishing a presence in India and participating actively in the software export game. The MNC sector emerged as an important segment contributing more to the total exports of 27 per cent share. India can be an ideal offshore destination due to a variety of advantages it has over other countries. The major categories being:

STRENGTHS

India, the hottest destination today for offshore IT outsourcing beats the other destinations with its unique strengths. No doubt, offshore outsourcing to India is expected to reach $50 billion by 2008 as per a report published by Brean Murray Institutional Research on June 16th, 2003.

The Indian Advantage for Offshore IT Outsourcing Includes

Process and Quality Emphasis

Indian companies with their high technical skills, are able to deliver quality and on time. India has 24 CMM Level 5 certified companies out of the 49 worldwide. According to NASSCOM, India will soon have the highest number of ISO-9000 software companies in the world.

Government Policies

The Indian Government has been proactive to meet the increasing needs of the fast emerging Indian software services and ITES-BPO sector in India. Indian Government has always been pro-IT, formulating its policies and laws to promote the IT industry's growth. Some of its initiatives include:

- Setting up of specific commerce zones including the Software Technology Parks (STPs);
- Making the existing laws more liberal;
- Giving tax exemption for exporting IT enabled outsourcing services;
- Deregulation and liberalization policies;
- Enactment of Cyber Legislation;
- Working on a stronger data protection and privacy law in association with NASSCOM.

Skilled Talent Pool

India has a large base of highly talented, qualified and easily available human resource in the field of Information Technology. Adding to this, India has the largest English speaking population amongst the developing countries. The government institutes like IIT (Indian Institute of Technology), IIM (Indian Institute of Management) and a number of other reputed institutes (both private and public) every year add to this pool.

Indian Education System

India has one of the most advanced and developed educational systems in the world. The educational system is modelled to nurture analytical and scientific talent. Besides education is much more affordable in India as compared to the western nations.

With all the above-mentioned strengths, India has and will continue to have a growing number of vendors successfully working on complex projects across all areas of software and services, and performing at levels comparable to those of leading global players, as per a McKinsey & Co. report. India is definitely emerging as one of the most suitable IT outsourcing destination.

Economy

By realizing its long-term potential, the Indian IT and IT-enabled services industry could be one of the most powerful drivers of India's economic growth.Apart from a powerful economy, India would also need a tremendous infrastructural development to realise this dream.

GDP Growth

The ITS and ITES industries are being recognized as the largest contributors to incremental market capitalization in India. However, it is still small in terms of contribution to GDP—especially when compared to other large sectors in the economy like agriculture and manufacturing.

This is likely to change quite substantially over the next six years. As per the NASSCOM-McKinsey study 2002, by achieving its long-term potential, the industry will dramatically boost the

Indian economy. If the industry achieves its long-term potential, it will become one of the largest sectors in the Indian economy. The share of the Indian IT and ITES industries in the GDP will increase from 1.4 per cent (in 2001) to 7 per cent by 2008. Moreover, the analysis predicts that it will contribute 19 per cent of incremental GDP growth between now and 2008.

Increase in Foreign Exchange Inflows

In addition, revenues from ITS and ITES exports are likely to grow at a significantly higher rate than other exports and invisibles and by 2008 will exceed all other invisibles combined. ITS and ITES exports, which currently account for 8 per cent of foreign exchange inflows, will contribute more than 30 per cent of foreign exchange inflows in 2008.

Enormous Employment Opportunities

Also, the industry will create enormous employment opportunities in the country. The IT industry which currently employs 0.5 million people, will employ over 2 million people directly and create indirect employment opportunities for at least an additional 2 million people by 2008.

In ITES exports, some of the segments creating the greatest number of jobs will be customer care (contributing 370,000 to 390,000 jobs), HR (contributing 140,000 to 160,000 jobs) and administration (contributing roughly 80,000 to 100,000 jobs).

Similarly, IT services will create employment for 450,000 people; the products and technology services opportunity will contribute around 140,000 jobs and the domestic market will employ about 650,000 people.

Not only, will the industry provide direct employment to 2 million people, it will also create significant entrepreneurial and employment opportunities in support services. Training, food/ canteen, transport, housekeeping and security will be some of the biggest areas.

The industry will employ more than four million people by 2008

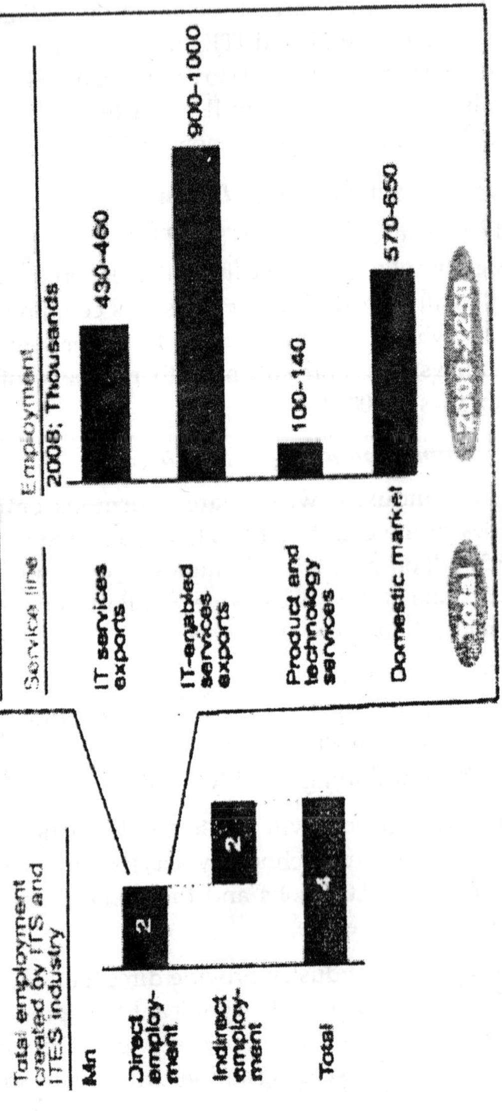

Source: McKinsey Analysis

Market Share

Technology and manufacturing hubs have emerged across many industries. India has already effected the cycle for customized application development and has succeeded in capturing a 15 per cent market share. Since India possess the ingredients and knowledge to repeat the cycle, it has the potential to emerge as a hub for other IT services like packaged software installation and support, and systems integration, IT-enabled services and technology services like embedded software development and ISV back-ending.

In terms of market share, the long-term potential for India translates into a 4 per cent market share in IT services and IT-enabled services.

Quality

In the past few years, the Indian IT industry has pursued the goal of attaining the highest international standards of quality. A World Bank funded study conducted as early as 1992 to discuss Indian software strategies had concluded that more and more vendors in the US prefer to get their software developed undertaken in India for its quality and cost advantage.

Indian players have created a strong value proposition in the IT software and services arena. India enjoys advantages of people sophistication in terms of a very large pool of English speaking scientific personnel, varied and extensive skill sets in terms of technology, and offering services at globally competitive costs. India also boast vendor sophistication—with more than 200 companies being quality accredited and serving the needs of over 255 Fortune 500 companies. Today, the world looks towards the Indian IT software and services industry for its good quality and high price performance.

According to McKinsey Co., India has and will continue to have a growing number of vendors successfully working on complex projects across all areas of software and services, and performing at levels comparable to those of leading global players.

As of 31st March 2002, India had 42 companies at SEI CMM Level 5 assessment. The quality maturity of the Indian software industry can be measured from the fact that already 316 Indian software companies have acquired quality certifications and more companies are in pipeline to do so.

The other heartening feature has been the growing acceptance and adoption of the newly emerging People-Capability Maturity Model (People-CMM) by the Indian software industry. For a country like India, with its large assets in the form of skilled human resources, the relevance of People CMM needs no emphasis. A large number of Indian IT software and services companies have been quick to realize this and have either implemented or initiated programmes.

Infrastructure

Infrastructure that is of importance in the IT industry includes telecommunications, electricity, access to computers, number of Internet hosts, number of ISP's and available bandwidth and broadband access.

Communications

Communications is one of the critical infrastructure requirements of a country. India, with its one billion people, over 500 districts, around 5,000 villages and large metropolitan cities having population equivalent to that of many countries needs an extensive infrastructure to serve such a population.

Power

Power availability has also improved dramatically and has become more consistent throughout the country. All 21 Software Technology Parks (STPs) across the country have installed dedicated substations and genstations for 100 per cent backup. Non-STPI locations have readily available generators and UPS. Most state governments have plans for power reform (e.g. privatised distribution in Mumbai (BSES)) and are becoming power surplus, e.g., Andhra Pradesh.

Education System

India has emerged as one of the top IT resource providers, mainly due to its ability to churn out highly skilled workers every year. The Indian school education system places great emphasis on mathematics and science, resulting in a large number of sciences and engineering graduates. The English medium of education also helps in nurturing top class English speaking resource.

Government institutes such as Indian Institute of Technology (IIT) and Indian Institute of Management (IIM) churn out quality graduates every year. There are a large number of other government and private institutes, all over the country, which help augment this process.

Country Competitiveness and Knowledge Professionals

There has been a healthy growth in the number of India's IT professionals over the last decade.

From a base of 6,800 knowledge workers in 1985-86, the number increased to 522,000 software and services professionals by the end of 2001-02. It is estimated that out of these 522,000 knowledge workers, almost 170,000 are working in the IT software and services export industry; nearly 106,000 are working in the IT enabled services and over 220,000 in user organizations.

INDIAN IT SECTOR: KNOWLEDGE PROFESSIONALS EMPLOYED

Category	1990-91	1996-97	1999-00	2000-01	2001-02 E
Software exports sector			110,000	162,000	170,000
Software domestic sector			17,000	20,000	22,000
Software-captive in user organizations			115,000	178,114	224,250
IT enabled services			42,000	70,000	106,000
Total	**156,000**	**160,000**	**284,000**	**430,114**	**522,250**

Source: Nasscom

MODEL FOR EFFICIENT MANPOWER PLANNING FOR IT

There is no single approach to developing a Human Resources Strategy. The specific approach will vary from one organization to another. Even so, an excellent approach towards an HR Strategic. This approach identifies six specific steps in developing an HR Strategy:

1. Setting the strategic direction;
2. Designing the Human Resource Management System;
3. Planning the total workforce;
4. Generating the required human resources;
5. Investing in human resource development and performance;
6. Assessing and sustaining organizational competence and performance.

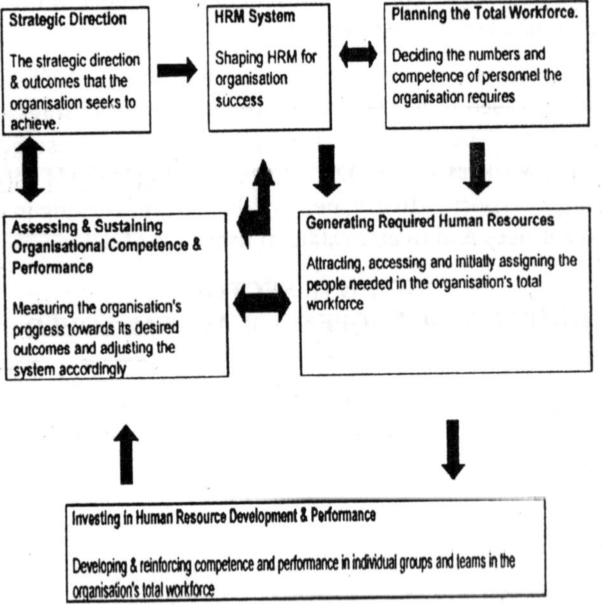

The above Model has Six Interconnected components consists of Three Planning steps and Three Execution steps.

1. Setting the Strategic Direction

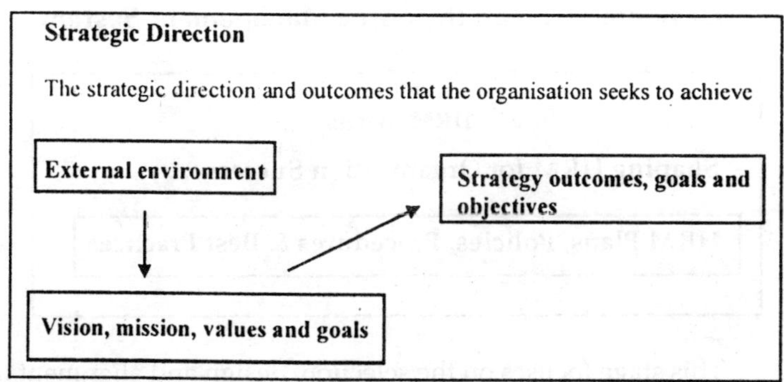

This process focuses on aligning human resource policies to support the accomplishment of the Company's mission, vision, goals and strategies. The business' goals sit at the heart of any HR strategy and in order to align business and HR we need to answer one key question, "Can organization's internal capability deliver the organization's business goals?"

Many organizations cite their people as their primary source of competitive advantage. Successful companies continuously identify and adopt innovative human resource management policies and practices to sustain that advantage. More importantly, they structure work and design training, performance management, pay, and reward policies to help members of the organization succeed in achieving desired organizational outcomes. In other words, they integrate and align HRM policies and practices to reinforce employee behaviours that can best realise the leaders' strategic intent. In the most successful companies, the set of policies and practices that collectively make up a company's HRM system is the critical management tool for communicating and reinforcing the leaders' strategic intent. The recommended action may be:

- Conducting of external environmental scan and evaluating its impact on the organization;
- Identifying the organization's vision, mission and guiding principles;
- Identifying the mission's outcomes and strategic goals;

- Consulting all relevant stakeholders
- ·Evaluating the impact of legislation on the organization

2. Designing Human Resource Management System

HRM System

Shaping HRM for Organisation Success

HRM Plans, Policies, Procedures & Best Practices

This stage focuses on the selection, design and alignment of HRM plans, policies and practices. Various options may be open to the organization such as drawing on industry best practices.

Emerging HRM policies and practices range from outsourcing certain non-core functions, adopting flexible work practices (telework, work from home) and the increased use of information technology. Not every industry trend may be appropriate for a specific organization. In addition, it is essential that a cost-benefit analysis of implementing new HRM policies and practices be undertaken. For example, the costs (monetary and in allocation of resources) of implementing a new job grading system may outweigh the benefit of such an undertaking. There may be more cost-effective alternatives available to the organization at this point in time.

Particular HRM policies and practices may be necessary to support strategic organizational objectives, such as improving the retention of women in the organization or promoting diversity, especially the representation of designated groups amongst senior management.

A good approach in selecting the appropriate HRM policies, procedures and practices is to identify the appropriate HRM practices which support the organization's strategic intent as it relates to recruitment, training, career planning and reward management. The recommended actions are:

- Identify appropriate human resource plans, policies and practices needed to support organizational objectives;
- Identify relevant human resource best practices;
- Conduct an employment systems review

3. Planning the Total Workforce

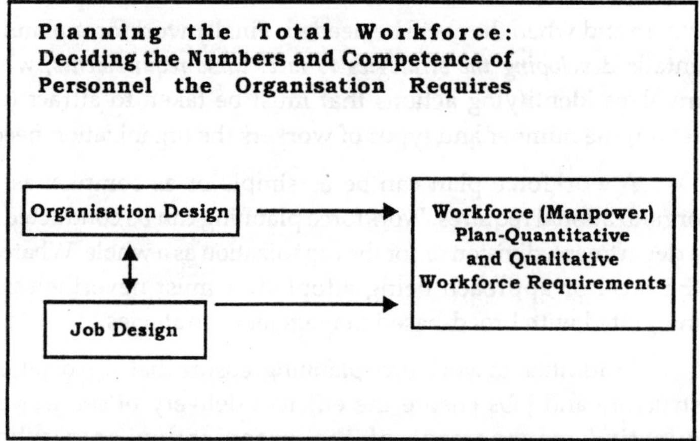

Determining future business requirements, especially those relating to manpower requirements, represents one of the most challenging tasks facing human resource practitioners.

The development of a workforce plan is a critical component of any human resource strategy and one of the expected outcomes of human resource practitioner's activities. Despite this, manpower or workforce planning, as well as succession planning, has only recently enjoyed resurgence in popularity. To some extent this has been prompted by the need to develop employment equity and workplace skills plans and set numerical employment equity targets. The failure of many organizations to develop and implement workforce planning is rather indicative of the lack of strategic planning itself.

Workforce planning is a systematic process of identifying the workforce competencies required to meet the company's strategic goals and for developing the strategies to meet these requirements. It is a methodical process that provides managers with a framework for making human resource decisions based on the organization's mission, strategic plan, budgetary resources, and a set of desired workforce competencies. Workforce planning is a *systematic process* that is integrated, methodical, and ongoing. It identifies *the human capital required to meet organizational goals,* which consists of determining the number and skills of the workers required and where and when they will be needed. Finally workforce planning entails d*eveloping the strategies to meet these requirements,* which involves identifying actions that must be taken to attract (and retain) the number and types of workers the organization needs.

A workforce plan can be as simple or as complex as the organizational requires. Workforce planning can be conducted for a department, division or for the organization as a whole. Whatever the level or approach being adopted, it must nevertheless be integrated with broad-based management strategies.

In addition to workforce planning, ensure that organizational structure and jobs ensure the efficient delivery of services and effective management of the organization as a whole. Recommendations are:

- Determine the appropriate organizational structure to support the strategic objectives;
- Structure jobs (competencies, tasks and activities) around key activities;
- Develop a workforce plan designed to support the organizations strategic objectives;
- Compile workforce profiles, identifying designated groups, an inventory of current workforce competencies, competencies required in the future and identified gaps in competencies.

4. Generating the Required Human Resource

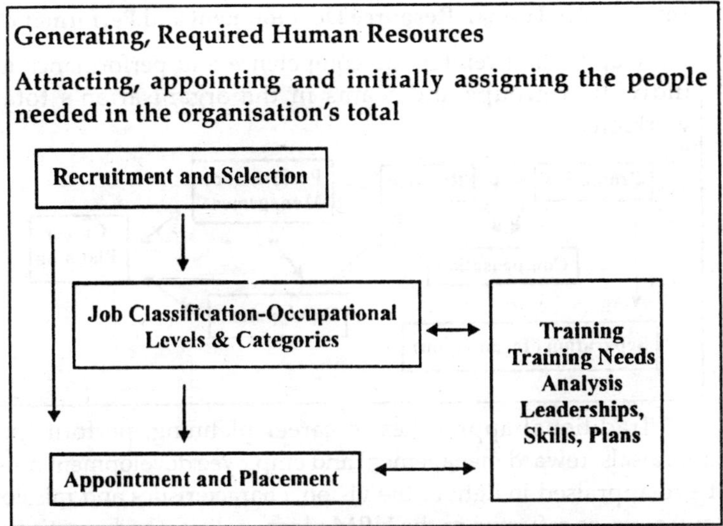

This process focuses on recruiting, hiring, classifying, training and assigning employees based on the strategic imperatives of the organization's workforce plan.

A comprehensive workplace skills plan will identify appropriate training priorities based on the organizations workforce needs now and in the future. New recruitment practices may need to be adopted to increase the representation of designated groups, or securing essential skills in the organization. A comprehensive "learnership strategy" may assist in developing future workforce needs, identified either in terms of the organizations workforce plan or required in terms of industry black economic empowerment charters. Recommendations are:

- Evaluate recruitment and selection practices in light of the organization's strategic objectives;
- Develop and implement a comprehensive workplace skills plan (with a thorough training needs analysis);
- Implement a learnership strategy;
- Adopt or clarify occupational levels and category classifications.

5. Investing in Human Resource Development and Performance

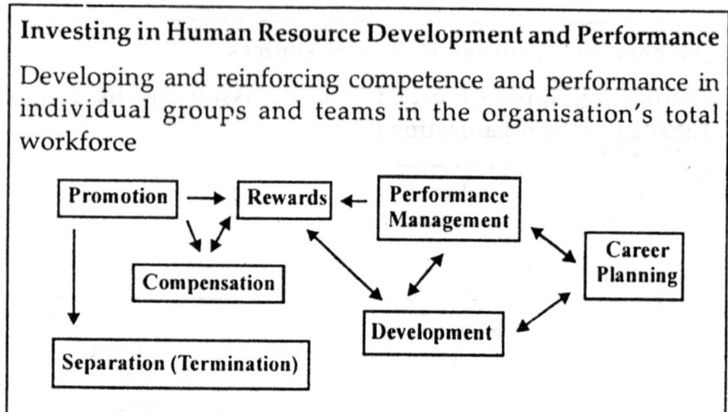

Traditional approaches to career planning, performance appraisals, reward management and employee development must be re-appraised in light of the vision, characteristics and mission outcomes as reflected in the HRM plans, policies, and practices.

Development responses will aim to increase business skills, the application of business skills (sometimes called competencies) and the behavioural elements—all of which contribute to an organization's effective performance. In many ways, the Skills Development legislation has required organizations to re-engineer their developmental methods and practices. New concepts such as lifelong learning and recognising prior learning should form an integral component of the process of investing in employees.

Clearly, where a workforce planning exercise reveals that there is little projected growth in the workforce or that promotional or career development opportunities are limited, strategies aimed at employee retention will be very different from organizations which are experiencing considerable growth and expansion.

Investment initiatives for the individual, team and organization are all geared to achieve high levels of organizational performance. It is important that at an individual level, particularly for senior staff, that they feel their development needs are agreed and that they are provided with the skills to do their jobs. At a team level, it defines the individuals' ability to work flexibly with others and align individual and team skills and activities to business goals—all of which ensures that the organization is equipped to achieve its goals.

Reward strategies aim to align the performance of the organization with the way it rewards its people, providing the necessary incentives and motivation to staff. Its components can be a combination of base pay, bonuses, profit sharing, share options, and a range of appropriate benefits, usually based on market or competitor norms and the organization's ability to pay.

6. Assessing and Sustaining Organizational Competence and Performance

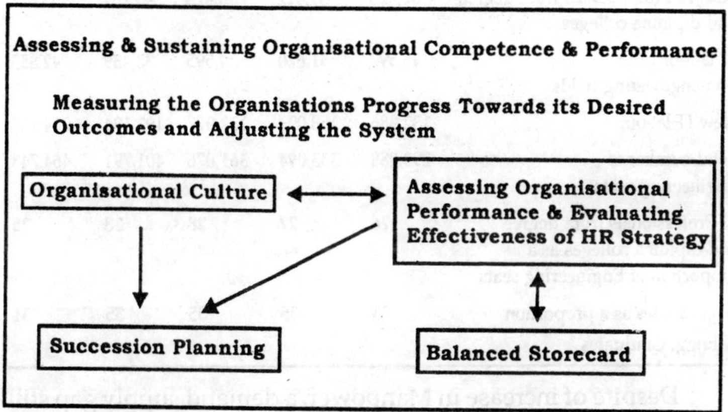

Finally, few organizations effectively measure how well their different inputs affect performance. In particular, no measures may be in place for quantifying the contribution people make to organizational outcomes or, more important, for estimating how changes in policies and practices, systems, or processes will affect that contribution. Implementing clear quantifiable measures, identifying milestones in the achievement of specific organizational goals, and using concepts such as a "balanced scorecard" will articulate the results of the HR Strategic Plan in measurable terms. Regular evaluation of the plan will also assist in fine-tuning the HR strategic plan itself. The recommended actions are:

- Evaluate organization culture and climate;
- Implement succession planning;
- Evaluate HR strategy using quantifiable measures, e.g. balanced scorecard;
- Revise and adapt HR strategy.

STRATEGIES FOR MATCHING THE DEMAND AND SUPPLY OF HUMAN RESOURCES IN IT INDUSTRY

India's New IT Labour

Category	2000-01	2001-02	2002-03	2003-04	2004-05
IT Professionals from degree and diploma colleges	74,364	90,867	99,959	110,495	115,533
Non-IT Professionals from degree and diploma colleges	32,025	35,612	38,423	43,261	55,877
IT labour from non-engineering fields	26,597	31,620	34,595	38,439	42,853
New IT labour	132,986	158,099	172,977	192,194	214,263
Total number of Engineering seats	290,088	333,094	361,076	401,791	464,743
IT Professionals from degree and diploma colleges as a proportion of Engineering seats	26	27	28	28	25
IT graduates as a proportion of Engg. Graduates	33	35	35	35	31

Despite of increase in Manpower, a demand supply gap still exists in IT Manpower market. India will have to educate at least 2 million additional knowledge workers over the next 8 years. Though the quantity of workers is important, it is the quality of this knowledge base that will ultimately play a crucial role in deciding the fate of the IT industry in India.

Mostly in IT sector,Manpower planning is done based on projects and Hours of Project completion The Supply of IT profesionals is high in Job Market, whereas Demand is purely based on Skill set and personal characterstics on oneside and Project demand on other side. Also, in current scenario, the Arbitration

Rate (Turn Around of Manpower) is very high in IT industry, thus, it also plays a vital role in the Manpower plainning for this industry.

To equate Demand and Supply, Manpower has to be trained effectively with uptodate issues and concerns and the following strategies can be given consideration:

Integration of Educational Institutes

The universities, engineering colleges, medical colleges, and other educational institutions in the states as well as Research and Development Organizations should be networked for a supplementary programme of distance education for improving the quality of education. This will facilitate the sharing of high quality and faculty and also provide access to the library resources in all the institutions.

Campus Recruitment

IT Companies go in for campus recruitment and select the manpower well before the actual requirement based on arbitration rate in the company. The freshers are trained for the current technologies in order to use them for manpower shortage due to arbitration.

Industry Experts Re-Training

The software and related services industry will increasingly need experts to lead and support IT projects in areas such as CRM e-CRM implementation (including front office automation, supply chain management, customer relationship management, etc.), and to provide ITES such as finance and accounting, HR, engineering design, etc.

IT Modules to Every Graduation Course

It is proposed that training in Information Technology, i.e. computer related courses should be made mandatory in every graduate course in the country. In other words, diverse courses like B.Sc, B.Com also should be taught computers. Special IT modules can be made available at the state level. The aim of these courses would be to impart the ability to use computers/IT as productivity-enhancing tool in a wide range of work situations.

To meet this need for domain and functional experts, industry professionals with a basic understanding of IT should be provided with the training to build the necessary expertise. This training would range from areas as CRM/EAS packaged software, Internet applications, and legacy/client server maintenance to better support development, implementation and consultative selling. Some companies have already implemented programmes to fill this capability gap.

CONCLUSION

Manpower Planning has become crucial stage for every organization and as a whole country thus, present IT workforce in India and strategies for matching the demand and supply of human resources in IT industry has to be known to overcome all hindrances in future and walk with success. While Manpower strategies must be developed to support the achievement of the organization's objectives, it is a two-way process. Manpower strategies can themselves be critical inputs in determining the strategic initiatives for the organization. A fatal error, however, is to develop and implement Manpower strategies without having regard for the goals and objectives which the organization has explicitly or implicitly identified. A common mistake is the development of workplace skills plans which are not linked to any strategic goals or objectives or which have no affirmative action components. Hence, a good HR planning and effective strategic model for planning effective Manpower is key to success.

23

Human Resource for Health Development

*P.K.Kamaraj**
*R.Selvam***

ABSTRACT

Much has been written about the disparity of manpower and money between the research communities in developed and developing countries. The well-known 10/90 gap summarizes this situation. Only 10 per cent of research money is spent on research that affects 90 per cent of the "Global Burden" of Disease, most of which is in developing countries. There have been a number of reports since that time and at present two groups. Health research is essential so that countries can develop "national autonomy" in health and this in turn will contribute to economic and social development. Science must be taken to where the problem lies and those most familiar with the society are more likely to correctly define its needs and priorities. If national research capacity remains stunted, the public health and scientific priorities of those nations will be controlled

* **Final Year/Dip. Printing Technology, Arasan Ganesan Polytechnic College, Post Bag No. 27 Sivakasi - 626123, Tamil nadu, Ph.No. 04562-230616, Email: agpoly@eth.net**

** **Final Year/Dip. Printing Technology, Arasan Ganesan Polytechnic College, Post Bag No. 27 Sivakasi - 626123, Tamil nadu, Ph.No. 04562-230616, Email: agpoly@eth.net**

by international organizations and outside consultants and scientists. A few words need to be said about the meaning of research capacity. "To support research capacity implies funding the multiple prerequisites to performing research; including technical skills and technology, career paths and computers, peer review, and publication. There are a number of elements necessary for the strengthening of research capability, which are interrelated and inter-dependent:

- *government support for research*
- *improving the capabilities of scientists through local and international training activities to undertake quality research*
- *providing institutional support in the form of careers, advancement, monetary compensation, and equipment and logistic support.*

Key Words: Global burden, National Autonomy, OECD

INTRODUCTION

In the face of rising demand for medical services due to ageing populations, physician migration flows are increasingly affecting the supply of physicians in Organization for Economic Co-operation and Development (OECD) countries. This chapter offers an integrated perspective on the impact of physician migration on home and host countries and discusses international regulation and policy approaches governing physician migration.

Information about migration flows, international regulation and policies governing physician migration were derived from two questionnaires sent to OECD countries, a secondary analysis of EUROSTAT Labour Force Surveys, a literature review and official policy documents of OECD countries.

OPPORTUNITIES

The much has been written about the need for additional training for developing country scientists and there are a number of institutions/organizations that have stepped forward to support this training. These include (though certainly not restricted to) the Rockefeller Foundation, The Gates Foundation.The Wellcome Trust, WHO (especially the TDR programme), various government aid organization (USAID, SIDA, GTZ, JICA etc), the Fogarty

International Programme of the National Institutes of Health (USA), ORSTOM, The Pasteur Network etc.

There are elements to any training programme that will improve research capacity and the retention of scientists who have trained outside their country, often at great cost. The selection of institutions and candidates for support is the first step in the process. Individuals selected for training should have a solid record of accomplishment at their home institution. Selection must be based on merit and such factors as family, and political or other non-academic considerations must be dismissed. If they become factors scientific integrity will be undermined. If training is more than a couple of years, strategies should be developed to allow the student to return home to reacquaint them with the local problems (and possibly to develop a research proposal). This may be problematic in a country such as the US where travel restrictions on students have markedly increased since the events of 9/11/01.

Faculty mentors are very important to ease the transition period and to set standards for the student. The strongest correlation with good scientific practice—methodologically and successful mentor-student relationships will endure a lifetime. If possible reciprocal faculty appointments should be made between institutions in developed and developing countries. Throughout the training process, students must be given the opportunity and guidance to give oral and written presentations. These are learned skills that are often neglected in the drive to develop good practice and technique.

THE ADDR PROJECT-RESEARCH DEVELOPMENT PROGRAMME

Research capacity can be built from two different ends: the developing country scientist can conduct studies designed by others or he/she can design, implement, analyze and write up their own study. The Applied Diarrheal Disease Research (ADDR) Project (of the Harvard Institute for International Development) with which I was involved for many years, had as its primary goal Cash 2. The development of research capacity in developing countries through the second of the two options. We had two principles: research supported by ADDR was to be owned by the host country national; and the research had to have the potential to contribute to at the very least to local or national disease control programmes. This was to be achieved through the awarding of grants to developing country scientists. It became clear early on in the process, that although a number of the scientists had received prior training (long and short-term) in the west, they had not been trained in how to develop a research proposal. They had done others research.

We decided to begin the process by conducting proposal development workshops which lasted 8-10 days during which time the investigators produced a proposal that we would consider funding. Pre-proposals had already been vetted through the ADDR scientists (background scientific literature could then be collected and sent). There were always two persons per team and about 6-8 teams per workshop. Senior members of the department were encouraged to send younger investigators to the workshop. The first task was to identify an important research question that could be done in a manageable amount of time (which we defined as one year). "Insufficient attention paid to problem identification can cause researchers to investigate trivial problems, work toward unattainable research objectives, develop excessively complex designs, or produce results that are not or cannot be compared with other work done on the same topic." (Trostle 1992) Some of the investigators had never written a budget, or a work plan and first attempts were often unrealistic (budgets that were too low as well as too high). The ADDR project then developed a system of scientific review and support for the investigators.

But support for research cannot end with the awarding of a grant. Where appropriate, technical expertise was provided to the investigator, but on their terms. After groups completed their data collection, they were brought together for another workshop that focused on data analysis and manuscript preparation. In addition to assisting in the best possible analysis of the data, facilitators helped investigators define the most important questions to present in their papers and identify the programmatic significance of their work.

Too often research results are reported in internal documents which are available only to funders and those fortunate enough to visit the investigators. This led to the emphasis on publication in either the local or international literature. The very publication of a paper was a confidence builder for junior investigators and it helped to legitimize results that might find their way into policy. Much of the international literature is in English which was often the second or Cash3.

Third language of the investigators. We provided editorial assistance following the first or second draft as dictated by the investigators English language skills. It is only recently that a number of the international journals have begun to address the language issue as in the past a number of manuscripts from non-English speaking scientists were turned down because of problems with the written word. Funders should try to take first-time investigators from proposal development to the final manuscript as there are lessons to be learned all along the way.

Lastly we explored how best to take research to policy and implementation. This is critical if there is to be in country support for research. Too often policy makers complain that research is a luxury. That it does not help to solve local problems. We conducted research on this issue and held an international workshop to explore how best to move research to policy. The major conclusion, not surprisingly, was that policy makers need to be part of the process from the beginning. Updating them on the progress of the research is very helpful. Though the policy makers who began the process with the investigators may have moved on by the time the results are ready for distribution, a precedent will have been established and there will be some familiarity with the work. Each proposal that ADDR funded had to have a section that indicated why the work was useful to the community and how the information would be disseminated to government, the institution, and practitioners.

Building on existing networks or researchers (Inclen, TDR, etc.) of researchers helped to support other efforts designed to enhance research capacity. Too often donors want to establish their own identity and thus fail to assist those who are struggling to support their research efforts. We gave second grants to some investigators who had successfully completed their first study especially if they had disseminated their results through publications and presentations. Funds were also provided to attend local and international meetings if appropriate. Where appropriate, investigators were asked to provide consultation to other young scientists. All of these support activities helped to build independent research careers and institutional capacity.

LIMITATIONS

There are significant limitations. Constraints can be examined from the perspective of the individual, the institution, the nation, however effective the training of developing country scientists/researchers may be, and the donor. How these constraints affect the long-term productivity of trained researchers is most important. We need to know just how many trainees are actively Casli 4 engaged in research in a developing country (their own or another) five years after they have returned from their training programme.

THE INDIVIDUAL

Because research often is not given priority by the host country, researchers receive low salaries and few financial incentives. As a consequence many physician-researchers (or other professions) maintain a private medical practice (in addition to their academic duties) and conduct research in whatever spare time they have. Donors should consider giving additional salary support to those who agree to conduct research on a full-time basis. There are other legitimate financial needs for investigators including: access to quality education for their children; and support to meet with other colleagues is at home or abroad and attend meetings. Returning researchers have usually been trained in the use of some advanced technology which often not present or has not been adapted to the local situation. Training sites need to consider this when developing country scientists return home. The use of a low-cost simplified method for doing PCR is one example of adapting technology to fit the situation. Reentry grants for returning scientists are becoming more common. Maybe additional money should be set aside to purchase the relevant equipment. Because of the uncertainty of salary support researchers may be tempted to put together mega-proposals with multiple objectives to secure long-term funding. Unfortunately these studies are often not funded or if they are never completed. Coupled with salary support is the need for distinct career paths for researchers. If this is not done there will be a tendency for investigators to be promoted to non-research positions for which they may be ill suited.

If research is to be valued, promotion must be tied to research quality not just the number of papers or the size of a grant or report. There is an unfortunate trend in US institutions where publications are valued over research application and where the quantity of publications trumps quality. Incentives systems have been created that give inordinate value to the amount of money that is generated by the researcher.

THE INSTITUTION

Most developing country institutions are severely lacking in good financial management. Other than a handful of institutions, few take any overhead which is often built into the contract even if not requested. Our experience is that grants may not reach the investigator once it enters the universities or government coffers. We often had to set up departmental accounts to get the Cash5 money to the grantee. There also is far too much dependence on donor money without an adequate assessment of what is available locally. Better communication between researchers, policy makers and planners must be facilitated by the institution if the investigator does not have enough political clout.

THE NATION

There must be a strong commitment on the part of government to support and fund research within their political constraints. Countries must recognize that research is not a luxury but a necessity, regardless whether in health, agriculture or other sectors. Political stability is essential if a viable research programme is to develop. Retention of researchers is very difficult if not impossible in the face of civil strife.

THE DONORS

Donors must move money, often times at a far greater rate than can be absorbed by the recipient country researchers. It is easier to give one grant for $300,000 than ten for $30,000 even though the smaller amount is all that is needed. And who can blame the researcher for accepting more, especially given that there may not be another chance as donor priorities may change the next time around. There may also be seasonality to when funds are disbursed; as the end of the fiscal year approaches, there are often excess funds to be given away, often without the same oversight that was present at the beginning of the fiscal year. This is not good development policy. Research priorities may quickly change or be dependent on political decisions without regard to local priorities. Are malaria, tuberculosis, and HIV/AIDS the research priorities for all societies? The amount of money available, however, may lead researchers away from other areas of importance towards these perceived pots of money.

Governments in particular tend to work in 5 year cycles which is far too short a time for significant capacity development where the support and nuturing of careers and institutions are as important as the need to produce research findings.

Donors are often in competition with each other such that scientists/researchers trained by others are not utilized by new projects that want to create their own stable of investigators. The scientific communities of some countries are so fragile that if an investigator goes without funding for a year he/she will drop out of research and follow a career as a practitioner, usually in the private sector. All the investment in training is lost. Just the opposite may happen, Cash6 however, where a researcher with a good reputation (deserved or not) acquires multiple grants there account for far more that 100 per cent of time. Double funding for a research project is not an unknown occurrence. There is a real need for networking among funders of research to identify promising but under funded investigators and prevent excessive funding of others. This competition may also put a drain on the limited supply of support staff for researchers—lab technicians, nurses, field workers, statisticians, managers etc. This competition may lead to inflation in wages which cannot be sustained once the donor leaves or moves to another area.

SOME SUGGESTIONS

Thought must be given as to how training opportunities can be maximized so that researchers will return to their countries and become involved in addressing the important health questions they face. Attrition must be minimized given the high cost of training. Proper selection of investigators for training involves a thorough assessment of the person and their institution. Support for researchers and research must cover all aspects of the process from proposal writing all the way to publication and dissemination of information. Efforts must be strengthened "towards increasing the ability of local researchers to monitor and identify salient problems in their regions, create their own research priorities, conceptualize and carry out research projects that will help to solve these problems, form local or regional collegial networks, and communicate their results to policymakers, scientific colleagues, and their public." (Trostle and Simon, 1992) All those involved in training must recognize the constraints that researchers face once they return home from their programmes and respond accordingly. This might involve long-term career awards, educational supplements, support for presentations and information dissemination, and assistance in networking different researchers within and between countries. This latter suggestion is especially true in supporting South-South exchanges. In addition, developed country funding agencies should nurture and provide support to those mentors who are committed to the training and support of developing country researchers. Lastly more thought must be given to establishing high quality training opportunities in developing countries. This would be for both long and short term training. This must be the trend of the future, Cash 7.

CONSEQUENCES FOR THE HOME COUNTRY

In assessing the impact of physician migration on health care provision in the home country, it is crucial to consider the issues of physician supply and the duration of migration.

A number of countries such as Cuba, India and the Philippines systematically train more physicians than they need and send them abroad to benefit from remittances. Remittances, the money that migrants earn working abroad and send back to their home country, can be a crucial source of foreign exchange and aid the long-term development of the home country. For instance, a study focusing on physicians from the Philippines who practise overseas estimated that remittances were large enough to compensate for the economic losses associated with emigration[4]. The impact of emigration on health care provision in the home country is limited, as these countries have an adequate supply of physicians.

However, many host countries are developing countries that face physician shortages themselves. In this case, emigration represents a brain drain from home countries and is likely to lead to a deterioration in the working conditions of remaining physicians. Moreover, it may affect access to and quality of care, and impair the ability of the health care system to achieve health objectives for its population[1]. Migration may also influence the capacity of the home country to provide quality training to new physicians and the research capacity of medical schools. For instance, in Nigeria and other countries in sub-Saharan Africa, most medical research institutions have collapsed from the massive emigration flows of highly-skilled physicians[5].

It is also important to distinguish between permanent and temporary migration. Whereas temporary migration of physicians may produce benefits through an upgrading of skills, technological and financial transfers, permanent migration represents a net transfer of human capital from the home to the host country. In the case of permanent migration, the home country incurs two types of costs: the first corresponds to resources spent to educate a physician; and the second represents the value of the health care services that the emigrating physician would have rendered to his/her country in the absence of migration. Permanent migration might improve the prospects of individual physicians, but substantial and lasting emigration flows may weaken the capacity of the home country's health care system. These consequences are most important in the poorest countries that are not able to attract substitutes from other countries.

Temporary migration may be inspired by the desire to acquire higher professional qualifications or to gain experience with new techniques not available in the home country. If the host country subsidises the education of foreign students and these migrants return to their home country after they graduate, temporary migration of physicians can contribute to a general upgrading of skills in the home country. Yet there may be certain limits to this. If the skills that migrants have acquired during their stay abroad are too specialised, the home country may not be in a position to take advantage of them.

CONSEQUENCES FOR THE HOST COUNTRY

In OECD countries, foreign physicians are predominantly used as a supplement to local labour. This is because foreign physicians are more willing to practise in certain organizational settings and in certain geographical areas that domestic physicians tend to avoid. This is sometimes referred to as the 'safety-net' role. In the United Kingdom, general practitioners who graduated in South Asian medical schools (Bangladesh, India, Pakistan and Sri Lanka) are concentrated in less attractive areas with large patient lists and relatively deprived populations. In the United States, international medical graduates contribute significantly to care in rural areas. However, in Canada, policies requiring foreign physicians to practise in pre-specified areas have been legally challenged as a violation of basic human rights and have been judged against the Canadian Charter of Human Rights.

Increased supply in the host country might bring benefits to consumers. Consumers may benefit from improved access to care and may gain from reduced medical care prices. Estimates of the gain to consumers from immigration in the United States, measured as a percentage of total expenditures on physician services, ranged from near 1 per cent in 1966 to over 12 per cent by 1971 increased competition between physicians may raise the quality of health care services provided in the host country. On the other hand, immigration may endanger the safety and quality of health care provision if the physicians concerned have a lower standard of medical practice. Concerns that qualifications are not equivalent across countries and differences in practice patterns have been used by professional associations to exclude foreign physicians.

CONCLUSION

Although OECD countries generally favour long-term policies of national self-sufficiency to sustain their physician workforce, such policies usually co-exist with short-term or medium-term policies to attract foreign physicians. As this is likely to continue, there is a need to create a global framework that enforces physician migration policies that confer benefits on home and host countries. In the long term, OECD countries need to put in place appropriate education and training policies rather than rely on physician migration to address their future needs. OECD countries increasingly perceive immigration of foreign physicians as a way of sustaining their physician workforce. As a result, countries have entered into international agreements regulating physician migration, although their success has been limited due to the imposition of licensing requirements and the protection of vested interests by domestic physicians. OECD countries have therefore adopted specific policies designed to stimulate the immigration of foreign physicians, whilst minimising its negative impact on the home country. Measures promoting immigration have included international recruitment campaigns, less strict immigration requirements and arrangements that foster shared learning between health care systems. Policies restricting the societal costs of physician emigration from developing countries such as good practice guidelines and taxes on host countries have not yet produced their expected effect or in some cases have not been established at all.

24

Technical Manpower Planning in the Services Sector

The Opportunities Ahead

*C.D.Balaji**

ABSTRACT

Nearly 42 million job seekers have registered in employment agencies and by 2020 nearly 846 million people will be in working age group (15 to 59 years). Though there has been increase GDP, employment has not increased. The Report of the Task Force on Employment Opportunities points out that 70 per cent of the growth in employment opportunities in the next decade will be in the service sector. According to reports, the manpower shortage is projected at one million by 2008 in the IT sector and in ITES nearly 3.3 million service jobs are expected to be off shored by 2008. Tourism and entertainment are two sectors which hold great potential for economic growth and employment generation.

Key Words: Services Sector, Jobless Growth, IT sector, Hardware, BPO, Tourism, Entertainment.

* **Panimalar Insti...e of Management Studies and Computer Science, 20, Railway Colony Second Street, Nelson Manickam Road, Chennai - 29. Email: cdbalaji2004@rediffmail.com**

INTRODUCTION

By 2020 India's population would touch 1.34 billion; over 237 million will be in the school going age group of 5 to 14, 846 million will be in the working age of 15 to 59 and 132 million in the 60 plus age group. That is 6 out of 10 Indians (a rise of 42%) will be below 35 and 846 million would need jobs. By 2040 India will be the third largest economy in the world according to the recent Goldman Sachs study titled "Dreaming with BRICs : The Path to 2050".

The Report places Brazil, Russia, India and China (identified as BRIC countries) among the Fastest growing economies in the world. A major reason for this is the increase in the working age population in these countries whereas the working age population in other developed countries shows a secular decline. It stated that India has the potential to show the fastest growth rate at more than 5 per cent in the next 30 to 50 years and even after 2050 India would be one country showing GDP growth rates of over 3 per cent.

SERVICE SECTOR—THE STAR PERFORMER

India's service sector has emerged among the top four fastest growing segments in the world during 1990-91 recording a higher growth than the 1980's. According to the World Development Indicators, 2003, released recently by the World Bank Indian service sector grew at 7.9 per cent in 1990-01 against a world average of 3.1 per cent.

Table—24.1 Top four economies in service sector growth

Country	1990-91	1990-2001
Azerbaijan	-	10.3
Botswana	15.9	8.1
China	13.5	8.9
India	6.9	7.9

Source: World Development Indicators, 2003

If one compares the post-reform period's (1992-93 to 2001-02) average growth, agriculture has shown a 3.4 per cent growth, while industry has grown by 6 per cent and services by 7.7 per cent. On the other hand in the prereform period, agriculture grew by 3.9 per cent while industry grew by 6.4 per cent and services by 6.4 per cent. In other words, on a comparative basis, the agricultural sector and industrial sector's growth declined in the post-reform period whereas the service sector's growth increased.

Table—24.2 Average sectoral growth rates (in %)

Sectors	80-81 to 91-92	92-93 to 01-02	04-07 (Projections)
Agriculture	3.9	3.4	4
Industry	6.3	6.0	9
Services	6.4	7.7	10

THE CONUNDRUM OF JOBLESS GROWTH

Higher output growth and acceleration of GDP which is normally accompanied by growth in Employment has not happened in India's case. On the contrary employment growth has actually declined with increase in GDP. Growth rate of employment declined from 2.7 per cent p.a. during 1983-94 to 1.07 per cent during 1993- 2000 when GDP accelerated from 5.2 per cent to 6.7 per cent.Employment elasticity has fallen from .52 during 1993-94 to 0.16 during 1993-2000.

The organized sector has failed to create jobs and the falling trend in employment in the organized sector in India has continued for the fourth consecutive year in 00-01, according to official data.

Table—24.3 Organized sector employment (in lakhs)

		Public Sector	Private Sector	Total
As of March	1995	194.5	79.3	273.8
	1996	194.7	80.6	275.3
	1997	194.3	85.1	279.4
	1998	195.6	86.9	282.5
	1999	194.2	87.5	281.7
	2000	194.2	87	281.2
	2001	193.1	86.5	279.6

Source: Ministry of Labour

EMPLOYMENT POTENTIAL IN THE SERVICE SECTOR

The Report of the Task Force on Employment Opportunities points out that 70 per cent of the growth in employment opportunities in the next decade will be in the service sector. Sectors such as IT, ITES, tourism and entertainment hold great potential for employing qualified technical manpower.

IT Sector

IT and IT services have heralded a revolution, especially during the last decade as brought out by the following table:

Table—24.4 Software and IT services exports

Year	Exports (Rs. In Crores)
1975	0.85
1984-85	30.00
1991-92	430.00
1994-95	1,535.00
2000-01	24,250.00
2001-02	29,400.00

Source: IPAG Journal and Dept. of Electronics

Table—24.5 Current employment figures for the IT & ITES industry

Sector	2001-02	2002-03	2003-04
S/W Exports	1,70,000	2,05,000	2,60,000
S/W Domestic	22,000	25,000	28,000
S/W-Captive in user organizations	2,24,250	2,60,000	2,80,000

Source: Nasscom

According to Meta figures 1/3rd of new IT development work for big US co., is done overseas with India being the biggest site. IT grew 24 per cent to touch Rs.92,924 crores in 2003-04 with the domestic market accounting for Rs. 33, 374 crores and exports Rs. 59, 550 crores. The Indian software industry is the number one exporter today, of the total merchandise exports of $ 60 million software exports accounted for $13 billion. The industry grew at

30 per cent last year and this year the projected growth has been pegged at 32 per cent. In 2003-04 around 4,35,000 people are employed in IT and IT related work up from 3,71,795 a year ago, a growth of 17 per cent.

Future Potential: A Nasscom -McKinsey study predicts that the turnover of the IT sector could touch $80 billion by 2008 of which $50 billion will come from exports. The following table points out the potential for further increase in business from the IT sector:

Table—24.6 IT services spending

Country	IT Services spending in $ billion	India's IT Export $ million	Indian Market %	Share in India's Exports
N. America	171.1	6685	3.92	67.7
Western Europe	109.6	2103	1.92	21.3
Japan	34.9	193	0.55	2
Latin America	17.5	583	3.33	5.9
Asia Pacific	16.0	311	1.94	3.2

According to the Tenth Five Year Plan (2002-07) estimates. It is assessed that IT will contribute to approximately 0.2 million jobs per year and around 1 million at the end of the Tenth Plan as additional direct employment. The manpower demand for IT Security Services which is a small portion of the IT industry points out the demand for IT professionals.

Table—24.7 Manpower demand for IT secutiry services in India

Service Category	2002	2003	2004	2005	2006	2007	2008
Consulting Services	1623	2778	4163	4498	5231	5425	5602
Implementation Services	2376	3552	5215	5609	6426	6574	6726
Management Services	827	1539	2626	2990	3608	4591	4682
S/W Services	13571	16790	22093	25378	39023	52875	60935
Total	18397	24659	34097	38475	54288	69465	77405

Source: IDC India 2003

IT in Manufacturing

According to an Accenture Report, IT in Indian manufacturing context has not been leveraged adequately - both due to inadequate investments and limited ability to leverage business value. IT investments in any co., remains focused on automating existing processes and hence limit the ability to extract business value. Lower priority attached to investments in IT relative to other investments and inadequate recognition of the need for world class IT infrastructure have been cited as reasons for this trend. But with Indian manufacturing reviving up its operations and gearing itself to become the manufacturing hub— a trend already witnessed in automobiles and auto components investments in IT and the demand for skilled IT professionals is bound to increase in the manufacturing sector.

HARDWARE GROWTH—THE PRE-REQUISITE

In every country where IT has been introduced and implemented extensively it has tremendously increased employment and job opportunities. In the US for example IT has contributed to half the productive growth and a third of the economic growth. Though we have done well in the software sector our hardware industry is not upto global standards.

Employment Creation Potential of the Hardware Sector

The achievement of $87 billion (Rs.4, 00,200 crores) target for software by 2008 would require cumulative imports of $120 billion (Rs.5, 52,000 crores) worth of hardware between 2001-08. The nation cannot afford such an import bill. Employment generation in the hardware sector for the same investment is much higher than other sectors. For every Rs.1 crore worth of sales, employment generation is greater than 10 for hardware against five - six for the engineering sector.

The hardware industry in India is at the point of inflection and Market Researcher IDC, known for its conservative numbers estimates that the corresponding market value estimate (for PC's, servers, handheld devices, traditional work stations, storage, peripherals and data communication) is Rs.75,000 crores. For such growth we need at least 5,000 micro-electronic engineers and the current turnout of 300 post-graduate engineers is highly inadequate.

BPO'S

India is emerging as a global hub in the BPO market and even during the slow down in software services growth it is the IT enabled services segment that propelled the country's growth engine in the services sphere. Types of operations currently outsourced are Customer Care, Bill Processing, Medical Transcription, Translation and HRIS. The range of services being outsourced is expanding to include equity research, software testing, infrastructure management, chip designing and market research.

Table—24.8 The booming Indian BPO market

Particulars	2002	2003	2004	2005	2006	2007	CAGR
Offshore BPO revenue	1322	1825	3017	6439	12563	24230	78
Indian BPO revenue	912	1205	1961	3928	7412	13811	69.35
Total BPO market	110167	121687	131171	143090	157033	173070	

Source: Nasscom

India's Position

In relation to the world spend of $800 billion on BPO last year; India's market share of $3.6 billion is miniscule. According to IDC estimates the global market is projected to grow at an overall CAGR of 11 per cent and reach $1.2 trillion by 2006.

Table—24.9 Worldwide ITES-BPO spending in select sectors (Figures in US $Million)

Vertical	2001 (Actual)	2006 (Projections)	Inc %
HR	7,373	25,555	246
Logistics	1,40,700	3,08,651	119
Purchasing	5,288	12,185	130
Engg/R&D	69,798	1,23,882	77
Legal	1,11,273	1,63,962	47
Fin/Acg	36,356	64,872	78

If India achieves at least 2 per cent of this market it could achieve revenue of over $20 billion. Job Potential: For the beleaguered millions of Indian college graduates, the BPO segment is a godsend as it is a volume employer.

Table—24.10 Manpower by horizontals

Service Lines	No. of People 2002-03	2003-04
Customer Care	65,000	95,000
Receivables Management	11,000	21000
Administration	25,000	40000
Finance	24000	40000
Total	**171000**	**245000**

Source: Nasscom

Employment Projections

Nasscom estimates that BPO's would generate 1.1 million jobs by 2008 as compared to 5 lakh jobs created by the IT industry in the last 20 years, making it a 20 times bigger opportunity than the latter.AT Kearney predicts that IT services and back office work in India will swell five fold to a $57 billion annual export industry employing nearly 4 million people. According to Gartner, the worldwide HR outsourcing market is projected to grow to $58.5 billion by 2006.

Backlash-Impact

According to Evalueserve 1 out of 6 persons in the US will be over 65 years by 2008. This would lead to a demand supply gap of 5.6 million jobs in the country's labor market by 2010. Factoring in the cumulative immigration of 3.2 million persons until 2010, the US needs to address a shortfall of 2.4 million workers leading to a GDP loss of $884 billion. These demographic trends clearly point out that US cannot sustain its economic growth without outsourcing.

TOURISM'S EMPLOYMENT POTENTIAL

Tourism is a sector though hitherto neglected which holds great potential for employment generation—both technical and non technical jobs. Tourism is the largest sector in the worldwide export of goods and services and accounts for 12 per cent of global income. Nations around the world have realized the potential of tourism in generating employment and contributing to economic development. Tourism contributes 13.9 per cent of national income in Thailand, 9.2 per cent in Indonesia, 8.6 per cent in China and only 5.6 per cent in India. In terms of employment, tourism's share in total employment is 11.2 per cent in Thailand, 7.4 per cent in Indonesia, 7 per cent in China and only 5.8 per cent in India. Every tourist directly or in directly creates 11 jobs. According to estimates, for every million of rupees invested, the agricultural sector creates 45 jobs, manufacturing only 13 jobs, whereas tourism can create 89 jobs i.e., job generating potential of tourism is twice that of agriculture and 7 times that of manufacturing.

The Country's Position

In 1964, the number of tourists worldwide was 100 million. It increased to 700 million in 2001. The disturbing fact is that though the number of tourists globally has recorded a manifold increase, India's share of global tourist traffic which was 0.54 per cent in 1950 has actually declined to 0.38 per cent. It is a sad commentary that it is placed in a low 47th position in the list of the top 60 tourism destinations in the world.

The Way Forward

A research forecast by the World Travel and Tourism Council pegs tourism industry growth at 4.5 per cent over the next 10 years with India having a growth potential of 9.7 per cent and prospects of creating 7 million jobs. During 2003-04, the tourism industry has registered a robust growth of 18.5 per cent (estd) in foreign tourist arrivals compared with the modest growth of 1.7 per cent registered in 2002-03as brought out by the following table:

Table—24.10 Foreign tourist arrivals and foreign exchange earnings

Year	Foreign Tourist Arrivals (in lakhs)	Growth (Percentage)	Estd. Foreign exchange earnings (in millions US$)	Percentage change
1999-00	25.05	4.5	3036	1.4
2000-01	26.99	7.7	3168	4.3
2001-02	24.28	-10.2	2910	-8.1
2002-03	24.7	1.7	3029	4.1
2003-04	29.25*	18.5*	3833*	26.5*

* Estimated

Source: Ministry of Tourism

ENTERTAINMENT

The Indian entertainment industry is today worth $4 billion. Leading chambers of commerce such as FICCI and CII have identified entertainment as a fast growing industry. Revenues are projected to increase to $10 billion in 2005 from $3 billion currently. A recent report of KPMG indicates that the Indian entertainment industry is expected to grow at more than 20 per cent annually. The Indian film industry is the largest in the world in terms of number of movies produced. India produces 800-900 movies every year in 52 languages and provides direct and indirect employment to 5 million people. Revenues from the entertainment industry are expected to touch $1 trillion in 10 years. This includes Film, Radio, TV, Music, DVD, videogames and new technologies.

Entertainment demographics (population in age groups that are the highest consumers of entertainment) are more acute indicators of the future of the entertainment business: North America has 65 million in that demographic, while China and India have almost 700 million. In India alone over the next 10 years, 40 per cent of our existing population will come from this demographic. The corresponding figure for the US is just 15 per cent. Aided by the large number of Asians in the West, Asian culture will make inroads into the West.

Animation is another area in the entertainment sphere where India has already made a visible impact. The country is increasingly becoming an attractive destination for 3D animation content especially outsourced content.Pentamedia Graphics has just completed an animation film of Lord Buddha, Toonz animation, Paprikaas animation and Crest Communications have all received jobs from abroad for producing 3D animation films. The entertainment industry as a whole is expected to exceed $3 billion by 2005. Of this, the animation industry is estimated at around $70 billion. Even if India is able to address 1 per cent of this $70 billion market it is a huge opportunity, but it is doubtful whether the country can handle it. The greatest constraint is the lack of talent..

According to a study by Andersen Consulting, India's animation industry(domestic and exports) will touch USD 2 billion and create employment for around 3 lakh professionals including content developers and animators by 2008.Today we have only 15,000 trained professionals. India has the largest number of technologists in the world today and also the highest number of trained entertainment technologists. If their skills are combined, then the opportunity to capture the market and generate employment is enormous.

CONCLUSION

At this point of our nation's history we don't suffer from the lack of options but from a surfeit of choices. Our share in global services is only 1.5 per cent. The emerging favorable global demographic trends would throw up immense opportunities for millions of Indians in the services sector. We need to make a paradigm shift from providing support services to serving global customers. India can be the world's leading health care provider, the preferred tourist destination and leading centre for creativity and innovation. A phenomenon observed throughout the world is the substitution of mental power for muscle power and India with its abundance of human capital should harness their capabilities in the optimum manner to join the league of developed nations by 2020 or even earlier.

25

Total Quality Management

A Case Study

*V. Kailasababu**

INTRODUCTION

Consequent to the adoption of the new policy, the present scenario of globalization and liberalized economy in the changed industrial scenario prevailing globally, the country faces challenge to improve industrial production both quantitatively and qualitatively to augment exports in order to compete in the international market, the industry has to import, adopt and adapt technologies suiting to the local manufacturing conditions and for this purpose high level of up-gradation in the skills is called for the technical manpower. Keeping in view of the same it has been envisaged to organise technical manpower development activities in consultation with the industrial experts. The important programmes thus to be made part of the technical manpower development invariably consisting of the areas e.g. *Total Quality Management*, ISO 9000 series concept, building skills, financial management, quality management for global competitiveness, personality development for professional success, implementation

* **National Technical Manpower Information System, (Nodal Centre), Board of Apprenticeship Training, (Western Region), Mumbai -400 022, Telefax - 022 -25292502/Email: ntmis@bom5.vsnl.net.in**

of new technology concept, vigilance in industrial sector, preventive maintenance, importance of effective communication etc.

Manuscript

The TQM philosophies which are translated to specific actions are in the following areas:

(i) Quality Programmes

(ii) Standardisation

(iii) Quality Control Circles

(iv) Education and Training.

A "Total Quality Council"—an apex body comprising Senior Executives and Directors of the company—overseas progress of the Company's TQM efforts. A full-fledged "Total Quality Council Secretariat" (TQCS), headed by the Technical Senior Executive, gives necessary guidance to the TQM activities in the company and monitors the same.

A brief of the four specific activities are given below:

Quality Programmes

The company has divided quality process in three segments

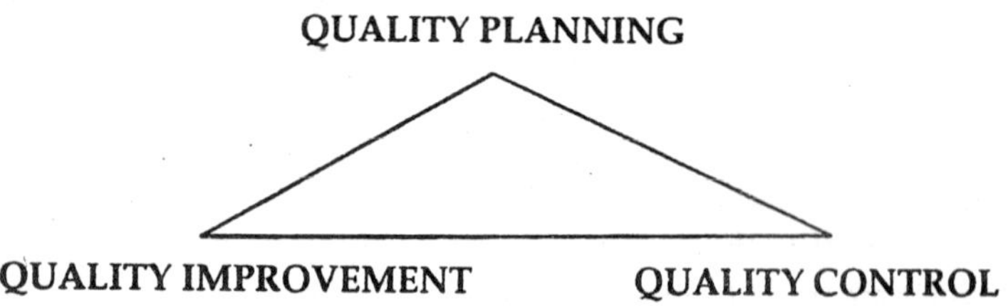

TRILOGY

The Trilogy is somewhat comparable to the three processes of financial management: Planning, Control and Improvement. This is the exact methodology that one needs to follow in each of these three segments involved in the quality process.

The objective of the Quality Improvement programme is to make the habit of annual improvement in quality and annual reductions in quality related costs. The methodology for Quality Management is that all quality related problems must be broken down to a number of projects, and each project should be attended to an organised manner.

The QI process consists essentially of two "journeys".

- Diagnostic Journey
- Remedial Journey

The diagnostic journey relates to the stage from symptom to cause while the remedial journey covers from cause to remedy for each of the quality related symptoms.

Separate project teams are made with persons with well defined roles, and problems are solved project-by-project, passing through the above two journeys. An apex body oversees the progress of the projects and guides the teams.

In the company, every functional area has formed an apex team, called "Quality Council". There are a number of Quality Councils operating and each guides project teams related to their area. Many employees are currently participating in different projects and a great amount of enthusiasm has been generated to bring out tangible results.

Standardisation

The International Standards Organization has brought out ISO 9000 series of standards after years of background work put in by ISO and the standards Organizations of several countries. The basic purpose of these standards is to make the supplier more aware of his responsibilities in ensuring quality both in process and at product stage. Many countries, including India, have adopted these standards word-by-word.

Some of the companys' executives have gone through rigorous training programmes for understanding these standards, and plans for implementation of these standards.

Quality Control Circles (QCC)

The QC Circle concept can be traced to Japan wherein small groups of people, doing similar work, voluntarily meet to analyse causes of problems and find solutions. Several senior executives, officer, supervisors and workmen of the company had undergone systematic training on the QC Circle Concepts. Today they have many QC Circles functioning and these have so far given excellent results.

Education and Training (E&T)

The fourth pillar of TQM is E & T and is considered to be the most important part of the corporate TQM programme. Only by proper training of employees both for quality culture and for skills, that a company can be a technological leader.

The great emphasis is laid by the company in training employees. Training, in fact, is a way of life and the programmes include involvement of all managerial and operative levels in the company—right from the top management to workforce.

Training modules are periodically designed to imbibe quality-related aspects in employees. Meetings with customers and also lectures by them are conducted as an on-going process.

The company has been launched 'with the objective of not only making quality products but also ensuring that high level of quality is maintained by each employee in every sphere of work. The company with this approach, hopes to grow qualitatively from strength to strength, retain its technological lead in the country and establish firm base as a company of world standard.

26

Human Resource Planning (HRP)

An Activity Profile of HRM Functionaries

*S.F. Chandra Sekhar**

ABSTRACT

Human resource planning as strategic issues of business management has been a crucial and much demanding activity on the part of management of people. HR functionaries from 57 companies in the twin cities of Hyderabad and Secunderabad participated in this research to raise their views on how they are practising one of the most important issues of strategic HR in their concerns in a conference on HRD in Hyderabad city. Results reveal certain startling findings of their HRP orientation and practices when compared them across public and private type of organizations, while controlling for their levels of functions. Public sector HR functionaries were found to be little more active in their HRP activities than their counterparts. However, the variations in their HRP activities have not reached statistical levels of significance indicating that HRP orientation and activity profile are of global in nature. Implications are drawn for practice of the HRP activities.

* **Professor of HRM, Siva Sivani Institute of Management, Kompally, Via.Hakimpet, Secunderabad- 500 014, Email: sfc@ssim.ac.in**

INTRODUCTION

Human resource as an integrating factor of production process has been much recognized for its significant role in transforming organizations these than ever before. Further, owing to the changes in the business environment and the advances in technology, communication and consumerism, planning of human resources has become an incessant activity on the part of HR functionaries working in services and manufacturing organizations. Broadly, human resources planning (hereinafter referred to as HRP) are not only to maintain the people as resources, but also to enhance the capability of the organization through its competent people. Thus, HRP should be used efficiently and effectively in order to realize the main objective of organizational effectiveness.

HRP—Concept

HRP means different things to different people. For an economist, it is a macro perspective issue of analysis the demand for and supply of human resources across length and breadth of the country over a period of time. For a sociologist, it assumes the connotation of size of population available in the form of individuals, groups and communities for the perpetuation of a society. For a manager, it is at a micro perspective understanding as a process by which his/her organization determines how to move from its current human resource position to its desired position. There are a plethora of definitions detailing the contents of tasks, and activities to be performed by HR functionaries in carrying out HRP. One such definition which deserves attention is give by John et.al (1983) that included a series of activities to be performed. They are i) forecasting the human resource requirements through mathematical projections, judgmental estimates etc., ii) making an inventory of current HR and assessing its optimal utilization, iii) anticipating HR problems when the forecasted requirements are implemented, iv) planning necessary programmes of recruitment, selection, training and development, etc. thus, in this chapter, it is conceptualized as the extent to which various activities related to the assessment of demand for and supply of human resources done by the HR functionaries in organizations for arriving at the reconciliation of the demand and supply side of human resources leading to their optimal utilization.

Determinants of HRP

There are various reasons for carrying out HRP. These reasons are categorized into i) external, ii) internal and iii) HR assessments.

External environment includes those elements which are beyond the control of the management/ for example, the liberalization, globalization and privatization processes initiated in the early 90's have triggered a greater sense of emergency for the HR functionaries to keep reconciling with the need for and supply of human resources. Further, the ecological issues demanding adoption of automation and computer based production technologies, the scarce population of technical human resources and the migratory character of knowledge workers, the ever raising aspiration of competent people in the economy, the changes in lifestyles growing consumerism, demands for quality goods and services have all unleashed their clout on the HRP practices.

The internal environments which include those issues that are under the control of the management were constantly altered in tune with the external environment. The long term and short term business planning, the financial commitments, the production planning and the strategic decisions have necessitated the resurgence of interest and intensive involvement in the HRP activities.

Finally, the process of reconciliation of demand for and supply of HR has been influenced by the HR assessments of the number of people attaining superannuation; voluntary and compulsory separations like retirement, resignation, termination, dismissal, suspension, deaths, long term leaves, besides employee turnover, absenteeism, accidents and so on have made the HRP functionaries job easy for their day to day act of balancing the HR needs.

THE PRESENT STUDY

In a recent provocative column, Thomas Stewart (1999) says "We as HR professionals have a terrible indictment of the HR function, and more importantly, of the profession we practice". In rush to reduce the costs, organizations are taking very hard look at HR function. They are critical in their assessment of large staff who appear to do nothing related to either core competencies or added value or unresponsive, non-strategic HR functionaries who always subscribed to the policing personnel approach in their day to day decision making, besides their expression of disillusionment with the democratic process of partnership by the line and participation from the staff. On the other hand, organizations have been downsizing and outsourcing the HR function owing to the relative importance attached to the people management processes. Therefore, there is a need to look at the HR functions in a renewed manner in these times of competing economies. The value of operating functions of HR has been questioned many a time in the context of the budgetary provisions by the corporations. Therefore, the professionals are constrained to be careful in redesigning their functions in order to attract the provisions of funds. One such function is acquisition function under which the HRP activity which has drawn significant attention across the world and also in our context. Thus, the first axe that falls on any budgetary provisions is on the HR budgets, more so, on the specifics of downsizing which eventually leads to the design of compensation packages. Thus, to that extent this study intends to explore the activity profile of HR functionaries of select organizations in the twin cities of Hyderabad and Secunderabad. It further attempts to understand to what extent the activities of HRP are carried out by the HR functionaries in the study organizations. However other operative functions of HRM are beyond the confines of this chapter. However, the HRP activities suggested by Dale Yoder (1984) have been adopted as the standard activity profiles. For more details about the HRP activities, conceptualization, and scale for their assessment, please refer to Table 26.1. The research question raised in this chapter is "are public and private companies' executives different in their HRP activity profile?" This question forms the guideline for the entire discussions in this chapter.

METHOD

HR executives from 57 public and private sector companies in the twin cities of Hyderabad and Secunderabad, while attending

Table—26.1 HRP dimensions, scale items, reliability coefficients

Sl. No.	HRP Activities	Conceptualization	Items	α
1.	Formulating Human Resource Strategies	Extent to which the quantitative and qualitative status of human resources maintained in the light of business strategy	5	0.73
2.	Managing Relationships with Managers	Extent to which the line managers were contacted while obtaining the status of quantitative and qualitative aspects of HR	10	0.74
3.	Personnel Professional Activities	extent to which the HR functionaries are conscious of the status of human resources on a day to day basis	9	0.80
4.	Manage the Human Resource Planning Function	Extent to which the function of assessing quantitative and qualitative status of human resources in a company	10	0.89
5.	Collecting and Analyzing Data	Extent to which executives are involved in collecting and analysis human resource data pertaining to surplus and losses on a day to day basis	10	0.79
6.	Designing and Using Forecasting Systems	Extent to which the mathematical, and assumptive forecasting models evolved, adopted and utilized	10	0.88
7.	Managing Career Development	Extent to which the career policy, path and counselling and development activities initiated in order to retain the employees	11	0.93
8.	Other Allied Activities	Extent to which the associated HR activities balanced in the light of managing HRP activities.	15	0.84

a national conclave on HRD participated in this study. A structured questionnaire which includes a 79-item standardized 4-point scale to assess frequency of HRP activities carried out by the HR executives and their demographic profile was administered to them. Data processed with the help of statistical software and analyzed using means, standard deviations and *f-values* to present the results of the study. Details of the HRP dimensions, scale items, reliability coefficients are presented in Table 26.1.

It is evident from the table above that in all there were 79 items used to assess the extent to which the HRP activities were carried out by the HR functionaries from the select public and private sector undertakings. The coefficient of alpha computed for the sub-scales of the HRP activities scale show that all the scales have higher internal homogeneity.

Profile of the Executives

The average age of the senior functionaries is 40 years, with 18 years of service. Their average span of control is 6 with an average of 2 promotions utilized by them. As regards the middle level functionaries, the average age of them is 34 years with 10 years of service having supervised four subordinates. They were promoted on an average for two times. Lastly, with regard to the lower level functionaries, the average age of them is 29 years with six years of service, followed by around three subordinates under their supervision. On an average, they were promoted once so far. Half of the executives from public sector undertaking are Post-graduates. Whereas a large number of them (45 per cent) of their counterparts are also Post-graduates.

RESULTS AND DISCUSSION

Formulating Human Resource Strategies

As per the norm evolved, if respondents obtain an arithmetic mean of 7.5, they are assumed to be formulating the HR strategies on an average frequency. It was interesting to note from Table 26.2 that both the public and the private sector executives have stated that they formulate HR strategies more than the expected standard as evident from their uniform mean scores. This indicates that HR

Table—26.2 Means, SDS and *F-Values* of the HRP sub scale scores

Type	Level of Functioning		Formulating Human Resource Strategies	Managing Relationships with Line Managers	Personnel Professional Activities	Manage the Human Resource Planning Function	Collecting and Analyzing Data	Designing and using Forcasting Systems	Managing Career Development	Other Allied Activities
Public Companies	Senior	Mean	12.83	24.33	20.00	**19.67**	18.67	18.17	25.83	35.17
		SD	3.49	6.28	5.18	**8.43**	8.24	7.57	7.99	6.31
	Middle	Mean	12.80	25.00	17.80	**22.20**	18.00	17.00	21.20	32.40
		SD	2.49	3.80	5.83	**6.16**	5.78	7.00	9.91	13.17
	Lower	Mean	10.22	18.78	13.00	**12.33**	15.22	11.00	15.22	24.22
		SD	3.15	5.32	5.90	7.79	6.24	7.94	10.07	11.03
Private Companies	Senior	Mean	11.71	22.29	18.00	19.71	16.57	16.00	23.71	30.43
		SD	2.87	4.54	4.28	7.93	7.23	5.72	6.05	4.72
	Middle	Mean	11.21	22.95	17.79	21.32	17.53	17.37	23.00	33.16
		SD	3.84	2.97	3.38	6.43	5.27	6.74	7.90	7.56
	Lower	Mean	9.00	18.82	13.82	12.18	13.73	16.09	22.45	26.73
		SD	3.44	5.21	3.74	8.20	5.87	3.59	6.12	3.93
	F_Values		1.07	.09	.07	.33	.19	1.31	1.84	0.24
	D.F		1.56	1.56	1.56	1.56	1.56	1.56	1.56	1.56
	P =		.30	.75	.79	.56	.66	.25	.18	.61

strategies are being devised by both of them irrespective of their ownership. This is also supported by the *f-value* presented in the table.

Managing Relationships with Managers

The norm for assessing how frequently HR functionaries manage relationship with line managers is 15.0 scores. Therefore, if they obtain a mean score above 15, they perform the said activity more than expected. As it is evident that all the executives have obtained mean scores more than the expected mean scores indicating that they have been practising the activity of managing relationships with line mangers more than expected. It is also found that the executives of public companies reported that they have been managing relationships with the line mangers more frequently than their counterparts. Surprisingly, the lower level executives were found less practising such activity than their superiors. Nevertheless, the variations in their mean scores have not reached statistical levels of significance as evident from the *f-value* presented in the table.

Personnel Professional Activities

As regards this activity, 13.5 scores is the norm. All the respondents have obtained the mean scores on this activity more than expected, indicating that this activity of HRP is also practised more frequently than expected. It is also found that the seniors and middle level executives of public sector undertakings obtained more scores on this activity than their counterparts. However, in both cases, the lower level executives were found to be practising this activity just on an average. However, such variations in their means scores have not reached statistical levels of significance as indicated by the *f-value*.

Manage the Human Resource Planning Function

It was established that the standard norm is 15.0 scores. It was found that though all the senior and middle level executives from public and private sector undertakings have obtained uniform mean scores which are above the expected mean scores, indicating that the 'managing the human resource planning function" is carried out more frequently. However, the mean scores obtained by lower level executives have not reached the expected mean score of 15.0. This shows that the lower levels of executives are not carrying out more of this activity than expected. The *f-values* also suggest that the variations in their mean scores are not statistically significant. This shows that this particular activity is a global activity of HR functionaries in all types of companies, but exists among top and middle levels only.

Collecting and Analyzing Data

The norm for understanding this activity is 15.0 scores. It is noticed that the executives in public sector undertaking have been carrying out this activity more than the expected frequency though the lower level executives have just reached the expected frequency. Whereas, in case of private companies' executives, though they just surpassed the expected mean scores, the lower levels have not reached such expected mean score. This indicates that the private sector companies are relatively low in carrying out this activity. Nevertheless, the *f-value* also suggests that the variations in the mean scores of their activity have not reached statistical level of significance.

Designing and Using Forecasting Systems

As regards this activity, the norm is 15.0 scores. In public companies, the top and the middle executives were involved in designing and using forecasting systems more frequently than expected. Whereas, the lower level executives have not reached the expected score of 15.0. Interestingly in case of private company executives, even the lower level executives were involved in carrying out this activity more than the frequency expected. However, the mean variations in their activity scores have not reached statistical level of significance. This indicates that though the public sector executives are more frequently using this activity than their counterparts, yet their lower level executives are not involved in this activity like their counterparts. Nevertheless, the mean variation in their scores has not reached statistical level of significance, indicating that the designing and using forecasting systems has been a uniform experience of all the executives.

Managing Career Development

In this regard, the norm is 16.5 scores indicating average utility of the activity. It is interesting to note from the table that the private companies' employees have surpassed their counterparts in managing career development of their employees by scoring above expected standard scores. Whereas, among the public companies, only the top level executives were found practising this activity more than expected. The *f-value* shows that such variation in their mean scores has not reached statistical level of significance.

Other Allied Activities

The norm evolved for interpreting this activity is 22.0 scores. It is very surprising to note that all the executives irrespective of their type of company and levels of functioning were found to have surpasses the standard score, indicating that the allied activities which support HR planning are carried out more than the expected frequency. Therefore, the *f-value* also suggests that the executives are uniform in their practice.

IMPLICATIONS

As the results pertaining to the activity profile of HR functionaries from the public and private companies with regard to Human resource planning, reveal that though in most of the HR planning activities, the executives were found to be practising more frequently than expected, none of the activity has noticed any variations when it comes to the cross-organizational and cross-functional comparisons. This indicates that HRP activities in these times of post liberalized environment have been more of global concerns for all the corporations. Secondly, the HRP activities are more linked to strategic function of the business entities, therefore, the top and the middle level executives were found to be more frequenting in using these activities.

Thus, what does these results convey to the corporations and to the theory building. It is suggested that since HR planning influences corporate strategy, firstly, the HRP should be a continuous activity with provision for control and review. Secondly, the lower level functionaries should be extensively involved in collecting, analyzing and projecting the data for making HRP activities more accurate and effective when carried out by the top and the middle level executives. Thirdly, since, the forecasting activities forms the most important of all in the gamut of HRP activities, usage of computers and canned software packages could be encouraged. Predicting the right number and quality of human resources will be done with more precision and accuracy when softwares are utilized. This way, corporations with their tight budgets will be able to have the right people for the right positions.

From a research context, there is a need for replication of these kinds of studies so that theory could be strengthened with new forecasting techniques based on mathematical models and judgmental models. Further, these kind of studies need to be carried out in order to know not only the frequency of activities in HRP domain carried out, but the intensity of such activities also need to be studied. More specifically, using non traditional methods like focused group discussions, participative appraisal also could be more useful in understanding the domains of HRP activities in the years to come.

CONCLUSION

Human resource planning is a strategic function of HR functionaries. In the wake of post 1991 business environment, this function has become a serious concern for all at the top levels of management, compelling the HR functionaries to re-look at this activity with more rigour. This study attempted to answer a research question "are public and private companies' HR executives different in their HRP activity profile? The study revealed that the public and private companies' HR executives are not different in their HRP activities profile. This means that HRP activities, though important, their execution is global in nature. Whether the companies are of public or private in nature, the external business environment compels these companies to carry out this function with special concern. Implications for corporations and future research considerations have been drawn.

REFERENCES

1. Fitz-Enz, Jac. A New Vision for Hr: Defining the Human Resource Function By Its Results. Crisp. 1999

2. John et.al. Manpower Planning, NewYork, John Wiley, 1983.

3. Stewart, T . As Quoted in Ashmita N.Rao . The Human Resource Profession: Insurrection or Resurrection, HRM Review, May 2004.

4. Yoder D. Personnel Management and Industrial Relations, New York, Prentice Hall, 1984.

27

Forecasting Employment
A European Approach

*Ajit R. Thete**
*S.M. Nilangekar***

PREAMBLE

Education and labour market policy are dependent on some notion about the future i.e. on possible future developments and structural changes in employment and qualification requirements. Forecasts of this kind may be of a quantitative, or of a qualitative nature. The determination of future "innovative" qualification and skill contents, on the other hand, is an area covered by occupation related pedagogic and curricular research. An alternative to quantitative forecasting is scenarios, which are based on past trends and (more or less subjective) expert estimates concerning different socio-economic developments.

The European Commission (1994) conducted the forecasts for the national, regional, local and firm level in the context of, 'Vocational training and its coordination with the needs of enterprises and individuals". The following questions were raised during forecasting:

* **Assistant Director(T), Directorate of Tech. Education, Regional Office, Aurangabad (M.S.)**

** **Assistant Secretary, Maharashtra State Board of T.E., Regional Office, Aurangabad (M.S.)**

- How these needs could be considered?
- How changes of demand could be identified and how foreseeable changes could be anticipated? And
- On which level."?

"As a tendency, there are indications that improved demand forecast are required and hence changes have to be anticipated better, concerning the national, regional, local and enterprise level."

The Delphi technique and the method and the procedures used for forecasting the manpower have been discussed in this chapter.

DELPHI TECHNIQUE IN FORECASTING AND ITS OUTCOME

Taking account of the uncertainties in all spheres of social and economic life, manpower and labour market scenarios indicates the increase in the awareness of the complex relationships. A Delphi technique has been adopted in forecasting the manpower as stated below:

- A "Delphi-enquiry" among European experts on policy need for research, study and experimentation in European education and training, carried out by SCIENTER (1996) on behalf of the European Commission/DG XXII;
- An examination of economic, social and cultural trends in Europe, carried out by de Jouvenel (1996) on behalf of the European Commission/DG V;
- A Delphi-enquiry on the future of adult education in 14 European countries, carried out by Leirman (1996);
- Infratest on behalf of the German Federal Ministry is currently conducting a Delphi-enquiry among mostly national experts concerning long-term trends in education and training in Germany and their implications for policy for Education, Science, Research and Technology. (1997/98).

The Delphi-enquiry addressed to around 100 experts and considering some 100 trends (e.g. flexibilisation, ageing, mobility, technology, employment structures, regional developments, etc.) The experts were asked for written statements on three "environments" relevant to education and training and considering the trends in the:

- Economic and technological environment;
- Employment environment;
- Training and knowledge environment.

As a result of the expert rating, several common trends have been identified:

- Increasing individual responsibility for training;
- Growing importance of specialization;
- Continued importance of schools for lower social groups;
- A strengthening of the relation between education and other knowledge institutions;
- Growing importance of tax relief for training.

The analysis of first round in the enquiry aimed at providing an empirically reliable and theoretically founded reduction in the variety of trends considered. In a second round, some more specific trends—linked to several factors of influence—were presented to the experts once again. Their statements served as a basis for the construction of four scenarios. These were the result of a matrix combining the items "employability life-cycle work" and "dependence of the economy on knowledge interaction structure" with each other.

Based on these scenarios, a range of strategies were formulated which are supposed to have a high degree of certainty:

- Increasing individual responsibility for training;
- Increasing importance of training courses organized by industrial branches;
- Growing division of responsibility; functionally oriented training for the industry;

Decreasing investment of industry in lower educated people.

METHODS AND PROCEDURES

The forecasts in European countries are based on the "Manpower Requirement Approach" (MRA) and the "Social Demand Approach" (SDA), which both have a long history and need not be described here in detail.

The *Manpower Requirement Approach* calculates the future demand for manpower, i.e. the future number of jobs available, by different job characteristics (mainly by industrial sectors, occupations or work activities, levels and subjects of qualification).

The basis of the MRA is a macro-economic or econometric forecast of future economic growth, productivity and other economic factors, from which future employment in the whole economy and by sectors is derived. In general, these macro-economic forecasts include the estimation of a more or less large number or relations within the economy and their change due to expected developments of certain parameters. In most cases, alternative forecasts are being made in order to illustrate the scope of expected employment changes.

In further steps or modules, the macro-economic and sectoral forecasts are broken down by job characteristics. Since the relationships between the numerous economic parameters and job characteristics are too complex and, in addition, require a huge quantity of empirical data not available in most countries, most forecasts of the job characteristics apply a *structural approach* in which employment figures by sectors are further broken down by occupations, qualifications and subjects. These specific structures are extrapolated by trend regressions.

Figure 27.1 illustrates the traditional procedure of manpower requirement forecasting.

The *replacement demand* is calculated by using flows of workers out of employment, (e.g. retirement, deaths, migration, etc.), usually differentiated by qualifications, occupations, age, sex, etc. It is assumed that persons with similar characteristics will fill the vacant jobs. Thus, the number of persons remaining in employment during the whole projection period represents the *residual stack.*

For estimating the *recruitment demand*, i.e. the number of jobs available for future graduates, and thus for estimating their employment prospects, the replacement demand and the net change in total demand are added up.

Supply projections normally use the *Social Demand Approach* and estimate the future flows of persons through education and training and their entry into the labour market. By adding up all new entrants during the projection period, the total *new supply* of persons (by qualification, etc.) is determined as shown in figure 27.2.

The new supply and residual stock add up to the total supply of manpower in the projection year. Structure *labour-market balances* compare the total number of available jobs (MRA) with the total supply (SDA).

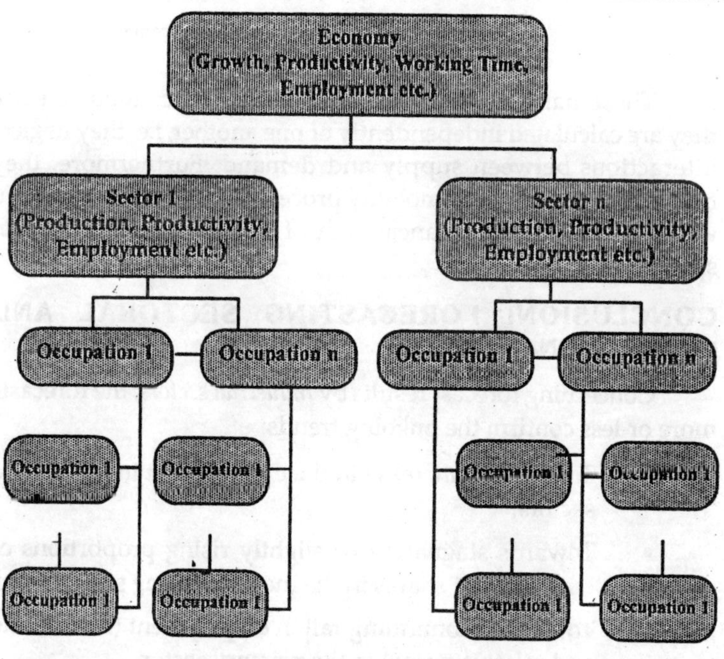

Fig. 27.1: Procedure of Traditional Manpower Requirement Approach

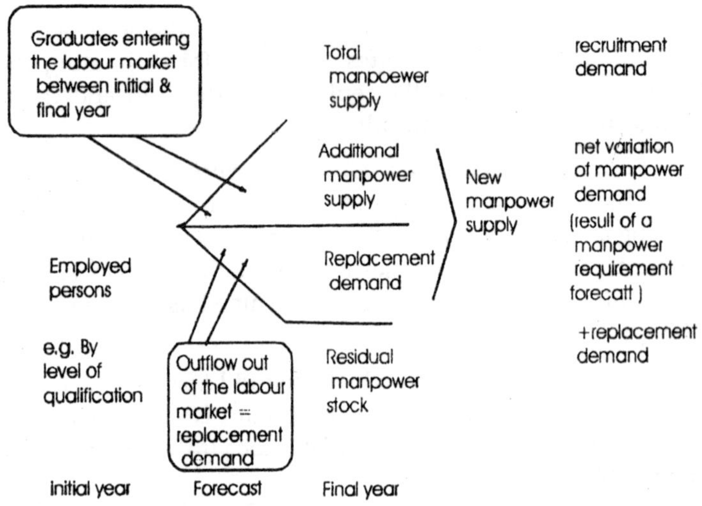

Fig. 27.2: Forecasting Manpower Requirement

Those balances, however, are interpreted cautiously since they are calculated independently of one another, i.e. they neglect interactions between supply and demand. Furthermore, they neglect substitution and mobility processes on the labour market, which may lead to a balancing out of surpluses or shortages in specific job areas.

CONCLUSION: FORECASTING SECTORAL AND OCCUPATIONAL CHANGE

Concerning forecast results by *industrial sectors,* the forecasts more or less confirm the ongoing trends:

- Towards an increase in the employment in the service sectors;
- Towards stagnating or slightly rising proportions of employment shares in the manufacturing sectors; and
- Towards a continuing fall in employment (in absolute and relative terms) in the primary sector.

Thus they widely confirm the theory of Fourastie and the hypotheses of a post-industrial society discussed above.

Available evidence on future demand trends for the *occupational structure of jobs* indicate a significant growth in professional and technical occupations and in administrative and managerial occupations.

The basis of the MRA is a macro-economic or econometric forecast of future economic growth, productivity and other economic factors, from which future employment in the whole economy and by sectors is derived. In general, these macro-economic forecasts include the estimation of a more or less large number or relations within the economy and their change due to expected developments of certain parameters. In most cases, alternative forecasts are being made in order to illustrate the scope of expected employment changes.

REFERENCES

1. Training for the Changing Society: European Study (1998), Germany.
2. Education and Employment in Developed Countries—Dr.A.R.Thete (2000), The Article Published for Search Conference (CDC-MSBTE, Mumbai).

28

Catch Them Young

New Paradigms of Manpower Planning

Sk. Azmal Hussain[*]
Tejovati S Prabhu[**]

ABSTRACT

Planning for human resource is more important than planning for any other resource. Organizations should concentrate not only on quality but also on quality when they are moving from current manpower position to required manpower. A manpower plan gives an overall picture for identification of surplus or shortage of personnel. Thinking of it, in terms of demand and supply, could do manpower planning. External and internal environmental changes create an imbalance that leads to wide variation between the availability of technically trained manpower and actual demand. Academicians, industrialists, and bureaucrats together have to develop manpower for the current requirements. Usually higher knowledge skills and ability are required for operating and maintain new technology and for participating in innovative process. Today organizations are expecting multi skilled and qualitative manpower to meet their organizational goals. This chapter is focusing supply of technical manpower concentrating on pre-recruitment education and training.

* **MBA, LLB, Lecturer, Vathsalya College of Business Management, Bhongir.**

** **Senior Lecturer, Department of Commerce, MK Amin Arts & Science College, Padra, Baroda, Gujarat.**

TECHNICAL MANPOWER PLANNING

Introduction

Manpower Planning is a vital sub activity of employment function. In fact employment process begins with manpower planning. But it never ends with this function. It pervades through number of activities after the process of manpower planning. Those activities include searching for prospective human resource, attracting them to the work in organization, and finding out their suitability to the job and organizational requirements and finally taking steps to absorb those human resources as organs of the company.

Importance of MPP

The government undertakings have too many employees than they need. Absence of succession planning has resulted in a situation where many organizations function without chief executives.

Manpower planning enables an enterprise to cope with changes in competitive forces, markets, technology, products and governments regulations. Such changes generate changes in job content, skill demand and number and type of personnel. Shortage of people may be noticed in some areas while surplus is the other areas may occur.

Jobs are becoming highly intellectual and incumbents are getting vastly professionalised.

Determining Manpower Requirements

Manpower requirements are determined by comparing the supply against the predicted demand and looking for manpower requirements in future.

Manpower planning is by thinking of it, it terms of demand and supply. Demand can be forecast from the corporate plans of the organization. Supply can be forecast by working out the stock of manpower currently employed, calculating the shortfalls and surplus, if shortage are anticipated, companies have a varicty of options to consider:

1. Better training;
2. Better retention of staff;
3. Better relations with local schools and colleges;
4. More flexible use of labour;
5. A positive attitude towards minority and ethnic groups.

Demand for the skilled manpower increases due to expansion, diversification and technological changes.

Non-availability of suitable manpower results in postponement of or delays in executing new projects and expansions of programmes which eventually leads to inefficiency and lower profitability.

A manpower plan could give an overall picture at corporate level an identification of surplus and shortage of personnel. If there is underutilisation through over manning, there will be unnecessary high labour cost and low profit margins.

Factors Affecting MPP

Manpower planning is affected by several considerations. Type and strategy of organization, organizational growth cycles and planning, environmental uncertainties, time horizons, type and quality of forecasting information, nature of jobs filled. Government policies, Business environment, level of technology, HR policy and trade unions.

Approach to MPP

Many executives are convinced that companies productivities can be increased through better management of employee performance. To strengthen managerial practices companies are modifying their planning and appraisal systems, making them simpler and easier to overcome difficulties experienced in the past.

Experiments to improve the quality of work life have pointed towards a flexible job design, flexible working hours, flexible benefits and compensation, more open communication and other innovations.

CURRENT POSITION

Organizations need to learn to forecast HR needs more effectively. In many countries including India there are wide variations between availability of technical manpower and actual demand for such personnel. Despite the high level of their development efforts, the developed countries still have critical manpower shortages. Their may be severe shortage of technicians and engineers on one hand, their may be a surplus of certain types and levels of personnel on other hand.

IN INDIA

While planning manpower organizations focuses both on quantitative and qualitative aspects it is said that engineers of today find it difficult to handle a machine, they are also not equipped to tackle human problems and the knowledge of about to tackle this country. Many engineering graduates from reputed institutions despite their expert theoretical grounding, are inept at handling shop floor conditions in the Indian scenario. This is because of, lack of high emphasis places upon practical apprenticeship courses in their curricula. These aspects can be analysed by our academicians and technocrats and government for developing appropriate curricula to meet the present needs.

A successful company can differ from an unsuccessful company from the aspect of, quality of its manpower.

It is necessary to translate the objectives of the company into the personnel activities, which make them achieveable. In addition, the companies plans are failing due to not having the right people in the right place at the right time is also obviated.

Impact of Technology

Advances in technology have offered organizations new opportunities to enhance and streamline their processes.

Changes in technology results in a change in occupational and skill profile of manpower.

Introduction of new technology can affect the working life of workers responsibilities, skill requirements, job content, and workload.

EDUCATION SYSTEM

Usually higher knowledge, skills and ability are required for operating and maintaining new technology. The present education system of our country is inadequate to match the technological needs, the syllabus is outdated, and teachers are not fully competent and lack of infrastructure facilities. So the companies, to add these skills to their employees focusing more on training and development after recruitment process is over.

Technical Education

Currently India has 300 universities including deemed universities and so many institutions. Technical people are architects of society. Technical education is vital part of higher education in the country. Much of the development in defence, manufacturing and information technology sectors directly depends upon quality of manpower generated by these institutions.

There are a number of academic, engineering and research centers that offer the education across India. Over four lakh students opt for engineering education annually. Success is not determined by how we are doing compared to others. But we are doing compared with what we are capable of doing.

Emphasis should be placed on quality of education and in Research and Development to meet the challenges presented by globalization and advancement of science and technology. Human development will be vital in order to harness science and technology for sustainable development. We should not forget the preparation of human resources to meet the challenges of the future. Because development in the future will be knowledge intensive and brain intensive.

The most important factor is the mind of human resource, how to invest in these minds in terms of higher education learning and how to develop the industry, which is brain intensive.

Technical education helps, transform students into professionals, capable of handling specialized jobs. In today's world technological application pervade the day to day life of human beings this has resulted in the rise in demand for technically qualified professionals so with an intent to cater these professionals to the society but with one major difference i.e., professionals with human touch and social logical concern.

Today educational institutions should be establishing with a motto to grow into a new world of excellence in technical education in research to promote expertise in engineering and with an aim to equip the students the understanding culture, values and appreciate creativity with human and inquisitive mind.

The institutes have to adopt the different approach in designing the curriculum that should be designed by the experts in academic, industry and government

Only a few premier institutes have been producing the qualitative graduates. The well qualified experienced and component teachers are seen in a few institutions. Their scope is limited.

The big challenge is: What about the other institutions?

Time has come. The experts from ACADEMIC, INDUSTRY AND GOVERNMENT as a part of social responsibility, have to concentrate much on *Pre-recruitment training, i.e., on education institutions* to produce qualitative and effective graduates to meet the ever growing organizational requirements. Otherwise, we will be responsible for unemployment, frustration and further consequences.

REFERENCES

1. P. Subba Rao (2004). *"Essentials of Human Resource Management and Industrial Relations"*.
2. Biswajeet Pattanayak (2002) *"Human Resource Management"*. PHI Publications.
3. *"The Hindu"*, Classifieds August 1st, 2004.

29

Manpower Planning

Going Western or Staying Indian?

*Anitha Kumar**

*P. Murali Krishna***

In a run for fancy and new concepts, the HR professionals and academicians are ignoring the basic concepts of HR, like Human Resource Planning, which is like backbone to HR area. Of late, are we not restricting HR Planning as a routine task of a personnel manager and mere teaching material for management students in their junior classes? Basically without HR Planning all our efforts of introducing newer concepts that we draw from either Western culture or Japanese, do not sustain for long, which we know through experience. This discussion further leads to the question of drawing various HR concepts from other countries time and again. We mainly have two management styles, Western and Japanese.

Though we all agree that the Japanese management style is more successful and effective in the long run, a fact which is vouched by even Western management Gurus, are we not

* **Associate Professor, Sri Krishnadevaraya Institute of Management, S K University, Anantapur (AP).**

** **Associate Professor, Sri Krishnadevaraya Institute of Management, S.K. University, Anantapur (A.P).**

following most of Western management practices? This leads to another important question, which is being emphasised by most of the authors of management—Do we have a management style of our own? As we Indians always tend to do, we are actually mixing up these two styles. But these two management styles are poles apart. They are two extremes. Then how possibly can we mix these two practices and be successful? The management concepts are nothing but outcome of the social, cultural practices of that particular society. The economic, social and cultural background of these two societies largely varies. Japanese society is mostly tradition bound. They stick to tested methods of self-discipline, respecting seniors, group work, quality consciousness etc., whereas the Western society has altogether different set of social values. For them personal growth, excellence, advancement, dynamism are more important. If we take human resource management practices alone, Western management style in case of human resource is largely an impersonal and materialistic one. In spite of claiming the contrary, human resource by Western managers is still treated as a commodity. Whereas, Japanese managers does everything for human resource with an objective of developing the individual.

Though the ultimate objective here is also profit, they are fulfilling this along with a twin objective of developing human resource. Now, let us think for a while, as to which of these two styles are we nearer? In India, like in most of the Asian countries, including Japan, family orientation and influence of family institution stretches to all professions and all walks of our life. In the institution of family, father and mother always strive for well being of their children without any heed to their own benefits. And in long run, even if the parents do not expect any thing in return, the children always take care of them. Whereas in Western culture, the institution of family was never as strong, nor is it now. From above discussion, is it not quite evident that we are closer towards Japanese management practices, than Western? But, probably, for the reason of more transit between Western and Indian business managers, more business transactions, cropping up of more US multinationals, we tend to adopt most of Western practices with fair modifications than Japanese. Let us discuss a little as to how effective are the concepts that we have drawn from these two management styles which are relevant to manpower planning. This can be better explained with the help of an example. Western managers depend upon performance of employees for promotions. They are less dependent on experience. In fact, the factor of experience and age are more or less irrelevant there. Can that practice be adopted by Indian managers and make manpower plans accordingly? As we couldn't, we have a system of 'merit cum experience'. In other words, we neither can completely adopt Western practices nor are sincere enough in adopting the Japanese practices which require utmost loyalty, sincerity and hard work. As such, wouldn't it be better, if we develop an exclusive Indian management practice? To continue with the previous example, in case of career advancement, we can give more weight to experience as our values and culture dictate. But this can be possible only if those with experience are capable and suitable for the given job. As such, in India, through manpower Planning, we can plan for organizational requirements in such a way, that not only quantity, but also quality is stressed. Suitability of a person should not only be constrained to the present job, but also for succession of jobs that he is likely to hold. As we can see, in Indian organizations, the subordinates treat younger boss with hostile attitude. Whereas elderly person is looked upon and is being accepted as boss. As such, in India, human resource planning has to be done keeping in view, the values, culture and ethics of our country. It is time when we come out of the shackles of the two most important management styles in the world and have an independent practice. Especially, in the areas like human resource planning, extra care and caution has to prevail as it is the foundation, on which lays the entire organizational human resource structure. We can never adopt the practices of adhoc planning successfully in our context. As such, it is time to evolve an Indian management style, which caters to the needs of people, respect their values and culture and impart ultimate success to the organization.

30

Employment Scenario in Punjab

Shaheed Ahmed[*]
M C Sharma[**]

OBJECTIVE

In the northern part of India, the state Punjab is most successive in the field of Agriculture as well as Industry. Even during the spell of 15 years of terrorism from 1982 to 1995, the industrial products in Punjab has never seems to be underestimated. The main objective of study is to evolve the employment scenario in Punjab state. Total male and total female ratio among total employment. Sector wise bifurcation of male and female employment for six successive years starting from 1997 to 2002. Also for the same period total technical manpower employment pattern and then study of four major branches of Engineering i.e. CIVIL, MECHANICAL ELECTRICAL, and ELECTRONICS.

OBSERVATION

In Central govt. sector there were only 23 establishments in the year 1997 and increased to 25 in the year 2002, but State govt

* **Project Officer, Nodal Centre NTMIS, Board of Apprenticeship Training(N.R.), Kanpur.**

** **COCP, Nodal Centre NTMIS, Board of Apprenticeship Training (N.R.), Kanpur.**

sector there were only 69 establishments covered in 1997 while in year 2002 total establishments covered were 91. In Private sector 33 per cent increase in establishment covered in Punjab with total 235 in 1997 to 312 in 2002. Line graph also indicates successive growth in industries in Punjab. With total 327 in 1997 to 428 in 2002.

	Central	State	Private	Total
1997	23	69	235	327
1998	23	75	238	336
1999	25	81	241	347
2000	24	81	248	353
2001	24	85	259	368
2002	25	91	312	428

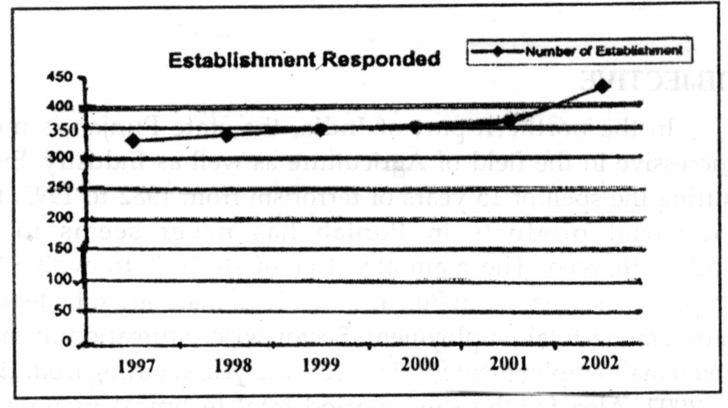

Year	Central	State	Private
1997	38410	73955	116039
1998	38119	81881	113218
1999	28534	81737	111681
2000	40032	83369	111804
2001	38539	84045	114698
2002	26399	85291	126716
Average	35005.5	81713	115692.7

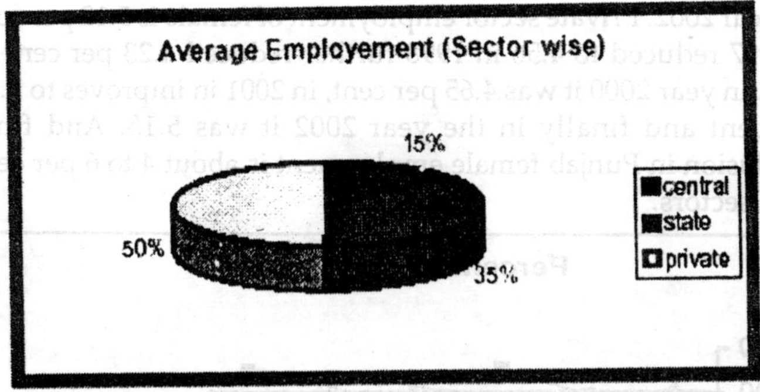

Average employment in Punjab (sector wise) evolved 15 per cent in Central govt. with 35000, 35 per cent in State govt. and Private sector employed 50 per cent of total employment while total employment through contractor was not included into the figure. Although the employment shown in table is for male only but the average percentage of employment with female is also 15 per cent, 35 per cent and 50 per cent.

	Central		% of Fem	State		% of Fem	Private		% of Fem
	Male	Female		Male	Female		Male	Female	
1997	38410	1765	4.39	73955	3257	4.22	116039	6263	5.12
1998	38119	1796	4.50	81881	4242	4.93	113218	5413	4.56
1999	28534	1456	4.85	81737	4796	5.54	111681	4929	4.23
2000	40032	2150	5.10	83369	4528	5.15	111804	5453	4.65
2001	38539	1926	5.00	84045	4756	5.36	114698	6185	5.12
2002	26399	1353	4.88	85291	4950	5.49	126716	6525	5.15

The table above indicates Male and female employment scenario in Central, State and Private sector in Punjab. There were 1765 female employed in 1997 in Central govt sector which was only 4.39 per cent of total employment, it gradually increased to 4.50 per cent, 4,85 per cent and 5.10 per cent in the successive years 1998, 1999, 2000 respectively and reduced to 5.00 per cent in 2001 and 4.88 per cent in the year 2002. In State govt. sector percentage of female employees were 4.22 in the year 1997, 4.93 in year 1998, 5.54 in 1999, 5.15 per cent in 2000, 5.36 in 2001 and 5.49 per cent in the year 2002. Private sector employment of female is 5.12 per cent in 1997 reduced to 4.56 in 1998 further reduced 4.23 per cent in 1999. In year 2000 it was 4.65 per cent, in 2001 in improves to 5.12 per cent and finally in the year 2002 it was 5.15. And final conclusion in Punjab female employment is about 4 to 6 per cent in all sectors.

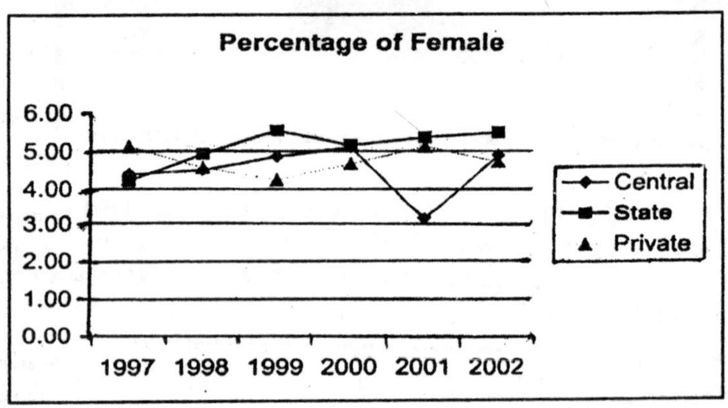

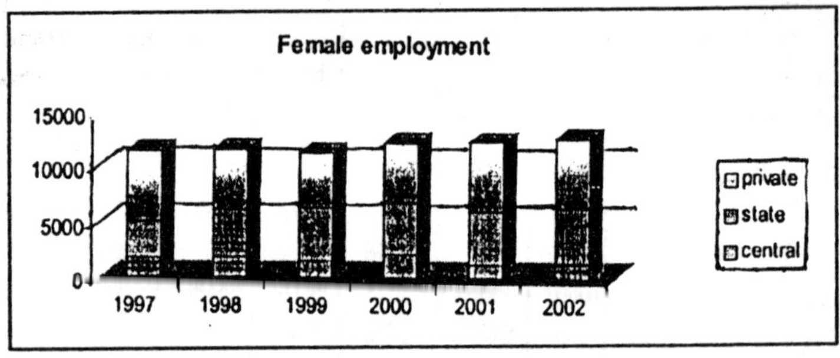

TOTAL ENGINEERS EMPLOYED

Year	Central	State	Private	Total engineers employed
1997	3823	7037	6266	17126
1998	3952	7200	6395	17547
1999	3284	6948	6548	16780
2000	4231	7381	6294	17906
2001	6657	7552	6676	20885
2002	6522	7507	7100	21129

The table shows Sector wise employment of engineers in last six years starting from 1997 to 2002, Total number of engineers employed in Central sector were 3823 in 1997 which increased to 3952 in 1998 and a little decrease in 1999 to 3284 while again increased to 4231 in 2000, and rises sharply to 6657 in 2001 and 6522 in 2002, total number of engineers (Including Diploma and degree engineers) in year 1997 were 17126, with regular increase in 1998 to 2002 it reached to 21129 in all the sectors.

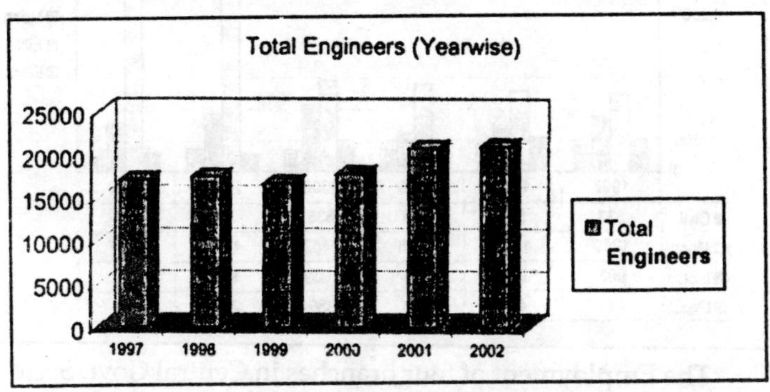

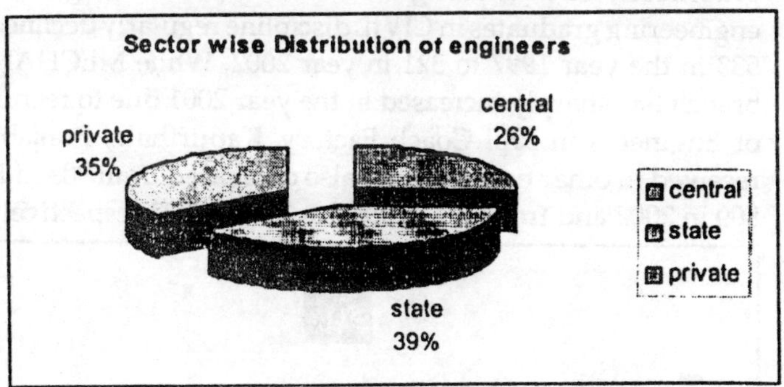

Total Average percentage of engineers during last six years starting from 1997 to 2002 , it is very clear that Central sector employed 26 per cent of engineers in the State and Private sector employed only 35 per cent of engineers, while State sector employed 39 per cent of total engineers employed in the state.

ANALYSIS OF FOUR ENGINEERING BRANCHES I.E. CIVIL, MECHANICAL, ELECTRICAL, AND ELECTRONICS

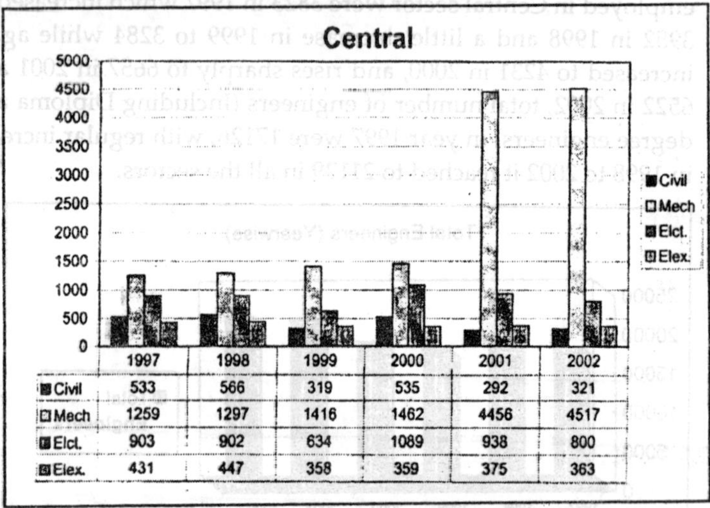

	1997	1998	1999	2000	2001	2002
Civil	533	566	319	535	292	321
Mech	1259	1297	1416	1462	4456	4517
Elct.	903	902	634	1089	938	800
Elex.	431	447	358	359	375	363

The Employment of four branches in Central Govt. Sector is graphically shown along with table. In Central govt. sector engineering graduates in CIVIL discipline regularly declined from 533 in the year 1997 to 321 in year 2002. While MECHANICAL branch has sharply increased in the year 2001 due to recruitment of Engineers in Rail Coach Factory, Kapurthala, Punjab. Data received in other two branches also decreased from 903 in 1997 to 800 in 2002 and from 431 in 1997 to 363 in 2002 respectively.

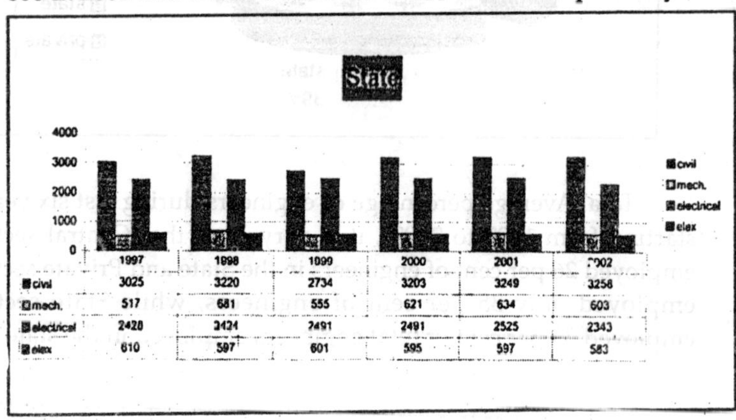

	1997	1998	1999	2000	2001	2002
civil	3025	3220	2734	3203	3249	3258
mech.	517	681	555	621	634	603
electrical	2428	3424	2491	2491	2525	2343
elex	610	597	601	595	597	583

In *State govt.* sector CIVIL and MECHANICAL engineering branch has a little gain in employment, while Electrical engineering reflected reducing from 2428 in 1997 to 2343 in 2002, and ELECTRONICS is also more or less lower side in comparison to 1997.

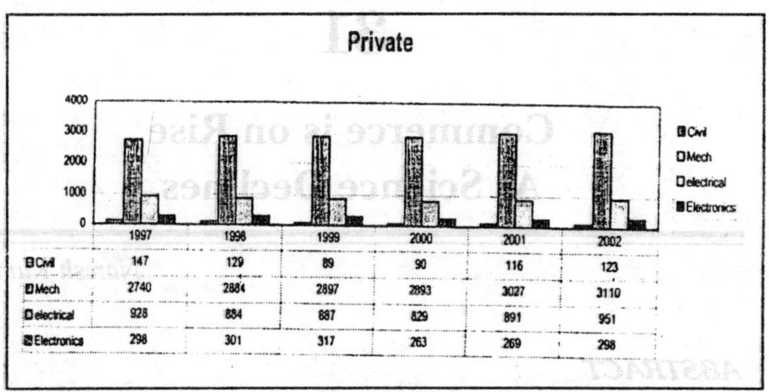

	1997	1998	1999	2000	2001	2002
Civil	147	129	89	90	116	123
Mech	2740	2884	2897	2893	3027	3110
electrical	928	884	887	829	891	951
Electronics	298	301	317	263	269	298

In *Private* sector for the same duration Civil engineering branch has reduced from 147 to 123 but employment in Mechanical Engineering branch has increased to 3110 in 2002 from 2740 in 1997, while employment in Electrical engineering decreased in 1998 to 2000 from 928 to 829, then increased to 891 and finally 951 in 2001 and 2002 respectively.

In the 21st century growth of employment of technical manpower from 1997 to 2002 in the state of Punjab is seen very nominal, hence accordingly technical manpower is not required to be produced, instead of opening new technical institutes for Degree/Diploma level in an unplanned manner alternatively country needs to generate more employment by establishment of new industries. Thus the growth of employment of Engineers in the Punjab state analyzed is very nominal during the period 1997 to 2002.

31

Commerce is on Rise As Science Declines

*Naresh Kumar**

ABSTRACT

Stock of scientific and technology (S&T) workforce plays an imperative role in the advancement of science and technology. Productivity of doctorates (Ph.Ds.) in the field of science and engineering/ technology influences the development in science and technical competitiveness. Shortage of outturn in S&T stock can slow down the process of growth and advancement and if shortage arises it may persist for a long time. As emerging trends of education and S&T manpower outturn are indicating a shift in doctorates, an analysis of these trends will be appropriate for reshaping the future of tomorrow and for taking the desired course of action. In the present study the emerging trends among five disciplines namely science, engineering/technology, arts, commerce and education in India are analysed with the help of mathematical models. The results show a shift towards commerce, arts and education and a decline of science doctorates whereas the engineering/ technology is reaching at the stage of saturation.

* **National Institute of Science Technology and Development Studies, K. S. Krishnan Marg, New Delhi-110012, (India), Email: nareshkumar@yahoo.com**

Key Words: S & T stock, competitive substitution, productivity of doctorates, flow of doctorates

INTRODUCTION

Scientific and technological (S&T) capabilities are a driving force of a country's growth and development. Basic research, industrial research and patents constitute major indicators of science and technological capabilities. Economist have three reasons to study science[1] viz. (i) science is a source of growth, (ii) scientific labour markets—and the human capital embodied in scientists and (iii) reward structure involved in science. Another reason may be to study science relates to the resource of science and technological (S&T) manpower stock because it offers fertile ground for economic growth and development. In this context higher education particularly, doctorates (Ph. Ds.) degrees awarded plays a significant role that provides a basis of technological growth and competitiveness. It is also important to analyse and study doctorates stock because new economic policies introduced in the early 1990, have rigorously affected the pattern of Indian higher education. This has opened the doors to a global marketplace for highly educated personnel. Besides, it has also influenced the flow of doctorates from one discipline to another. This kind of shift may create an imbalance in education in future since every year thousands of doctorates (Ph.Ds.) in different subjects and disciplines are coming out from academic institutions and contributing in growth and development on the national as well as international level. To overcome from this dilemma the suitable employment of the S&T personnel is required. This lies in the effectiveness of planning the manpower requirement in desired areas of S&T to create a base for scientific and industrial research. Therefore, present study focuses on the emerging trends in the field of higher education particularly analysis of doctorates. This may contribute for the formulation of S&T policy and the development of S &T plans and programmes for higher education.

Several changes have occurred in the current trends in higher education that need to be understood as a part of the picture. A long-standing concern for India has been its brain drain. In addition to brain drain, interdisciplinary shift of students is a matter of serious concern. This may affect the structure of scientific and technological (S&T) manpower because science and engineering as a discipline are posing a slow growth rate[2]. Further, the decline in Indian science[3] is now a central issue in higher education. Therefore, objective of the chapter is to analyse the relative shift of new doctorates in the field of science, engineering/technology, arts, commerce and education. This analysis may provide an important information about the future pattern of the emerging trends among the scientific and technology (S&T) manpower and particularly supply of new doctorates produced. The estimates for future trends of doctorates produced will be supportive in policy formulation and proper planning. Indian scientific and technology (S&T) manpower is ranked as the third largest in the world; for this reason India is taken as a case study. This also implies that India has the potential to emerge as a significant player in the global technology market (GTM). Correspondingly, the findings may provide a helpful map to navigate the emerging trends of new doctorates produced in different disciplines by analysing the interdisciplinary shift of the Ph. D. students.

METHODOLOGY AND ANALYSIS

The framework of the study is to analyse the interdisciplinary shift of doctorates among five different disciplines namely science, engineering/technology, arts, commerce and education. Data used in this study belongs to doctorate degrees awarded during the period 1974 to 1999[4]. The data pertaining to doctorate degrees awarded in science, engineering/technology, arts, commerce and education is listed in Table—31.1. To analyse data and for making future projections a mathematical model proposed by Fisher-Pry[5] is applied. The Fisher-Pry model is studied and applied extensively for the analysis of competition between competing technologies. The model may be expressed in the following mathematical form:

$$\log\left(\frac{f}{1-f}\right) = a + bt$$

where 'f' is the share of the new technology at any time 't', and a, b are model parameters. The model is based on the following assumptions:

- Technological advances can be considered as competitive substitutions of one method of satisfying a need for another.
- If a substitution has progressed as far as a few per cent, it will proceed to completion.
- The fractional rate of fractional substitution of new for old is proportional to the remaining amount of the old left to be substituted.

Accordingly, assuming that the competition between different commodities is alike competing technologies and behave in the similar manner technology substitution model is applied for the study. Substitution studies show that substitution tends to proceed with a constant percentage annual growth increment or exponentially in the early years, and to follow a logistic (S-shaped) curve.

Table—31.1 Doctorate degrees awarded in different disciplines

Year	Disciplines				
	Science	Eng./Tech.	Arts	Commerce	Education
1	2	3	4	5	6
1974	1327	95	1093	58	60
1975	1515	163	1258	55	77
1976	1516	136	1282	41	82
1977	1671	152	1364	70	98
1978	1901	168	1677	96	92
1979	2044	134	1811	87	105
1980	2261	176	1831	118	120
1981	2792	189	2246	105	173
1982	2846	190	2347	173	178
1983	2892	160	2422	175	191
1984	2890	192	2678	177	187
1985	2922	210	2754	185	239
1986	2838	194	2886	263	219
1987	2814	224	2987	272	227

(Contd...)

1	2	3	4	5	6
1988	2790	256	2830	235	211
1989	3044	238	3346	336	242
1990	2976	252	3242	301	205
1991	3002	260	3327	346	261
1992	3226	299	3489	409	254
1993	3386	323	3621	453	247
1994	3467	329	4039	515	308
1995	3657	337	3829	537	290
1996	3861	374	3957	612	295
1997	3498	298	4245	502	295
1998	3894	744	4058	541	342
1999	3896	696	4256	517	310

A non-linear least square method is applied to estimate the model parameters using SYSTAT package[6]. Model parameters are obtained by Quasi-Newton iterative technique for '*log(f/1-f) = a + b*t*' and fraction '*f*' separately and are listed in Table 31.2 and Table 31.3 respectively. Using values of the parameters for fractions, forecast have been made for the doctorate degrees awarded in different disciplines up to the year 2010 AD. Using the projected values of fractions '*f*', percentage of doctorate degrees awarded in all five disciplines are calculated and listed in Table 31.4.

Table—31.2 Parameter estimates for log function*

Discipline	Parameters		
	a	b	CRS
Science	0.070	-0.019	0.874
Eng./Tech.	-3.327	0.009	0.075
Arts	-0.359	0.008	0.452
Commerce	-4.090	0.058	0.887
Education	-3.624	0.013	0.513

*log function represents here: log(f/1-f) = a + b*t.*

Table—31.3 Parameter estimates for fraction 'f'

Discipline	Parameters		
	a	b	CRS
Science	0.070	-0.019	0.874
Eng./Tech.	-3.378	0.015	0.114
Arts	-0.359	0.008	0.450
Commerce	-3.975	0.052	0.875
Education	-3.600	0.012	0.477

Table—31.4 Projection of shares of different disciplines

(%)

Year	Science	Eng./Tech.	Arts	Commerce	Education
2000	39.30	04.70	46.20	07.00	03.40
2001	38.50	04.70	46.30	07.40	03.50
2002	38.00	04.80	46.50	07.80	03.60
2003	37.40	05.00	46.70	08.20	03.60
2004	36.90	05.00	46.80	08.60	03.70
2005	36.40	05.10	47.30	09.00	03.80
2006	36.00	05.20	47.50	09.40	03.90
2007	35.80	05.30	47.70	09.80	03.90
2008	35.30	05.40	47.90	10.30	04.00
2009	34.90	05.50	48.10	10.80	04.00
2010	33.50	05.50	48.30	11.30	04.10

RESULTS AND DISCUSSIONS

Scientific and technology (S&T) workforce is a major factor in economic and technical growth and have multi-dimensional effect on the economy. Technology, patents, and education are the important indicators of science and economic development. Stock of higher S &T personnel in general and doctorates in particular is one of the most significant indicators for overall development of a country's prosperity, advancement and technological competitiveness. University Grants Commission (UGC) is a nodal agency to coordinate the responsibility of regulating the standard of higher education. UGC has been monitoring the growth of higher education to ensure that the trained manpower with appropriate levels of professional training, skills and specializations will grow according to the needs of the society and technological development. India has more than 250 central and state universities, a major source of Ph.Ds. producing institutions. Apart from universities, Indian Institute of Technology (IITs), and different engineering colleges also awarded Ph.D. degrees. The higher education in terms of doctorates in science and engineering/ technology is one of the major performers of research and development (R&D). Therefore, Department of Science and Technology (DST) has also been trying to quantify S &T manpower and financial resources devoted to research and development (R&D) in science and technology by launching a national survey regularly.

Doctorate degrees awarded by Indian universities are more or less constant or declining in recent years. The total number of research degrees (doctorate) awarded decreased from 11,107 in 1998-99 to 11,067 in 1999-2000. Out of the total number awarded in 1999-2000, the faculty of arts had the highest number with 4231 doctorates, followed by the faculty of science with 3832 doctorates. These two faculties together accounted highest proportion of total number of doctoral degrees awarded[7]. Comparative proportional shares of doctorate degrees awarded in each discipline are (science, eng./tech., arts, commerce and education) shown in Figure 31.1. From the figure, it may be noticed that faculty of science shows a

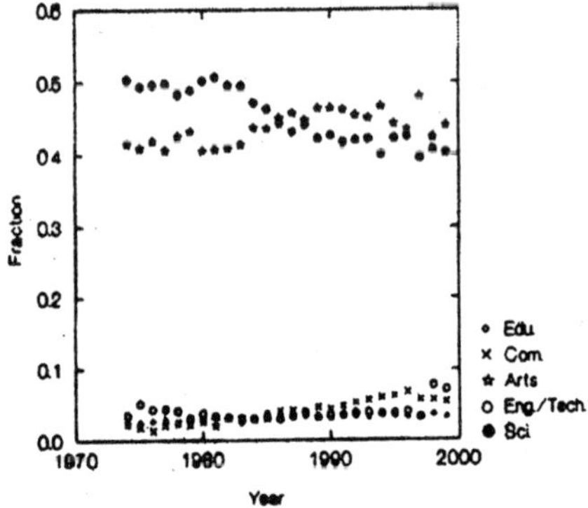

Fig. 31.1: Share of doctorate degrees awarded

relative declining trend among the studied disciplines. Faculties of education and arts exhibits marginal improvement and can increase in the future while steep sharpness in commerce indicates that major swing is expected towards commerce. Engineering/ technology on the other hand is reaching towards saturation level.

Results obtained in terms of logarithmic function for all five disciplines are given in Figures 2-6. From the graph presented in the Figure 31.2, for doctorate degrees awarded in science indicates substantial decline in science discipline whereas Figure 31.3, points out that engineering/technology may reach at saturation level in future. It may be noticed from Figures 4-6, that arts, commerce and education have probability for growth in future. Similarly, from Table—31.4, it may also be concluded that science is declining whereas commerce, arts and education are showing positive growth. However, science and engineering/technology is expected to reach up to 34 per cent and 6 per cent respectively by 2010 AD., whereas arts, commerce and education may capture 48 per cent, 11 per cent and 4 per cent respectively by 2010 AD.

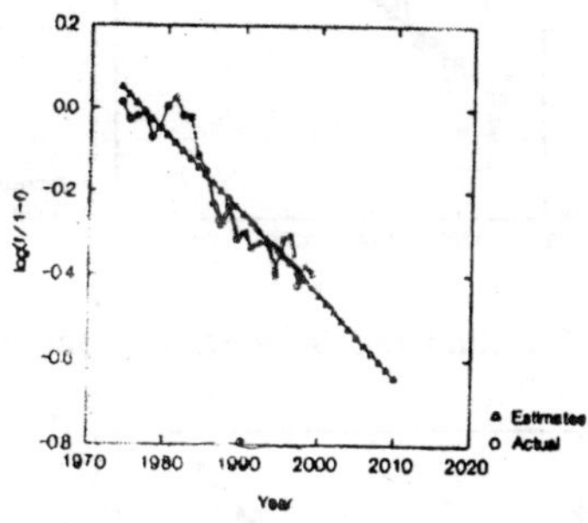

Fig. 31.2: Actual and estimates for science

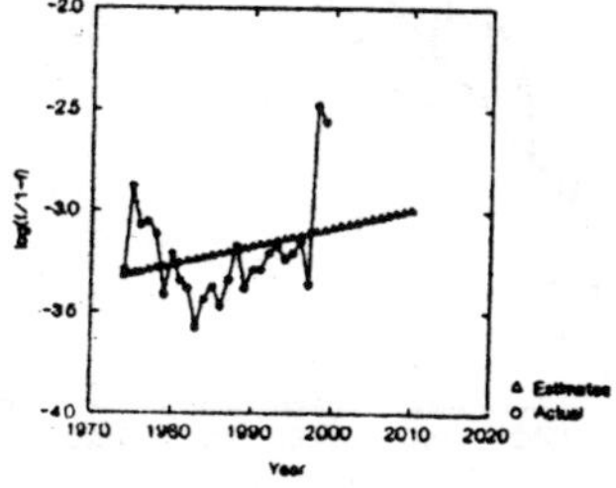

Fig. 31.3: Actual and estimates for enggineering/tech.

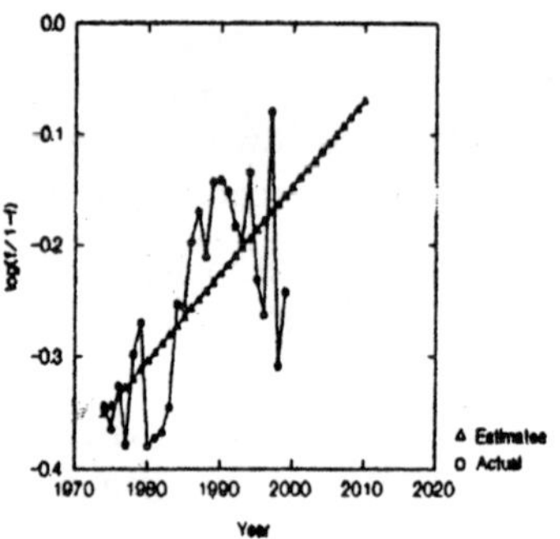

Fig. 31.4: Actual and estimates for arts

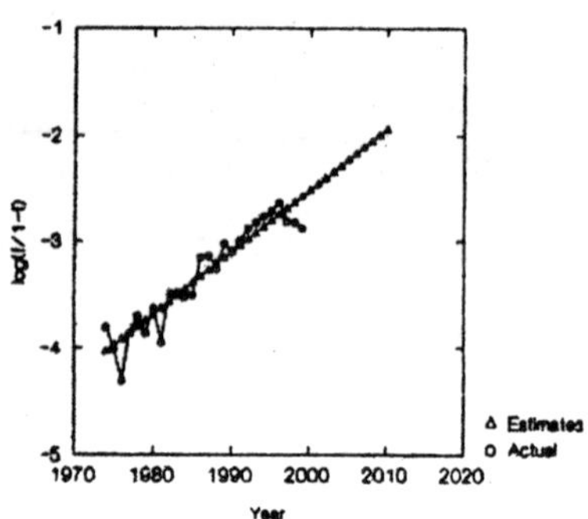

Fig. 31.5: Actual and estimates for commerce

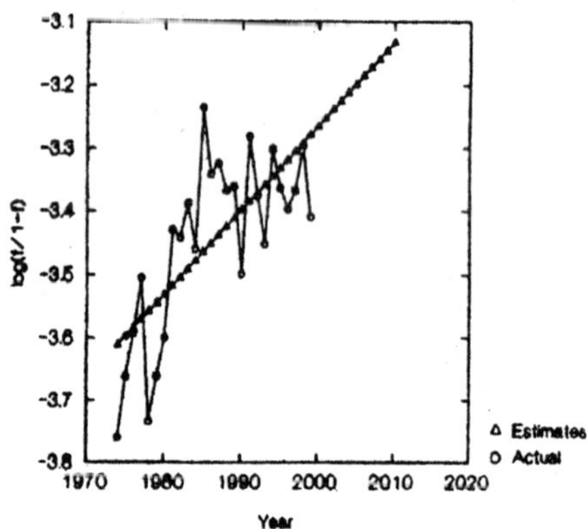

Fig. 31.6: Actual and estimates for education

CONCLUSION

The information regarding outturn of doctorates in India is an example of a change of attitude in researchers, where it may be noticed that science is not academic preference among the students. The analysis reveals that the major shift of new doctorates is towards commerce while arts and education also show growth trends. Engineering/technology gives the impression of saturation phase. This has also been pointed out by the AICTE[8] that advanced research has suffered and annual out-turn of Ph.Ds. in the field of science and engineering is declining. As a result the number of doctorates produced in science may decline in future which can slow down the process of contribution to fundamental knowledge. If this decline continues, it may persist for a long time and will create a gap in supply and demand of S&T professionals. The imbalance and shortage of supply of doctorates in science will generate a vicious phase in the field of research and development because technological developments depend to a large extent on scientific contributions. However, to these swings, annual production of new doctorates in science has remained more or less constant. It may because of that the students of science have job opportunities in other non-scientific fields. Further, increase in the number of doctorates in the field of commerce signifies that in the present scenario commerce has more job opportunities than in sciences.

The swing of doctorate students from science and engineering to humanities may be attributed to some degree to carrier opportunities and economic incentives. Decline of doctorates in the field of science shows, that science has less job opportunities in the changing economic perspective because economic incentive affects the higher education[9]. Lack of career choices is dwindling the linkage between students and scientific production. For this reason students are deviating from science and engineering/ technology and moving towards commerce and other disciplines due to variation of economic encouragements. The other reason may be the government policies of private investment in higher education. These new policies can affect the growth of graduates and doctorates in the field of science and engineering/technology due to fees structure. Therefore, it needs to make higher education in science and engineering/technology accessible to more people. To achieve these goals the emphasis must be given for improving public-private partnership. This may help to some extent to overcome from the problem of declining of doctorates in science and engineering disciplines. Moreover, research in science should not be encouraged not only to generate fundamental knowledge but also to support the technological developments. If these developments are ignored the shortage of doctorates in science and engineering/technology may emerge in future.

REFFRENCES

1. Stephan, P. E., The Economics of Science, *Journal of Economic Literature*, Vol. XXXIV, 1996, pp. 1199-1235.
2. Rai, L. P., Naresh Kumar, and S. Madan, Structural Changes in S&T Research in India, *Scientometrics*, Vol. 50, 2001, pp. 313-321.
3. Prathap, G., Indian Science Slows Down-III: While We Sleep, *Current Science*, Vol. 83, 2002, pp. 1056.
4. University Grants Commission, *Annual Reports from 1976 to 2001*, New Delhi.
5. Fisher, J. C., and R. H. Pry, A Simple Substitution Model for Technological Change, *Technological Forecasting and Social Change*, Vol. 2, 1971, pp. 75-78.
6. SYSTAT, SYSTAT Inc., Evanston, IL, 1988.
7. University Grants Commission, *Annual Report 2000-2001*, New Delhi, 2001.
8. Reshaping Post-graduate Education and Research in Engineering & Technology, *All India Council for Technical Education*, New Delhi, 1999.
9. Cebula, R. J., and J. Lopes, Determinants of Student Choice of Undergraduate Major Field, *American Educational Research Journal*, Vol. 19, 1982, pp. 303-312.

32

Principle of Budget and Manpower Planning

R. Ramesh Kumar[*]
M. Bala Kannan[**]

ABSTRACT

Budget and manpower planning is complicated by the fact that information on the availability of resources is often completely lacking, not only when projects are being formulated, but also during their implementation. As a result, planning is fraught with uncertainty and implementation must be continually adjusted as circumstances change. The central problem of budget and manpower planning is how to deal with this uncertainty. Careful formulation and monitoring are thus important in minimising this uncertainty—which also arises from the absolute and relative limitations in the availability of financial and manpower resources.

A number of principles are important in this respect:

- *We have to understand the relationship between capital and recurrent costs;*

* **Arasan Ganesan Polytechnic College, Post Box No. 27, Sivakasi - 626 123, Tamilnadu, Email: agpoly@eth.net**

** **Arasan Ganesan Polytechnic College, Post Box No. 27, Sivakasi - 626 123, Tamilnadu, Email: agpoly@eth.net**

- *We have to understand the relationship between staff and non-staff recurrent costs;*
- *We have to clearly identify those resources critical for success and seek consensus to ensure that they will be made available;*
- *If resources will not be made available, we have to modify the project accordingly;*
- *We have to understand the relationships between inputs;*
- *We have to include contingency allowances in budget projections.*

WHAT IS BUDGET?

Financial resources of every production concern are very limited and as such every management wants to keep the resources in check and use these for earning maximum profits. Budget is financial planning of resources for the future and as such a very useful instrument in preparing programmes of every business undertaking. It can be said as a financial statement, which is prepared for a definite period of time for the execution of some policies and programmes during that period. It concludes both the present and likely sources of income and expenditure during that period and if there are deficits how to meet these by raising additional resources of income. It is a device, which coordinates various departments of production and is an overall plan for the operation of business both in terms of sales, production and expenditure.

BUDGETING

Budget is concerned with forecasting, planning and predetermining financial resources. Budgeting is concerned with planning function of management. The art of budget making is called budgeting.

WHAT IS A GOOD BUDGET?

A good budget should help in stabilizing production and harmonizing both sales and production programmes, it should specify the units to be produced and should not be produced and should not be very rigid. It should have sufficient flexibility. It should control wastes and unwanted expenditure. Before finalization, it should analyze all such factors, which affect the business as a whole.

TYPES OF BUDGET

Today each and every enterprise tries to prepare a budget. Not only this but even individuals and families too prepare the budget. Budget can briefly be categorized as: (a) fixed budget (b) Variable budget and (c) functional budget. Functional budget can again be studied under different heads like:(i) Sales Budget; (ii) Production Budget; (iii) Labour Budget (v) Financial Budget (vi) Capital Expenditure Budget (vii) Administrative Budget; (viii) Material and Purchase Budget; and (ix) Master Budget.

LABOUR BUDGET

Every production work and manufacturing activity can be carried out with the help of labour, which is employed by a factory. A labour budget indicates how much manpower at different levels, i.e. unskilled, semiskilled and skilled labour will be needed for achieving production targets. It will also indicate whether the required labour is an available or will have to be employed and if so to which extent. It will also show whether it is better to employ the labour by making recruitments or getting the work done through contractors. For this a good budget will use work-study method for calculating standard time for each operation, i.e. the operations involved and number of workmen needed for each department and for the factory as a whole.

MANPOWER PLANNING—DEFINED

It is wish and desire of every industrial undertaking that available manpower should be properly utilized so that there is no under utilization of available material and manual resources. Needless to say that where there is proper manpower utilization, there will be more production at lower cost and proper person shall be put on right type of job. This will obviously reduce idle hours of work and volume of work every worker is supposed to do and is actually doing on scientific lines can be assessed to some extent. When everyone will have equal workload, there will be no grudges and misunderstandings but spirit of cooperation among the workers will increase. There will be better understanding of each other. In brief, it can be said that manpower planning means scientific process of allocating the right quantity of work for right type of person. Without proper manpower planning estimates of human resources needed for accomplishing a job are reduced to get work.

GUIDELINES FOR MANPOWER PLANNING

It is thus by now amply clear that manpower planning is not an easy task. It is both time and energy consuming task and as such it is very essential that some guidelines should be followed and help of the data already available should be taken. It should be seen that time is not washed in re-collecting the already collected data. Some of the important facts, which can be collected from the available records and can also provide good guidelines for future planning, are briefly discussed below:

Form the available records, it can be found out whether available machinery has in the past been fully utilized of it has been under-utilized and of so to what extent and why for. This will help in finding out the percentage of idle time of the machines in a particular department and in the factory as a whole. The records also show the past record of the workers. It is expected of an old experienced worker to reach 85 per cent efficiency standard and if a new worker in the beginning reaches 60 per cent efficiency that can be tolerable. It can be illustrated from the example given below. In this it has been presumed that a worker in a week of 6 days works 8 hours in a day. Machine efficiency is 90 per cent and worker efficiency is 80 per cent. Thus in a year the actual working hours shall as under;

Total days in a year	365
Sundays	(-) 52

MAN POWER PLANNING

Other holidays (like casual leave, medical leave, earned leave)	(-) 35
Balance of working days	278

Total available working hours:

$$278 \text{ days} \times \frac{8}{\text{Hours Per day}} \times \frac{90}{100 \text{ (Machine efficiency)}} \times \frac{80}{100 \text{ (Workers efficiency)}} =$$

$$= 278 \times 8 \times \frac{9}{10} \times \frac{8}{10} = 1601.28 \text{ Hours}$$

This in a year, machine and operator efficiency is 1601.28 hours and the rest of the time is wasted either because of inefficiency of the workers or that of the machine.

TECHNIQUES OF MANPOWER PLANNING

Two main techniques of manpower planning are: (a) work measurement; and (b) work sampling. By work measurement, we mean measuring the time required to do each detailed element of an industrial operation to obtain standard time required to complete the job and also to ascertain how many machines can an operator run. In this method, an analysis of the job, as a whole, is done and thus total output is obtained. For calculating manpower requirement total output is divided with the standard time needed to complete the job. Since this method is very simple, therefore, it is very much in use.

The other method is work sampling method which is also called activity sampling, It is based on being increasingly increasingly felt, therefore, some useful in repetitive operations. This theory is based on the principle that the percentage of observations recorded in an operation is a reliable estimate of the percentage of the time needed or taken in the operation in that state provided sufficient numbers of observations are taken at random. As the number of sample increases with that the percentage of error comes down.

CONCLUSION

The process by which management determines how the organization should move from its current manpower position to its desired manpower position is the basis of manpower planning through manpower, management strikes to have the right number and right kind of people at the right place, at right time, doing things which result both in the organization and the individual receiving maximum long run benefits. Thus he has also said that the sole aim of manpower planning is two-fold, i.e. the manpower which an industrial establishment has and it should have. Secondly, it aims at finding out right type of work for right type of persons at the right time.

Thus it can be said that manpower planning helps in future assessing of manpower needs of an industrial establishment including internal and external economies taking into consideration social and nature of work and quality and quantity of its production.

33

Role of Government, Society, Institutions and Industries in Empowerment of Women to Facilitate Their Participation and Involvement in Science and Technical Areas

H. R. Shah[*]

Nimish Shah[**]

Ankita Dave[***]

ABSTRACT

The beginning of the third millennium has already evidenced unprecedented changes in the domain of Science and Technology. While the gender gap has narrowed, the full gender equality in engineering careers still seems elusive with women being remarkably absent from

* **Chemical Engineering Department, Institute of Diploma Studies, Nirma University of Science & Technology, Gandhinagar- Sarkhej Highway, P.O. Chandlodia, Ahmedabad - 382, E-mail: hod_chemical@nids.edu**

** **Chemical Engineering Department, Institute of Diploma Studies, Nirma University of Science & Technology, Gandhinagar- Sarkhej Highway, P.O. Chandlodia, Ahmedabad - 382, E-mail: nimish_nirma@yahoo.com**

*** **Chemical Engineering Department, Institute of Diploma Studies, Nirma University of Science & Technology, Gandhinagar- Sarkhej Highway, P.O. Chandlodia, Ahmedabad - 382, E-mail: anmolb4u@hotmail.com**

senior positions. This chapter is a broad-brush view of Engineering education and the complexities which women Engineers have encountered in their work environment in the past and, thus affecting their career advancement. The present gender barriers are highlighted and the future is looked at with a hope that women Engineers shall be viewed as the fuel that powers the internal engines of socio-economic growth and development in Engineering.

Key Words: gender inequity, women engineers, under-representation, empowerment, technical workforce, paternalism, discrimination

INTRODUCTION

In its report to the UN Commission on Science and Technology for Development in 1995, the Gender Working Group called attention to *gender inequity worldwide in education and careers in science and technology*. It noted that there are serious obstacles to girls' and women's participation in scientific and technical education and careers, and there are relatively few women in science and technology decision-making bodies and advisory boards. Additionally it identified the gender specific nature of technical change, in that technical change aimed at benefiting people in rural areas in developing countries appears to have benefited men more than women. In 2001, the Commission noted that gender is a cross-cutting issue of "Technology development and capacity-building for competitiveness in a digital society", its current programme of work[1].

Woman is often described as the better half of man. But the actual condition of women in the world does not match with this description. By and large across the world, women have not achieved equality with men.

- Nearly 70 per cent of the world's 1.4 billion poor people are women;
- Of the world's 30 million refugees 80 per cent are women and children, of the world's one billion illiterate adults two third are women; and,
- Of the 150 million children world wide who are not in schools two third are girls[2].

Despite some concerted attention and resources devoted to recruitment and retention of women in engineering over the last couple of decades, they are still woefully under-represent in engineering and many related sciences. This under-representation is problematic from several perspectives: From the point of view of the science and engineering workforce, nearly half the potential talent for the technical workforce is missing. There is also cause for concern on the part of those seeking quality, talent, and creativity for the engineering and scientific disciplines and professions. And women themselves are missing out on opportunities to leverage learning and skills in interesting and rewarding careers, explore new fields, develop new knowledge, design new solutions, and benefit from the rewards of financial independence and economic equity[3].

It is believed that economic strength is the basis of social, political and psychological power in the society. Thus the lower status of women mostly stems from their low economic status and subsequent dependence and lack of decision making power. Therefore, if women gain economic strength, they gain visibility and voice.

Among the various approaches, the empowerment approach in development programmes is considered best. This approach is modeled to 'power' itself and gain control over the self, the resources and freedom to decide. This process of gaining control over the self, the resources and the decision making power may be termed as empowerment. Ideally, the empowerment process should aim at "women finding time and space of their own" and should provide mechanisms for their active participation in the development process. Further it should ensure their role in decision making and should foster self reliance both socially and economically[2].

The main objective of this chapter is to outline the Engineering Education among women and detail the challenges which women Engineers have faced in the past, which unduly burden women Engineers in their endeavours and, thus, in their advancement. The chapter concludes with the hope to empower women to facilitate their participation and involvement in Science and Technical areas.

PRESENT SCENERIO

When we consider why there are so few women in science and technology fields, it's important to understand a few facts:

- Women represent more than half the population, and 46 per cent of the U.S. workforce, but just 24 per cent of those working in science and engineering combined, and only 10% of the engineering workforce (NSF, 2002)[3].
- Women were 16 per cent of the U.S. scientific and engineering (S&E) labor force in 1988, they represented only 12.3 per cent (roughly 400,000 women) of the total number of scientists and engineers employed in industry[4].
- Since 1980, the percentage of women receiving bachelor's degree has slowly increased from about 10 per cent to nearly 20 per cent. But in some years the percentage remained flat, and in recent years, even when the percentage increased, the total numbers remained the same or decreased[3].
- July 2000 data from the National Science Foundation, US, put the percentage of women receiving bachelor's degrees in science and engineering at 50 per cent of the total. That seems pretty equitable until you unpack the story: NSF defines "science" as including social and behavioural sciences, including psychology (in which women represented 76 per cent of bachelor's degree recipients in 2000) and other fields where women are over-represented. In 2000, women earned about 20 per cent of bachelor's degrees in engineering, 33 per cent in mathematical and computer sciences, and 56 per cent in biological and agricultural sciences[3].
- In 1966, women comprised less than 24 per cent of the S&E bachelor degree recipients, less than 14 per cent of the S&E master degree recipients, and 8 per cent of the S&E doctorate recipients. By 1989, these numbers had increased to 40 per cent obtaining bachelor degrees, 31 per cent getting master's degrees, and 28 per cent receiving doctorates[4].

Those less engaged with developing the scientific and technical workforce may be lulled into complacency. Since the social changes of the women's movement and legislation removing barriers and addressing gender equity changed the landscape for women's opportunities 30 years ago, women have made considerable progress in participation a variety of professional fields. The percentage of women earning bachelor degrees or higher has increased dramatically in the past few decades.

Furthermore, the apparent "gains" in percentages are more reflective of the lower percentages of men entering these fields than increases in percentages of women: In 1980, 1.3 per cent of women earning bachelor's degrees majored in engineering vs. 11.1 per cent of men. In 2000, 1.7 per cent of women earning bachelor's degrees majored in engineering vs. 8.8 per cent of men. The gap in participation of minority groups is not as large as the gender gap, but race and ethnicity are also key factors in understanding the full spectrum of women's participation in science and engineering[3].

- In the US, women make up: 9 per cent of mid- to upper-level IT engineers, 28.5 per cent computer programmers, 26.9 per cent systems analysts, 85 per cent data entry workers[1].
- No European Union member state has more than 1/3 women researchers in engineering and technology, while the average is 10 per cent. If the current number of women computer programmers in Western Europe were to double to 94,000, women would still constitute only 7 per cent of the total workforce[1].
- In Asia, women constitute 20 per cent of programmers (mostly in lower-skilled, low-value-added positions), while making up the majority of workers in data processing (especially overseas work)[1].

In India, women constitute about 48 per cent of the population but their participation in economic activity is only 34 per cent. There is a continuing concentration of women in low paid and low status occupations which indicates that women are marginalised in the labour force. There is a common assumption that men are the bread winners and that most of the female work is either done in the leisure time or serves as the procurer of supporting income for the family. The major reason for this is social prejudices that women's world is required to be focused around family and household[2].

Almost half the population of our country comprises of women while businesses owned and operated by them constitute less than 5 per cent. This is a reflection on social, cultural as well as economic distortions in the decades of development. In fact, women's contribution and participation in economic activity and production of goods and services is much greater than statistics reveal, since much of it takes place in the informal sector and also in the households[2].

COMPLEXITIES ENCOUNTERED BY WOMEN ENGINEERS

Most recently, the outcomes document of Beijing+5 (2000) emphasized the importance to develop policies and programmes to enhance the employability of women and their access to quality jobs, through improving access to formal, non-formal and vocational training, life-long learning and retraining, long-distance education, including in information and communications technology and entrepreneurial skills, particularly in developing countries, to support women's empowerment in the different stages of their lives.

But female scientists and engineers remain underrepresented in industry, due to their choice of S&E field and of the employment sector. There is a tendency for female scientists and engineers to choose careers in life sciences, behavioural sciences, and social sciences, all fields where industry is a less likely source of employment than academe or government[4].

Why Girls Don't Consider Engineering Careers?

The fact that women tend to prefer jobs in other sections is consistent with a perception that working conditions for women are less favourable in industry. It may also be consistent with a number of other hypotheses, some of which involve decisions based on factors other than the nature of working conditions in industry. Another fact consistent with the working conditions explanation is the greater exit rate of women than men from S&E positions in industry, although there may be other factors contributing to this rate.

One of the main reasons why there are so few women in engineering is the often subtle but sometimes direct discouragement that girls and young women get from adults, their peers, and the media. One of the most important contributions that each of us can make to foster girls' interest in engineering is to challenge our own stereotypes of what is good for girls and women. Here are some commonly held myths that often discourage girls from pursuing engineering careers[5].

MYTH: Boys are better at maths and science than girls.

REALITY: There is no difference in ability to learn maths and science between boys and girls. In truth, these young women, who remain, have higher GPAs in these fields than young men.

MYTH: Competitive activities are the best way to motivate students to learn.

REALITY: Girls (and many boys) often respond better to cooperative/collaborative learning experiences than to competition.

MYTH: Girls don't like technology.

REALITY: Girls are very interested in technology, but cultural differences in the way boys and girls are raised typically limit the experiences girls have with different technologies.

MYTH: A woman engineer can't be feminine.

REALITY: A quick survey of the Gallery of Women Engineers provides proof that engineers are the same kinds of sisters, daughters, and mothers found in other professions.

MYTH: Women can't succeed professionally in engineering careers.

REALITY: Engineering is still a male-dominated profession, but women can and do build success careers in this field. As more women enter and work their way up through the engineering workforce, the profession is becoming more female-friendly.

There is no solid reason that young people would have to choose at age 17, before they ever go to college that whether they want to be an engineer or not.

Obstacles in the Path

Analysis of organizations and the past society identifies informal obstacles, which women Engineers confronted in their profession. Below are some of these obstacles:

1. Barriers for women in corporate culture at every stage of career development
2. The workplace environment is hostile to women
3. Paternalism in allotment of work assignments
4. Allegations of reverse discrimination
5. Sexual harassment
6. Different standards for male and female engineer employees
7. Misunderstandings due to different styles ofcCommunication
8. Specific, sometimes limiting perceptions of the role of women
9. Status of women viewed as "outsiders" or classified as non-engineering
10. women usually excluded from professional networks
11. Silent discrimination in offering jobs, salaries etc.
12. Difficulties in performance evaluation due to undefined guidelines
13. Lack of confidence
14. Social roles
15. Socio-cultural barriers

Any framework for technology development and enhanced competitiveness should therefore include guidelines for increasing the percentage of women in the national/international digital economy. It is suggested that three main benefits would result:

1. Increasing the pool of human resources in a country can only contribute to increased creativity, expertise and competitiveness in the technology sector.

2. Increasing the pool of potential and available expertise will allow a country to more quickly arrive at the "critical mass" of IT professionals who will facilitate a national information economy and attract FDI.

3. Finally, increasing the number of women in the sector will increase its ability to meet the concerns and interests of women, thereby increasing its potential customer base[1].

REMEDIES

UNESCO/ICSU World Conference on Science stressed that special efforts should be made by governments, educational institutions, scientific communities, non-governmental organizations and civil society to ensure the full participation of women and girls in all aspects of science and technology.

Why it is Desired, to have Women in Engineering?

There are several reasons why we should be encouraging girls and young women to become engineers:

1. There is a shortage of skilled workers
2. Society benefits from a more diverse engineering community
3. Businesses benefit from engaging women in research, design, and development
4. Engineering can be a rewarding lifetime career
5. It is an opportunity for advancement of career
6. Corporate initiatives to recruit and retain women scientists and engineers

Five attributes appear to be common to women who have earned S&E degrees and successfully pursued industrial employment[4].

1. Science and Engineering Expertise and Competence
2. Ability to Establish Goals and to Take Risks
3. Strong Communication Skills
4. Self-confidence
5. Openness to Change

Recruitment and Hiring Practices that Create De Facto Entry Barriers for Women

Recognizing the advantages of incorporating female scientists and engineers in the corporate labour force, some companies have developed aggressive programmes and strategies to recruit more women into these fields. Projections of the future work force indicate that 80-85 per cent of the net additions over the next 10 years will be minorities and women. These companies feel that they must recruit aggressively among these groups or the best will go elsewhere[4].

In India, Dr. M. Suriya had studied *"Strategies for attracting women into IT-enabled service sector (ITES): An empirical survey"*. The IT Enabled Service Sector is one of the fastest growing sectors of the Indian economy. The NASSCOM-McKinsey report projected that this sector will be the largest Revenue and Employment generator for the Indian IT industry. However, it is estimated (NASSCOM) that the job markets will be higher for women in this area of work since women possess the soft skills and qualities that are essential for this work environment. The central aim of the study made by Dr. M. Suriya was to investigate the employment potentials and the training facilities available for women to get into the ITES sector which generates millions of job vacancies. It is an empirical survey to be conducted in the ITES companies based at the metropolitans. The data conducted at two different levels: one set of data collected from the HR manager of the sample companies and the other one from the employees of these companies[6].

Who Can Make What Difference?

Girls' opinions about engineering are shaped by their interaction with parents, teachers, and other mentors. Here are some of the most important things you can do for girls and young women:

- *Parents:* Expect your daughters to achieve success in maths and science and encourage them to try new things.

- *Teachers:* Teach or present maths, science, and technology through activities and curriculum that engage girls.
- *Counsellors:* Encourage girls to take math and science and to explore engineering and other technology careers.
- *Mentors:* Be a role model for girls—encouraging them pursue engineering and technology careers.

STEPS TOWARDS DEVELOPMENT OF SOLUTION

Solutions to increase participation of women in science and engineering often initially focus on the problem of "How can we persuade more girls/women to enter/stay in these fields?" These interventions have been characterized as efforts that focus on a "deficit" model, in which it is assumed that these individuals lack something—ability, experience, interest, inspiration, motivation—that they need in order to succeed. In this model, attention is paid to mitigating that deficit, typically by providing programmes—summer camps, internships, remedial courses, special study groups, mentoring programmes, social opportunities, seminars, evening programmes, etc.

It is suggested that well-designed intervention programmes can definitely make a difference in increasing the numbers of women in science and engineering, at least for some portion of the population in some environments. But even on college campuses with longstanding, comprehensive programmes focused on women in engineering and/or science, the representation of women does not rise to parity. Some have criticized this approach for its development of "band-aid" efforts that address symptoms rather than tackling the roots of the problem[3]. Here are a few possibilities:

- A large-scale, multi-year public awareness campaign could be helpful in shifting public opinion about this issue.
- Be alert to what is encouraged—or not encouraged- by educational modes that are driven by performance assessment based on standardized tests. This type of

instruction often fails to impart important concepts and engage students' interests.

- When you're involved in discussions on how to solve the problem of women's under-representation in science and technology fields, be aware that many people focus on trying to "fix" the individuals who aren't choosing these fields. We must realize that the focus needs to be on changing systems, practices, and institutions, not on "fixing" the individuals.

Nancy J. lane, U.K. studied "Recent Developments in the UK for Women in Science, Engineering and Technology (SET)". She said that in the UK, the Greenfield Report in late 2002, recommended, three major schemes to improve the position of women in Science, Engineering & Technology, was called for by the Secretary of State in the DTI (Department of Trade and Industry).

- UK recognized this problem in 1994, when The Rising Tide report was published. Then, as a result, a Unit for Women in Science, Engineering and Technology was set up in the Department of Trade and Industry to encourage girls into science subjects at school.
- In 1999 Athena Project was established to promote the recruitment, participation and progression of women in Science, Engineering and Technology in Universities.
- It began with a series of grants to encourage Higher Education Institutes to instigate good practice as regards women and in 2002/3 culminated in four awards to those Higher Education Institutes, which had put best practice successfully into place.
- In Cambridge, they have the award-winning WiSET Initiative, which runs projects involving mentors, recruitment officers to seek out able women, confidence-building programmes and networking, with activities featuring high profile women lecturers and the setting up of codes of good practice, especially for short-term contract research staff, in science departments[7].

Nirupama Prakash of India had presented a study on "Status of Women in Indian Society—Issues and Challenges in Processes of Empowerment". During her study she shows that the post-independence period has seen a number of positive efforts by the Government of India to improve the socio-economic status of women. The National plans have focused on women's education and empowerment with thrust on gender friendly technology at rural level and encouragement of urban-based women technocrats in various domains of Science and Technology. There are disturbing trends in terms of decline in sex-ratio in 0-6 age group which indicate gender bias and unhealthy use of technology such as ultra-sound pre-natal test devices[8].

The Finance Minister of India, in his Budget Speech of 2000-01 had announced that the year 2001 will be observed as *"Women Empowerment Year"*. He had also announced setting up of a Task Force to chalk out specific programmes for observing the year 2001 as *"Women Empowerment Year"*. The announcement has been made in the context of an urgent need for improving the access of women to national resources and for ensuring their rightful place in the mainstream of economic development. The Government is committed to improve the status of women in India and towards this end, apart from the Constitutional guarantees; several schemes and programmes have been planned and executed from time to time. The declaration of the year 2001 as the *"Women's Empowerment Year"* is therefore, significant as it reiterates the Government's commitment to bring about equality for women in all walks of life.

The objective of the *Women's Empowerment Year* was to create large-scale awareness with the active participation of women themselves. The Department proposed to launch yearlong activities to bring about a change in the environment which will be conducive to develop self-confidence and assertiveness among women and children, especially girls. A list of month-wise programmes to be taken up during the Women's Empowerment Year[8].

RECOMMENDATIONS

A series of recommendations to increase the participation of women in science, engineering and technology disciplines and professions have been made in several important international and regional policy forums, including the World Conference on Science (1999) and Beijing +5 (2000) among others. The Gender Advisory Board of the United Nations Commission on Science and Technology for Development (GABUNCSTD) and the Global Alliance for Diversifying the Engineering and Science Workforce present in this document a summary of these recommendations, which are considered to be extremely important and pertinent to increasing the participation of women in computer science and engineering professions and research. Summary of Recommendation[1, 2, 3] actions are:

1. There is Need for systematic, reliable, and harmonized data on women in all sectors and levels of science, education and technology.
2. The Need for more research to understand the attrition of girls and women through all stages of S&T education and employment.
3. It is required to promote within the education system the access of girls and women to scientific education at all levels.
4. Establishment of Transparent and fair selection and recruitment practices.
5. Improve conditions for recruitment, retention and advancement in all fields of research.
6. Undertake research, supported by the collection and analysis of gender-disaggregated data, documenting constraints and progress in expanding the role of women in science and technology.
7. Provision for Career, fellowship and training support for women returning to the workforce after a career break.
8. Measure the effects of intervention programmes, and offer those that are effective as widely as possible.

9. Monitor the implementation of and document best practices and lessons learned through impact assessment and evaluations.
10. Bring effective programmes into the mainstream of everyday educational practice, and create more ways to institutionalize, replicate, and scale these efforts.
11. Support for networking among women in science and technology.
12. Invest in both treatment (support under current systems) and cure (systemic change).
13. Explore ways in which technology can support scale and achieve efficiencies for such programmes.
14. Support for role model and mentoring schemes.
15. An emphasis be placed on promoting role models and mentors for women in science and engineering—in school, in post-secondary education, in the workforce, and among high-tech business owners and executives.
16. Maths and science programmes should be designed to accommodate the learning styles of girls and young women and to make these subjects more relevant to their lives.

CONCLUSION

"When women move forward, the family moves, the village moves and the nation moves". These words of Pandit Jawaharlal Nehru are an accepted fact. Employment gives economic status to women. Economic status gives way to social status and thereby empowerment to women. From modern management research, it is evident that women contribute to special leadership characteristics which can promote social development in a more positive humanistic direction. Since societies are made up of equally large numbers of women and men, it is apparent that a greater integration of gender in leadership and management can only favour this positive development. In present scenario due to modernization, urbanization, globalization and development of education, with increasing awareness women are now seeking gainful employment in several fields.